MONTBÉLIARD IMMIGRATION

TO

NOVA SCOTIA, 1749 - 1752

Revised Edition

Terrence M. Punch, CM

Genealogical Publishing Company
Baltimore, Maryland

Published by Genealogical Publishing Company
Baltimore, Maryland, 2015

Library of Congress Catalog Card Number 2015935857

ISBN 978-0-8063-2014-4

CONTENTS

A NOTE ABOUT MONTBÉLIARD

What do we know about Montbéliard (Mömpelgard in German), the francophone Lutheran principality belonging to the dukes of Württemberg? In his *Meran-English Genealogical Dictionary* (Baltimore, 1992), Ernest Thode writes,

> Mömpelgard - Montbéliard district of France, (hist.) County, exclave of Wuerttemberg 1397- 1676 and 1679 - 1793, capital Moempelgard (frequently used as a haven for settlement by Anabaptists).

Fans of royal genealogy may be aware that Princess Mary of Teck, grandmother of Queen Elizabeth II, was a member of the royal family of Württemberg, and descended from the counts of Montbéliard.

Frederick of Württemberg-Mömpelgard visited England in 1592 and expressed a desire to be made a Knight of the Garter. Shakespeare wrote the play, *The Merry Wives of Windsor*, intended to be performed in spring 1597 to coincide with the investiture of the duke as a Knight of the Garter. The allusion is clear from the name of the Windsor hostelry: *The Garter Inn*. Shakespeare worked that contemporary news into Act IV, Scene iii, of the play, where Bardolph asks the host to lend three horses to the German guests so they could go to meet their duke at court. Later we learn that they nee not make preparations for the German duke as he did not exist! The real German duke was *not* expected to come to Windsor because Frederick was not invited in time to attend the investiture, a deliberate snub.

Those who enjoy interesting food discover *saucisse de Montbéliard*, made from pork, cumin and pepper, and smoked over the sawdust from resinous trees, usually evergreens. Another regional specialty is *cancoillotte*, made from *metton* (a runny cheese) cooked with water or milk, to which is added salt and butter, and sometimes garlic. It is similar to what Germans know as *Kochkäse* (cook cheese).

People was live near Montréal, Québec, perhaps know that a rue de Montbéliard exists in suburban Lorraine, just north of the golf course. The city of Greensboro, North Carolina, is twinned with the city of Montbéliard.

The point of making these apparently random references is to show that, somewhere on the margin of our knowledge, Montbéliard has a presence. In Nova Scotia and Maine, as well as beyond, it survives in the bloodlines of thousands of North Americans.

INTRODUCTION TO REVISED EDITION

Like time, research does not stay still; it moves onward as new information is discovered and assimilated. In the nearly two years which have passed since my genealogical investigations took place, several new sources of material have been found and put to work. A section introducing these may be found at the end of the book.

A number of church registers are now available on line. In particular, the records of the Temple St.-Martin in the town of Montbéliard may be consulted by anyone with a good reading knowledge of French and is willing to tackle the sometimes convoluted, handwriting, faded ink and smudged pages. Since these open in 1571 and appear to be complete for baptisms, they afford North American researchers the rare opportunity to trace people who lived over four centuries ago. Four other parishes reach to the 1590s.

For a researcher who takes the trouble to read them, the early eighteenth-century census records can greatly assist them in developing a milieu for their ancestors. The returns of poor people in 1750 will explain why some families took the plunge and emigrated a year or so afterwards.

The genealogies of a few families have been revised significantly: Carlin, Jacques, Jeanbas, Virpillot and Vuilquet. Several wives' surnames have been uncovered and some dates added or clarified. Amêt, Besançon, Bouillon, Calame, Carlin, Clemençon, Fevre, Jeanbas, Maillard, and Nardin have been followed to their exact place of origin. The Jeanperrin, Leau, Mettin, Morleau, Quidore, Rigoulot, Sertier and Veutilot families have been traced back a further generation or two. Several knots have been untangled and puzzles resolved. Some lines continue to defy attempts to track them down, which leaves the reader with the challenge of doing so.

Typographical or factual errors have been corrected whenever they have been detected. Footnotes have been added, removed or amended in line with new evidence. Statistics have been revised to reflect the added research, and fewer people fall into the "fate unknown" category.

My reward will be a feeling that at last this small group of settlers has a book written in English, allowing many people to bridge the Atlantic in the quest for their origins.

Terrence M. Punch, C.M.   Armdale, Nova Scotia, February 2015

MONTBÉLIARD TO ROTTERDAM
(VIA THE RHINE)

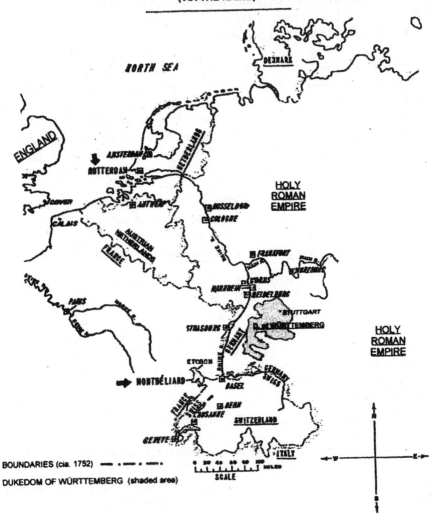

BOUNDARIES (cia. 1752) ·—·—·—·—·—·

DUKEDOM OF WÜRTTEMBERG (shaded area)

PREFACE

Dr. Winthrop Pickard Bell wrote his encyclopædic book about the Foreign Protestants and the settlement of Nova Scotia over forty years ago. It has remained the definitive study of the subject, and there seems little likelihood that his work will be superseded.

One might ask why anyone else would address the subject. There are several responses to that. In the present instance the author has had access to numbers of church records in Montbéliard that were not available to Dr. Bell in the post-war years (1945-1961), and the benefit of correspondence over a period of years with Professor Jean-Marc Debard of Besançon, then president of the Société d'Émulation de Montbéliard, a professional academic historian and author. More to the point, Bell did not study the Montbéliardais element *per se* among the Foreign Protestants, nor was he interested, except incidentally, in their genealogical history when he was writing his book.

Bell did, however, compile information about the several hundred Foreign Protestant families for the period 1749-1770, and the *Register* of his findings was published as two volumes in 2003 by Dr. J. Christopher Young of Guelph, Ontario, with the assistance, principally, of Fulbright scholar Dr. Kenneth S. Paulsen and myself.

What I have done here is to present the Montbéliard background of that portion of the Foreign Protestants who arrived in Nova Scotia between 1749 and 1752, discuss their fate at sea, in Halifax over the tragic winter of 1752/53, their arrival at Lunenburg in 1753, and their subsequent dispersion. The genealogical part of this book mainly covers the years between 1700 and 1815 to the extent that these could be ascertained. In the great majority of cases it has been possible to locate the specific communities from which the various families came.

In short, this work fills in one part of the wider story as outlined by Winthrop Bell in his book and his *Register*.

Terrence M. Punch, C.M.   Armdale, Nova Scotia, November 2013

Acknowledgements

My appreciation goes to Dr. Kenneth S. Paulsen, Carolyn Smedley and my wife Pamela for reading the historical sections of this book and I thank them for many valuable and helpful suggestions and corrections. Thanks are also owing to Norris Whiston for drawing some important documents to my attention. I shall be indebted always to my friend, Dr. Jean-Marc Debard, for many years president of la Société d'Émulation de Montbéliard, of which I have been un sociétaire since 1985.

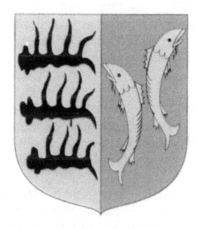

Cover Illustration: **Württemberg**, shown on the viewer's left (shield-bearer's right, or *dexter*): *D'or, à trois demi ramures de cerf de sable (*On a gold background, three stag's antlers of four branches, in black). **Montbéliard**, or Mömpelgard, shown on the viewer's right (shield-bearer's left, or *sinister)*: *De gueule aux deux bars adossés 'or (*On a red background, two gold fishes back-to-back.

I - MONTBÉLIARD, AN ANCIENT HOMELAND

Among the 2700 Foreign Protestants who came to Nova Scotia between 1749 and 1752 were about 440 people from Montbéliard, a francophone and Lutheran territory of the Duke of Württemberg .The tiny *Pays* is less than one-fifth the size of the Grand Duchy of Luxembourg: 55 kilometres at its greatest length, and 22 kilometres at its widest. The Vosges bound it on the north, Alsace and the Juras on the east, Franche-Comté and the Swiss cantons to the west and south. Until 1648 Alsace was part of the Holy Roman Empire of the German Nation, while Franche-Comté was Spanish territory down to 1678. France had not been an immediate neighbour until then. For the next 115 years French ambition to possess this strategic territory was one of the pressures felt by the Montbéliardais. In 1793 the French revolutionaries consummated the policy of absorption begun by Louis XIV. The territory which had formed the principality of Mömpelgard or Montbéliard was divided between the *départements* of Haute-Saône and Doubs.

The principality consisted of the County of Montbéliard with its dependent lordship of Étobon, as well as the four seigneuries of Clémont, Blamont, Châtelot and Héricourt. The towns of Riquewihr and Horbourg, enclaves deep inside Alsace, also pertained to the principality. It had been a typical small feudal entity until its heiress, Countess Henriette de Montfaucon, married Eberhard IV of Württemberg in 1397 vesting Montbéliard's sovereignty in that German dynasty.

The subjects of the territory possessed an advanced legal status for the time. The town of Montbéliard enjoyed a charter granted in 1283 which, in effect, created an urban republic with a middle class, guilds, and local self-government. Each new ruler was obliged to confirm these freedoms in a public ceremony prior to entering upon his inheritance, a custom that continued until France seized the state. Moreover, the widowed Henriette, acting as regent for her sons, had liberated her peasants. The ruler lived at Stuttgart, so that the day-to-day administration fell to a Regency Council which combined the functions of council of state, court of justice, board of finance and ecclesiastical tribunal. Citizens had a right to petition through the resident intendant to the Duke should the Council's decisions provoke objections[1].

The later history of Montbéliard may be divided into three parts. The earliest runs from the Reformation to 1620 and may be termed the years of establishment. The second span of years, from 1620 to 1723, is known locally as *les jours de détresse*, while the third period, 1723-1793, form the years of struggle.[2]

Duke Ulrich of Württemberg was an early supporter of Luther and had to flee Stuttgart. He took refuge in his county of Montbéliard and in 1524 invited the Protestant, Guillaume Farel, to preach there. Riots ensued between religious factions and Farel was driven away. By the time Ulrich regained control of Montbéliard, considerable destruction had taken place. Following his restoration in Württemberg, Ulrich sent to Montbéliard in 1535 the preacher Pierre Toussain, a man who sought a middle way between Lutheranism and Calvinism. The Regency Council banned the Catholic Mass in 1538, after which the Reformation spread to the lordships of Étobon and Blamont. The principality became the one and only francophone Lutheran state in Europe.

Ulrich preferred Luther's conservative attitudes to the more radical views of the Calvinists, and his brother Christoph bequeathed funding to send six Montbéliardais annually to the University of Tübingen. From 1560 until 1793 most theological students from Montbéliard studied in Württemberg, ensuring a steady flow of well-educated, bilingual, Lutheran clergy for Montbéliard. Yet, the duke did permit non-Lutheran religious refugees to settle in designated places within his realm .[3]

---

[1] Pierre Pegeot, "Montbéliard, origines et originalités d'une ville medievale," *Histoire de la Ville de Montbéliard*, Claude Voisin, ed. (Roanne, France, 1980), 20-21, outlines these conditions and privileges.

[2] Jean-Marc Debard, "La Principauté de Montbéliard (XVIᵉ-XVIIIᵉ siècles)", in Roland Fiétier, ed., *Histoire de la Franche-Comté* (Toulouse, France, 1977), 323-350.

[3] This phenomenon is discussed in Terrence M. Punch, "Montbéliard, 1523-1773; Homeland, Refuge, Way-Station," in *Deutsch-kanadisches Jahrbuch*, XVI (2000), 147-157.

Ulrich's nephew and successor, Frédéric, was Montbéliard's greatest ruler. He used the money from the sale of monastic and episcopal properties to endow schools and churches. Each parish fined non-attendance at church; such fines, together with alms in the poor box and bequests, were administered carefully for the benefit of those in need. A modern study shows not only that the system worked well, at least in normal times, but that the parish committees did their work honestly and diligently.[4]

Frédéric was intelligent and energetic, and lived for much of the time in Montbéliard. He introduced paper-making, printing works, iron mining, gypsum quarrying, a powder factory, a cannon foundry, and founded a local mint. He established schools, a botanical garden, new fairs and markets. Guild privileges were extended to drapers, tanners, apothecaries, physicians and surgeons. His most famous initiative was the forges at Chagey. Coal-mining was encouraged so that use of coal at the forges and the salt works would conserve timber from the forests.[5] The roads and bridges were improved and extended, while Frédéric's keen interest in agriculture resulted in the establishment of sheep farms, a stud farm to improve horse stocks, and the region's earliest vineyards.

Part of the duke's genius lay in recruiting, not only the talented architect and engineer Schickhardt, but people who could implement and operate his innovations. Frédéric encouraged settlement by any industrious, law-abiding Protestant. Religious persecution in nearby states provided a stream of refugee manpower seeking peace and employment. In the capital city alone, there were 555 adult male refugees

---

[4] Jean-Marc Debard, "Une institution charitable luthérienne 'La Boîte des Pauvres' dans la principauté de Montbéliard. Un exemple paroissial: Saint-Julien au XVIIIe siècle," *Bulletin et Mémoires*, LXXVIII (1982), 197-221.

[5] André Bouvard, "Heinrich Schickhardt, technicien des salines au XVIe siècle – Les salines de Saulnot," *Bulletin et Mémoires*, LXXIX (1983), 69-77, explains how there was a major search for a means of conserving wood by substituting other mediums to provide heat in the salt-making process.

between 1573 and 1588.[6] Two years after he established the forges at Chagey, the duke laid out a new village in his seigneury of Étobon (1588), and paid for the housing of the first sixteen families (86 people) himself. He did expect the Calvinist Huguenots to become Lutherans if they wished to remain in this village of Frédéric-Fontaine. The objects of the duke's charity obliged without much grumbling.[7]

Frédéric's five sons agreed that the second eldest, Louis-Frédéric, would succeed their father and govern Montbéliard. Should his legitimate line fail, the heirs of the oldest brother, Jean-Frédéric, would reunite the principality with Württemberg. From 1617 to 1723 a distinct line of princes resided in and reigned over Montbéliard.

In 1620 Montbéliard's sovereignty over the lordship of Étobon was recognized, but then a century of ill fortune beset the principality. There was a scandal involving the coinage, followed by a collapse of confidence. The Thirty Years War had erupted in the Holy Roman Empire, creating a shortage of supplies and galloping inflation. Between 1627 and 1630 there was an outbreak of the bubonic plague in the *Pays*. Prince Léopold-Frédéric (1631-1662) accepted French protection against the Spanish of Franche-Comté, only to turn the principality into a theatre of war. A recurrence of the plague in 1642 completed the work of devastation.

The events of 1622-1642 precipitated a demographic crisis in Montbéliard. Population losses due to plague, war and famine have been estimated at between 65 and 75%.[8] Some villages were totally destroyed or depopulated: Chenebier was wiped out, and Charmont as a distinct community disappeared forever. People fled to Switzerland, while others were killed or left to die of privation.

---

[6] Jean-Marc Debard, "Tolérance et intolérance; les refugiés huguenots à Montbéliard et dans la Principauté, 1537-1617 (seconde moitié du XVIème siècle), *Bulletin et Mémoires*, LXXXIV (1988), 78.

[7] There is a good summary of Frédéric's reign in Louis Renard, *Nouvelle Histoire du Pays de Montbéliard* (Montbéliard, 1950), 81-83.

[8] Jean-Marc Debard, "Immigrations, émigrations dans la principauté de Montbéliard du XVIe au XVIIIe siècle - Essai de synthèse," *Bulletin et Mémoires*, XCI (1995), 158-159.

Since people from the area of Héricourt and Étobon settled in Nova Scotia and New England in the 1750s, some reliable statistics about those areas provide useful background. Héricourt had 720 people in 1635, living in 165 houses. Three years later, only 40 houses were standing and just 170 souls remained to live in them.[9] The little lordship of Étobon, with its five forest villages, was home to over 500 people before the plague of 1627, and still had 435 inhabitants in 1638. By 1647 it was reduced to ten dwellings inhabited by eight families and two widows. At Étobon village, at Clairegoutte, at Magny Danigon, and at Belverne the duke's agent reported "all absent." All fifty survivors of the seigneury were huddled into Frédéric-Fontaine.[10] The capital, Montbéliard, saw its population drop from nearly 3,000 to below 2,000 between June and November 1635. The peace of Westphalia (1648) found *un pays ruiné, vide d'hommes et retourné à la friche.*[11]

Many of those who fled never returned, and the prince had to seek French-speaking Protestant settlers to populate his devastated lands. Recruitment was limited to the Swiss territories beyond the Juras: Vaud, Neuchâtel, the Priory of Moutier-Grandval, and that part of Bern which is now the canton of Jura. Many newcomers were Calvinists who were gradually assimilated as Lutherans, a tendency assisted by the absence of Calvinist clergy in Montbéliard. Swiss immigration raised their proportion of the population of Montbéliard to about one in nine (11%).[12]

A further immigration of Huguenots followed the revocation of the Edict of Nantes by Louis XIV in 1685, and these were readily absorbed. Less homogeneous were the German-speaking Mennonites who arrived from Alsace. They had sought refuge there in the 1670s, after the canton

---

[9] Lassus, François, et Jean-Marc Debard, "Une petite ville luthérienne: Héricourt, 1698-1721," *Bulletin et Mémoires*, LXXXVIII (1992), 360.

[10] Pierre Croissant, 'La population de la seigneurie d'Étobon du XVIe au XVIIIe siècle," *Bulletin et Mémoires*, LXXXVI (1990), 375.

[11] Debard, "Immigrations, émigrations . . .", 153-154. " A ruined country, devoid of people, returned to a wasteland."

[12] *Ibid.*, 160.

of Bern expelled them. By 1712, France controlled much of Alsace and many Anabaptists moved to Montbéliard within a year.[13] Despite some resentment directed towards them, the Mennonites persisted and still have a congregation in Montbéliard.

The parish of Héricourt is within one of the four lordships occupied by France. In the registers between 1636 and 1754, 754 households or family groups occur. At least 76 (10%) were immigrants or their children, in the order: 45 Swiss, 12 French, 9 Lorrainer, 7 Alsatian and 3 German. The next parish is Chagey and Luze, whose church was the scene of an affray in 1740 when the French attempted to install a Catholic curé following the death of the Lutheran pastor, Méquillet. Between 1620 and 1755, 683 households existed. Again 10% - 69 family groups - were newcomers or their progeny: 46 Swiss, 15 French, 8 German.[14]

France expanded to the western frontier of Montbéliard in 1648. Three decades later France had wrested Franche-Comté from Spain. Only the Swiss border was free from French ambition. From 1676 to 1697 French troops occupied Montbéliard and Louis XIV's lawyers obtained decrees that transferred the sovereignty of the county from the Holy Roman Empire to the Duchy of Burgundy, by then in French hands. The Montbéliardais had to swear allegiance to Louis XIV under penalty of having their property seized. The prince, George II, refused to take the

---

[13] Charles Mathiot et Roger Boigeol, *Recherches historiques sur les Anabaptistes de l'ancienne principauté de Montbéliard, d'Alsace et du territoire de Belfort* (Flavion, Belgium, 1969), 36, 38, 46. A few Mennonite families moved away in 1791 - *cf.*, Jerold A. Stahly, "The Montbéliard Amish Move to Poland in 1791," in *Mennonite Family History* (Jan 1989), 13 - 17.

[14] Terrence M. Punch, 'L'État-civil d'Héricourt, 1636-1754,' and 'L'État-civil de Chagey et Luze, 1620-1755' [Unpublished MSS in the fonds of the Société d'Émulation de Montbéliard]. Registers of the parish of Étobon and the village of Belverne, show that in 1681, 15 of Belverne's 38 inhabitants (39%) were Swiss, as were 19 of the 86 persons (22%) in Étobon. Chenebier shows the same pattern. The replacement population of the seigneury of Étobon was drawn heavily from Swiss regions. Many Montbéliardais emigrants to Nova Scotia and New England came from that seigneury, a fact reflected in the substantial number of Swiss references in the genealogy section.

oath and withdrew to Württemberg. The Treaty of Ryswick (1697) obliged the French to evacuate the principality. Prince George died soon afterwards and in 1700 the French king quartered dragoons in the four lordships of Blamont, Clémont, Châtelot and Héricourt. Louis cynically used religion as a lever and replaced some Lutheran pastors with Catholic curés.[15]

The illegal French occupation was still in effect in 1723 when Prince Léopold-Eberhard died without legitimate issue. Montbéliard and Étobon reverted to the Stuttgart branch of his dynasty. The new ruler caused a census to be taken, which revealed that the population had grown since 1671 by fifty percent, to 12,000 souls half a century later.

The presence of a garrison of Württemberg troops secured Montbéliard itself, and Étobon, but the remaining four lordships felt the weight of French oppression. There were clashes between local people and the French occupation forces, including a riot outside the church

---

[15] Jean-Marc Debard, "Réforme et dragonnades à Brévilliers (XVIᵉ - XVIIᵉ siècles)", *Bulletin et Mémoires*, LXXIX (1983), 184-188. Winthrop Bell to Gordon Haliburton (Avonport), 17 Sep 1954: "The entire principality belonging to the Duke of Württemberg as prince of Montbéliard consisted of the 'county' proper and four 'seigneuries' adjacent to it. The treaty of Ryswick . . . 'annulled' any recognition of a French suzerainty over those seigneuries, and declared the entire territory in 'possession pleine et libre' of the duke of Württemberg. Louis XIV . . . simply maintained his sovereignty over those seigneuries (not over the mere original 'county' of Montbéliard) and had one of his notorious 'chambres de réunion' declare that those seigneuries belonged to French tenure. The Württembergians were, of course, no match for the power of France, and ultimately the duke consented to hold those four seigneuries as fiefs of the French crown. This created considerable differences between conditions in that part of the territory of Montbéliard which had constituted the 'county' and the parts comprised in the adjacent seigneuries. And it was in the latter that the Protestants suffered, not exactly persecution perhaps, but certainly oppressions, disadvantages, etc., for the remainder of the time prior to the French Revolution."(NSA, MG 1, Vol. 117 # 532). "The French Crown tried to destroy Protestantism because the structure of French governing institutions and of society itself could not tolerate deviance of any kind." - Julian Dent, "Why Did the French Crown in the Seventeenth Century Attempt to Destroy Protestantism?" in *Canada's Huguenot Heritage* (Toronto, 1987), p. 34.

at Chagey in 1740.[16]

Despite the unstable situation, the population of the territories continued to increase. With eighteenth-century farming methods, the carrying capacity of the territory was reached when there were about 13,000 inhabitants and their livestock. In previous generations, essart (newly cleared of forest) lands provided additional arable fields, but the need to conserve wood for building, the forges at Chagey and the woodworkers at Audincourt seriously restricted such a solution. Soon after 1700 the cultivation of the potato had been introduced, but it had yet to supplant grain as the staple of the Montbéliard diet.

The Montbéliardais faced major adjustments in what has been described as the years of the struggle. People could remain, but would have to find new means of support. A man could plant potatoes in land

---

[16] Renard, 94, 149, tells of this incident. The story grew with the telling and passed into local lore among the Montbéliardais settlers along Northumberland Strait. George Patterson uncritically included the tale in his *History of Pictou County* (Montréal, 1877), 127-128. Recent research casts quite a different complexion on these events. Claude Canard, "Chagey, de la zizanie du culte simultané à la construction d'une nouvelle église," *Bulletin et Mémoires* of the Société d'Émulation de Montbéliard, No. 126 (2002), 57-76, portrays the struggle for the church at Chagey as what we would term 'an irresistible force meeting an immovable object', the orders of the French king being resisted by a group of agitated country folk. From Canard's study of documents submitted by *both* sides after the fight, we see that the confrontation was neither spontaneous nor can all the responsibility for what happened be assigned to one side or the other. Patterson wrote that fifty young men 'armed only with stones' resisted a detachment of troops. Contemporary sources agree that there were "600 au moins" [at least 600], and that "les revoltés répondent du haut des murs du cimitière par quelques coups fusils et part une grêle de pierres." [The rioters replied from high on the cemetery wall with several musket shots and a shower of stones.] Patterson comments that Peter Millard had participated in the affray in August 1740. It is unlikely he was present, since Pierre Maillard was not quite 14 years old when he was brought to Nova Scotia in 1752. He was baptised at Chenebier on 17 August 1738 (Archives de l'Inspection Ecclèsiastique de l'Eglise evangélique Lutherienne de France, P269-272). I believe Patterson was the recipient of badly garbled stories that had lost nothing in the telling and retelling, and which he appears to have accepted at face value.

formerly fallow; potatoes yielded four times the calories of grain grown in the same field. He could use fertilizer to increase productivity, or he might raise more livestock. Many people supplemented their farming by small-scale artisan activity: making nails, clocks or metal tools. Such diversification in part explains why men's occupations shown on ships' passenger lists differ from their trades according to tax, church, or census records. Men who appeared to shift from a trade to cultivation were in fact combining both to make a living. The Foreign Protestants who came here 250 years ago had grown up with that culture.[17] Such pursuit of multiple means of subsistence persisted into the twentieth century in rural Nova Scotia and elsewhere.

II - EMIGRATION TO NORTH AMERICA

Emigration was the alternative. The pressure was strongest in the four lordships where the French were slowly suffocating Lutheranism. While there was some emigration to nearby destinations such as Mulhouse in Upper Alsace, hundreds of Montbéliardais crossed the Atlantic to the British colonies in North America in the middle years of the eighteenth century.

We find the occasional name in the records of New York, Pennsylvania and Carolina, with rather more in Massachusetts.[18] About eighty Montbéliardais settled on the Kennebec River in Maine, including the Jacquin and Malbon families, who crossed to Halifax and then continued to the Frankfort Plantation in Maine. There they were joined by others who emigrated directly from Montbéliard to New England, landing

---

[17] Wolfgang von Hippel, *Auswanderung aus Sudwestdeutschland: Studieren zur württembergischen Auswanderung und Auswanderungspolitik im 18 und 19 Jahrhundert* (Stuttgart, 1984), 50-51.

[18] J.-M. Debard, "Les Montbéliardais au Nouvelle-Angleterre; une émigration protestante au milieu du XVIIIᵉ siècle (1751-1755); documents et lettres d'Amérique," *Bulletin et Mémoires*, LXXX, 251-288. For a reconstitution of most of the passenger list of the *Priscilla*, which brought Foreign Protestants to Boston, *1751, cf.* Charles W. Hurst, "French and German Immigrants into Boston 1751," *The American Genealogist*, 43:3 (July 1967), 168-177; and 44:2 (Apr.1968), 110.

at Boston, down to 1755.[19] Most Montbéliard immigration to Nova Scotia occurred in 1752, when 425 souls sailed in the *Betty, Pearl, Sally* and *Speedwell*. Five of the Laurilliard family had come to Halifax at its founding in 1749, while the *Ann* in 1750 brought over the Duvoisins, some Maillards, a further ten between them, giving a total of 440 Montbéliardais, with 20 of their names not being known.

Those intending to emigrate from the principality to America were obliged to sell all but what they could carry with them to a seaport such as Rotterdam. There were two routes one could use. One could take oneself and family overland in Swiss territory and from there take a river boat from Basel to the Netherlands. This required payment of the fare down the Rhine, which discouraged some of the poorer folk.

Those who were thrifty or less affluent walked across the Alsatian plain to the Rhine and followed the river to its mouth. This was slow, especially if one had small children or an elderly parent along. People risked being arrested as vagabonds or fugitives. Prudent emigrants made sure they obtained certificates of character or some form of passport as insurance against such circumstances.[20] The brothers Léopold and David Langille carried a document from Dampierre-les-Bois dated 3 April 1752, over six weeks before they sailed in the *Betty*,[21] while

---

[19] Charles Edwin Allen, *History of Dresden, Maine* (Lewiston, ME, 1931), 125-153. *Cf.*, especially 142, 208-210 for many of their names. Montbéliardais emigration to New England lasted until 1755, *cf.*, Debard, "Les Montbéliardais au Nouvelle-Angleterre . . .," 257-260.

[20] Remarkably few of these documents have survived, but see Terrence M. Punch, "Les Montbéliardais en Nouvelle Écosse: une colonisation par des protestants étrangers au XVIIIe siècle (1750-1815), *Bulletin et Mémoires*, LXXXI (1985), 202, 204-205, and NSA. MG 4, Vol. 99 # 6a (Langille brothers), and MG 100, Vol. 113 # 25 (Bouteillier).

[21] Léopold Langille and his wife are mentioned in the passport of 3 April, without children. The ship's list of the *Betty*, made on 16 May, following, counts a *free freight* - a child below the age of four - with them. Although a birth date of 28 May 1752 has been seen for their first child, Catherine, it is clear from the two documents that the child was born in the interval 3 April/16 May 1752. As the only 28th within that window is 28 April, I take that as the child's likely date of birth.

the certificate of Jean-George Bouteillier of Étobon was dated 7 April 1752, nearly eight weeks before he embarked in the *Sally* from Rotterdam. Evidently, people took some time preparing for the journey from Montbéliard to Rotterdam.

French officials at Héricourt reported that Isaac Veuilamet left in May 1752. He was in the *Betty* when it sailed on the 16th of that month, so he lost no time in getting to Rotterdam.[22] Veuilamet was 36 years old and had a wife and young family. The report of his departure states of *Isaac Willamier, âgé de 40 ans, tixerand,* that *il a vendu des fonds pour 500 livres qu'il a emportées 500 livres.*[23] Since his village was in French territory (the seigneury of Héricourt), Veuilamet may have used some of his proceeds to travel across French territory to the Netherlands, which would have been an easier and quicker trip than going via the Rhine.

A German contemporary, Gottlieb Mittelberger, who travelled from Heilbronn to Rotterdam in 1751, wrote of his experiences a few years later and mentioned that his party had passed through thirty-six customs and toll stations in about 350 miles.[24] The Montbéliardais who travelled by the river began about Basel, possibly some further downstream at Strasbourg. Even the latter would be stopped and obliged to make a payment at ten toll stations between Strasbourg and Mainz, eleven between there and Cologne, and a further nine between Cologne and the Netherlands border. That amounts to thirty customs posts, not to mention

---

[22] Archives départementales du Doubs, E589[1] (Pigallet) (formerly E 1821 Babey).

[23] *Ibid.* We have his baptism record so we he know was actually 36 years old and that the figure in the report of his leaving Échavanne is an instance of "age-heaping", a tendency noticed in older documents, such as census and passenger lists. *Cf.,* T. Lynn Smith, *Demography: Principles and Methods* (Philadelphia, 1970), 152-157. Note that he was a weaver ("tixerand"), but in the *Betty*'s passenger list he is a farmer, another case of the bi-occupationalism earlier noted.

[24] Gottlieb Mittelberger, *Journey to Pennsylvania. 1756.* Oscar Handlin, ed. (Cambridge, Mass., 1960), 17.

three or four more posts to pass after an emigrant had entered the Netherlands.[25] Apart from this official picking of the emigrants' pockets there was the ever-present danger of being robbed by bandits, shippers, fellow passengers, and later by the ship's crews. Some emigrants were diverted by agents of rival destinations,.[26] while others were lured by specious promises, to such an extent that the records where a traveller began his journey might indicate an intention to emigrate to a destination quite different from that in which he wound up In short, the overland/river journey from Montbéliard to the seaport was hazardous, though most of the perils were man-made rather than due to natural forces, as at sea.

There is no need here to relate the privations of the sea voyage on immigrant ships in that period, as these have been extensively described by Winthrop Bell and other authors.[27] We should, however, note in the case of the 1752 voyages of Montbéliardais that the experience varied from ship to ship. Probably the major factor was the length of the voyage which depended entirely on the weather encountered once the ships had left the coast of Britain onto the north Atlantic.The *Betty* and the *Speedwell* fared best, taking 68 and 82 days for the crossing, respectively. There were 321 Montbéliardais aboard the two vessels and 304 landed at Halifax, a mortality of 5.3% which, while shocking by modern standards, was not remarkable for an immigrant voyage at that time. The *Pearl* took almost thirteen weeks for the crossing, while the luckless *Sally* knocked about the ocean for four months! Of the 104 Montbéliardais who took passage from Rotterdam in these two vessels, just 81 disembarked at Halifax, a mortality of 22.1%, an exceptionally

---

[25] Marianne S. Wokeck, *Trade in Strangers; The Beginnings of Mass Migration to North America* (University Park, PA, 1999), 120.

[26] An instance of this occurred in 1750 and involved Swiss who meant to come to Nova Scotia. *Cf.*, Winthrop Pickard Bell, *The "Foreign Protestants" and the Settlement of Nova Scotia* (Toronto, 1961), 137-139.

[27] *Cf.*, for example, Wokeck, 129-137, or Andreas Brinck, *Die deutsche Auswanderungswelle in die britischen Kolonien Nord-amerikas um die Mitte des 18. Jahrhunderts* (Stuttgart, 1993), 200-213.

high rate indeed, though not unsurpassed in contemporary experience.[28] Collectively for the four vessels, the Montbéliard mortality rate was 9.4%, compared to 12.8% for the German and Swiss passengers.

The winter of 1752-53 in Halifax winnowed the numbers of the Montbéliardais far more than had the sea voyage. Between the landing of the settlers in the late summer of 1752 and their departure to found Lunenburg late in May 1753 at least 96 of the 385 remainder had died, representing 22.6% of the original group or one-quarter of the survivors who reached Halifax. The deaths peaked in March, leaving little doubt that both contagion and the privations of winter in relatively exposed circumstances (e.g., barracks at the isthmus - Dutch Village Road area -- and on Georges Island) were responsible for this serious loss of life.[29]

III - IN NOVA SCOTIA

Winthrop P. Bell told the story of the Foreign Protestant immigration into Nova Scotia in the 1750s in great detail in *The "Foreign Protestants" and the Settlement of Nova Scotia*, while information about the several families has more recently been made available in a two-volume facsimile of Dr. Bell's *Register of the Foreign Protestants of Nova Scotia (ca. 1749-1770)*, edited by J. Christopher Young (Guelph, 2003). I shall, therefore, only draw attention to a few details concerning the Montbéliard contingent among the settlers.

---

[28] Klaus Wust, "The emigration Season of 1738 – Year of the Destroying Angel," *The Report: A Journal of German-American History,* 40 (1986), 21-56, mentions mortality in that harsh year as high as 35%. The identification and age of many of those who died at sea coming to Nova Scotia in 1752 will be found in the statistical appendix to this work.

[29] For an earlier and somewhat less complete computation of these deaths, refer to Terrence M. Punch, "L'effrayante mortalité des Mont-béliardais à Halifax en 1752-1753," *Bulletin et Mémoires*, CXX (1997), 295-303. The names and age cohorts of these deaths may be found in a statistical appendix to the present work. Of twenty children left orphaned by the deaths of their parents at sea or over the winter of 1752-53, two died in the Halifax Orphanage, and of the eighteen others only three or four turn up in later records of Halifax or Lunenburg, so the attrition of the original 425 was probably about 35-36%, a number not very different from the proportion (36.2%) who definitely remained in Nova Scotia. Also see appendix 7.

Foreign Protestants worked at redemption labour at Halifax over the winter of 1752-53. Fewer than 250 Montbéliardais were alive and in Nova Scotia when the settlers were taken to Lunenburg in the spring. Their number is difficult to say as precisely as one could wish, due to the inadequacy of the records and the largely undocumented evidence that many people simply left Nova Scotia or signed up in the British armed forces. Nor is the historian's task rendered any easier by the tendency of clergy and anglophone officials to mis-spell or deliberately change foreign names. Most English speakers were unfamiliar with the common German and French practice of calling people by the second of their given names. This sometimes makes it impossible, or nearly so, to discriminate among individuals severally named, for example, Anne-Marie, Marie-Catherine and Catherine-Anne. They were known to their countrymen as Marie, Catherine and Anne, but perhaps entered in English records as Anne, Marie and Catherine, respectively.

Through a series of swaps, the 150-200 Montbéliardais who remained in Lunenburg after 1753 would concentrate themselves in the Northwest Range of lots, an area still known as Northwest and Fauxbourg (French *faubourg*, meaning a suburb; local people kept a hint of proper French and said *fobo*).[30]

Until the settlers permanently moved from their town lots after 1760, George-F. Bailly from Héricourt conducted a French school, and had sixty pupils in 1754. On 28 October 1765 at Bailly's request, the French people at Lunenburg signed a testimonial on his behalf.[31]

Nous Soussignez, habitant de Lunenburg et Communicants de l'eglise francoise:

Certifions a qu'il appartiendra, que Mr. Bailly notre maitre d'ecole,

---

[30] Kenneth S. Paulsen, "Settlement and Ethnicity in Lunenburg, Nova Scotia, 1753 - 1800: A History of the Foreign Protestant Community." Unpublished Ph. D. thesis, University of Maine, 1996, chapter 2, especially the figures on pp. 29 and 35.

[31] Bell, 607-611. *Cf.*, Terrence M. Punch, "A Genealogy: George-Frédéric Bailly," in *Journal of the Royal Nova Scotia Historical Society,* 5 (2002), 154-168.

Envers nos enfants, q'ils les a toujours bien Eleve dans notre sainte Religion & qu'il n'a Epargne aucune peine pour en faire d'honetes gens tous les hyverts [hivers] qui est le meilleur temps que nous pouvons Envoyer nos Enfants, il les a toujours [?] montre a lire et a Ecrire avec un Soin infatigable en foy de quoy nous avons signe avec plaisir ce testimonial qu'il nous a demand & que ne contient que la pure verite.

Jean Sagarie [Lagarce]	Jaques Viennot
Leopold Vienot	Christof J. Veinot
Jean Dauphnie	George Bisset
Jean urban jeanPerrin	Nicolas X [his mark] Daree
David X [his mark] Langille	I. [Jean] Biset
Marc Bourgogne	Jaque X [his mark] Jodry
Jaque Melmethut	Adam Boulion
George X [his mark] Gratot	Joseph Contoy
P. lonney [Pierre Joney]	Louis Gourdon
Frideric Mason	Henry Schuply
André Jaillet[32]	George X [his mark] Taterie

Bailly reported to the Society for the Propagation of the Gospel (SPG) on 21 September 1765 that he could not tell the exact number of his students because they lived 2 to 10 miles from the town and were never assembled at one time, so that sometimes he had but 10 or 12, and at others twice that number. When parents let their children attend in summer he held school for three hours in the morning and for two hours 'after dinner'. In the winters he taught from 5 to 9 in the evening.

---

[32] Society for the Propagation of the Gospel in Foreign Parts, "Letters received (Originals) - B.25, Nova Scotia 1760 to 1786, item 56; and NSA, MG 1, Vol. 115, Vol. 5 #206. Note that 19 of the 22 French were Montbéliardais. Contoy, Gourdon and Schuply were Swiss. The preamble reads, in English: *We the undersigned residents of Lunenburg, communicants of the French church, certify to whom it may concern, that Mr. Bailly, our schoolmaster, has always taught our children well in our holy religion, and that he has spared no trouble to make them honourable people, [doing so] during winter which is always the best time when we can send our children. He has always taught them to read and write with tireless care, in witness of which we have been pleased to sign this testimonial, as he requested of us, and which states just the simple truth.*

He told Burton of the SPG on 10 April 1766 that he did not know what to do for books in the future. He had to copy them for the children's use, because of *the great poverty of the settlement* [my italics]. Bailly thanked Burton on 2 October 1766 for sending small French catechisms. He says the school was very small in summer as the parents required the help of the children on their farms. Bailly was acting as clerk in church, bell ringer, and teacher of the children in reading, writing, psalm singing and the recital of the catechism.

In a letter of 8 October 1765, Bailly gave the SPG a picture of some of the miseries besetting early Lunenburg, particularly with regard to dissenting sects then, and Indian attacks a few years previously. The small number of francophones was particularly hard hit by the raids, as Bailly reports

Dans la derniere [guerre] nos avons eu trente deux personnes de Massacrés dans le seul district de Lunenburg, parmis lesquelle il y'avait deux familles francais, de dix sept personnes entierement detruittes.[33]

He adds regarding the German Lunenburgers,

Il y a parmis des Alleman toutes sortes de sectes; y'avait des Lutheriens, des Calvinistes, des Anabaptistes, des trembleurs, et des presbyteriens.[34]

Perhaps due to their small number in relation to the German speakers, who outnumbered them by a ratio of 8:1, the Montbéliard and

---

[33] Translation: *During the late war* [Seven Year's War] *we had thirty-two people slain in the one district of Lunenburg, among them were two French families of seventeen people completely destroyed.* The Huguenot Payzants and their servants named Riovant and Langlois, and the widow Alison (Mrs. Trippeau by then) and her younger daughter, were these two families. Jean-George, a 9-year-old son of the Jeauné family was carried away; his fate has never been ascertained.

[34] Translation: *There are all sorts of sects among the Germans: there are Lutherans, Calvinists, Anabaptists, shakers, and Presbyterians.*

francophone Swiss families quickly used the English language, and it is doubtful that one heard much French spoken in Lunenburg after 1800. The Germans had Lutheran and Calvinist churches after 1770 in which theirs was the language of service and record, whereas the Montbéliardais, having attended the Church of England from the time of their arrival until twenty years later, generally did not return to the Lutheran church. Having to choose between a German or an English congregation, most of the Montbéliardais opted for the Anglican church, perhaps because they were used to attending an "official" church, or perhaps they saw socio-economic advantages in doing so. There was no francophone pastor at Lunenburg once Rev. Peter De La Roche left in 1786.

Another factor which undermined the survival of the French language and reduced the influence of the Montbéliardais minority at Lunenburg was their relocation to areas removed from the original townships laid out for the foreign Protestants. Many of the 1750-1752 settlers had remained in Halifax Town or been drawn there by employment during the Seven Years' War (1756-63), but the Montbéliard element formed little of that group. The1792/93 poll tax lists for the town of Halifax reveal just two exceptions. Laurilliard had come in 1749 after living in England and was not really part of the foreign Protestant migration at all, while David Jeanbas was concealed under the English-seeming name of David Chambers.[35]

Far more significant in the dispersion of the Montbéliard contingent were J. F. W. DesBarres, lieutenant-governor of Cape Breton Island, and John Parr, governor of Nova Scotia. The former enjoyed a long life, blessed by excellent health. His outstanding accomplishment was *The Atlantic Neptune* (1774-84), a series of charts and views of the eastern coast of America from Newfoundland to New

---

[35] NSA, RG 1, Vol. 444 (Halifax Poll Tax, 1792 and 1793).

York.[36] DesBarres entertained the hope of establishing a European style manor in Nova Scotia. He formed various manors near Windsor (Fort Frederick) and at Minudie, but it was to his lands along Northumberland Strait that he attracted twelve or fifteen of the Montbéliardais with their families.

A list dated 20 June 1781 contains *"Le nombre des familie qui son sur le tairan de mon Seigneur Josette frederi valet desbar hatateMigouche delen 1780."*[37] Thirteen tenants, all of them Montbéliardais, representing a total of about sixty-six souls, are shown. They shared nine surnames, written binet [Bigney], boutelier, graito, Jodri, langille, menigos [Mingo], mettatale, ma liar [Millard] and tateras [Tattrie]. By 1795 the name Boutilier was gone from that area, while the name of George Patterkin [Patriquin] figures in a "List of Tennants on the Estate of Tatamagouche . . ." which had been "obtained on the spot by Capt John Macdonald . . ."[38]

John Parr was governor of Nova Scotia at the end of the American Revolution and is remembered as the administrator who was faced by

---

[36] R.J. Morgan, "Joseph Frederick Wallet DesBarres," in the *Dictionary of Canadian Biography,* VI (Toronto, 1987), 192-197, is a generally reliable account of the man's career. Jean-Marc Debard, "The Family Origins of Joseph Frederick Wallet DesBarres: A Riddle Finally Solved," *Nova Scotia Historical Review,* 14:2 (1994), 108-122, proves that DesBarres had considerable connection with Montbéliard and a rather unusual family background.

[37] NSA, MG 1, Vol. 1183, series 5, Vol. 19, item 3667 (NAC mfm. C1459). I am indebted to Norris Whiston for drawing this document to my attention. *"The number of families which are on the lands of M. Joseph-Freédéric DesBarres at Tatamagouche in the year 1780."*

[38] NAC, *Desbarres Papers,* Vol. 4. Mather Byles DesBrisay, *History of the County of Lunenburg,* 2nd edition (Toronto, 1895), 501-506, tells of the murder of George F. Eminaud by two Boutilier brothers who had been living in 1791 at Tatamagouche. For their crime they were hanged.

the influx of Loyalists in 1783 and 1784.[39] Under Parr, the settlement of the northern and eastern shores of St. Margaret's Bay commenced in earnest. On 8 August 1786 John "Dofiney" was granted land at Hackett's Cove, one of several Montbéliardais from Lunenburg who received land in an area that came to be known as French Village.[40] The poll tax lists of 1792 and 1793 name fifteen such settlers on that coastline, sharing the surnames *Boutilier, Dauphinee,* Jeanperrin, Jodrey, *Jollimore,* Mingo and Marriot. This represents about seventy to seventy-five people. While the italicized names remained at St. Margaret's Bay a quarter century later, the others had gone elsewhere, to be replaced by Montbéliardais named Burgoyne, Dorey, Grono and Mason, in all forming thirty-six households.[41]

The extent to which these out-migrations impacted on the Montbéliard presence in the Lunenburg area is made evident by comparing the number of Montbéliardais grown men in Lunenburg to those known to be elsewhere: St. Margaret's Bay 15, Tatamagouche 12, Halifax 2, for a total of 30. The poll tax for Lunenburg, Chester and New Dublin townships, together forming modern Lunenburg County, reveal about 45 adult males of Montbéliardais birth or parentage.[42] The absence of fully forty percent of the total number of Montbéliardais families rendered them a very small minority in a considerably larger pool of German-speakers living in a province that was rapidly acquiring, both from the British Isles and the new United States, a majority of native anglophones. It is scarcely surprising that within two or three generations,

---

[39] Peter Burroughs, "John Parr," the *Dictionary of Canadian Biography,* IV (Toronto, 1979),192-197.

[40] *Place-Names and Places of Nova Scotia* (Halifax, 1967), 223, 270.

[41] NSA, RG 20, Series "C", Vol. 88, item #174, return of settlers dated 27 June 1817. Servants aside, these households contained 138 family members.

[42] NSA, RG 1, Vol. 444, docs. 23, 24; Vol. 444½, docs. 1, 2 (various years 1791, 1792 and 1795).

none of the Montbéliardais descendants used the French language at all. In time, intermarriage with German and English families completed the process of assimilating the Montbéliardais.

The federal census of Canada, taken in 1901, recorded 7,029 residents of Nova Scotia who had one of fewer than thirty Montbéliardais surnames then in the province. More than half of these individuals bore the names Langille, Boutilier, Jodrey or Veinot. We do not know how many had mothers, grandmothers, or great-grand-mothers of Montbéliardais origins. A reasonable estimate would be that approximately 15,000 Montbéliard descendants lived in Nova Scotia a century and a half after the immigration of the 1750s. In 2006, following the passage of little more than another century, the total within Nova Scotia was more than three times the figure reported in 1901.

Considering the major emigration from Nova Scotia since the nineteenth century, the small Montbéliardais migration of 1752 probably planted the roots of well over 160,000 living people across North America.[43] The results justify an observation made by Colonel Charles Lawrence to Governor Peregrine Hopson in 1754, when he wrote that "The Montbéliard people are very tractable, and tho' not half so strong [i.e., numerous] as the others, perform double the labour."[44] The seed may have been small, but the harvest is plentiful.

---

[43] As one example of the outflow of Montbéliardais descendants from Nova Scotia to the United States, there was the emigration of two grandsons of Jean-Urbain Jeanperrin (p. 104), namely James John Perrin, born 6 Feb 1789, and his brother John Frederick Perrin, born 13 June 1792, in 1838. They sailed from Pictou, NS, and arrived in Bristol, Rhode Island, on 9 August 1838, with their wives and eighteen children, on their way to Ohio. See Maureen A. Taylor, compiler, *Rhode Island Passenger Lists* (Baltimore: Genealogical Publishing Co., Inc., 1995), 218-9.

[44] Bell, 441.

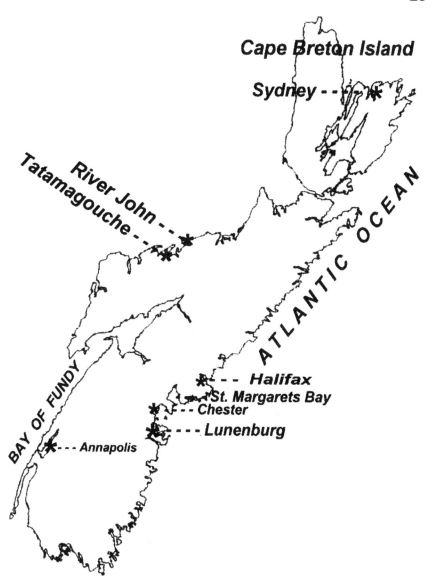

Map 1 - Some Montbéliard Locations in Nova Scotia

MONTBÉLIARD

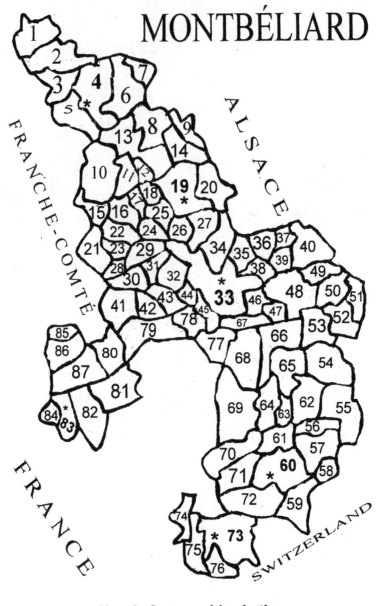

**Map 2: Communities in the
Principality of Montbéliard**
(Key on the facing page)

Key to communities on facing map of Montbéliard

1 - Magny Danigon
2 - Clairegoutte
3 - Frédéric-Fontaine
4 - * Étobon
5 - Belverne
6 - Chenebier
7 - Échavanne
8 - Chagey
9 - Mandrevillars
10 - Champey
11 - Coisevaux
12 - Couthenans
13 - Luze
14 - Échenans-sous-
    Mont-Vaudois
15 - Le Vernoy
16 - Trémoins
17 - Verlans
18 - Byans
19 - * Héricourt
20 - Brevilliers
21 - Désandans
22 - Aibre
23 - Semondans
24 - Laire
25 - Tavey
26 - Vyans
27 - Bussurel
28 - Échenans-sur-l'Étang
29 - Raynans

30 - St.-Julien
31 - Issans
32 - Allondans
33 - * MONTBÉLIARD
34 - Bethoncourt
35 - Grand-Charmont
36 - Nommay
37 - Dambenois
38 - Vieux-Charmont
39 - Brognard
40 - Allenjoie
41 - Ste.-Marie
42 - Présentevillers
43 - Dung
44 - Ste.-Suzanne
45 - Courcelles
46 - Exincourt
47 - Taillecourt
48 - Étupes
49 - Fesches-le-Châtel
50 - Dempierre-les-Bois
51 - Badeval
52 - Beaucort
53 - Dasle
54 - Vandoncourt
55 - Abbévillers
56 - Meslières
57 - Glay
58 - Dannemarie
59 - Villars-les-Blamont

60 - * Blamont
61 - Roches-les-Blamont
62 - Hérimoncourt
63 - Thulay
64 - Bondeval
65 - Seloncourt
66 - Audincourt
67 - Arbouans
68 - Valentigney
69 - Mandeure
70 - Écurcey
71 - Autechaux
72 - Pierrefontaine
73 - Montécheroux/
    * Clémont
74 - Villars
75 - Noirefontaine
76 - Liebvillars
77 - Voujaucourt
78 - Bart
79 - Bavans
80 - Lougres
81 - Colombier-Fontaine
82 - St.- Maurice
83 - * Châtelot
84 - Blussangeaux
85 - Brétigney
86 - Beutal
87 - Longevelle

Note: The main body of the *County of Montbéliard* consisted of twenty-six places (#30-52, 67, 78-79), as well as two detached exclaves: Abbévillers and Beutal, numbers 55 and 86 on Map 1, in all amounting to twenty-eight places. Its recognized seigneury of Étobon had six villages (#1-5,10). Héricourt lordship amounted to twenty-three villages (#6-9, 11-29); Blamont lordship nineteen communities (#53-54, 56-66, 68-72, 77); Châtelot lordship seven villages (#80-84, 86-87), while the tiny seigneury of Clémont had only four (#73-76). Communities marked with an asterisk (*) were the historic centres of the several seigneuries.

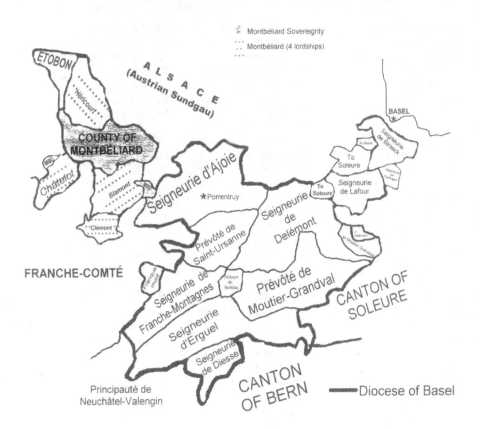

Map 3: The Relation of Montbéliard to its Neighbours, ca. 1675

Abbaye = Lands of an Abbey   Prévôté = Deanery
Principauté = Principality   Seigneurie = Lordship

Soleure = Canton of Solothurn

Map 4 - Part of Schickard's Map of Montbéliard (1616)

Wilhelm Schickhard was born at Herrenberg in Württemberg in 1592, and died of the bubonic plague in 1635. He received the degrees of bachelor (1609) and master (1611) of arts from the University of Tübingen, and was ordained a Lutheran minister in 1613. He became professor of Hebrew (1619) and of Astronomy (1631) at Tübingen. He made advances in map making, such that his work was a considerable improvement over earlier cartography. He was a noted engraver in both wood and copperplate. The map above is an example of his work. Despite some flaws, his designs for a calculator date from 1623, twenty years before Pascal made such a device. Schickhard was regularly employed by Duke Friedrich who ruled both Württemberg and Montbéliard.

APPENDIX A: TABLES & LISTS

1) MONTBÉLIARDAIS IMMIGRANTS OF 1752 BY VESSEL

The spellings of the names are those found in the primary document. The age and occupation are those given to the clerk at Rotterdam in 1752. Discrepancies and other observations are dealt with in the genealogical section. Those counted as *men* and *women* were full freights, i.e., they were over the age of 14 and had to pay the full fare. The *half freights* were those aged between 4 and 14, for whom half the fare was collected and half the quantity of rations issued. Those under 4 years of age travelled free, but were allocated no extra space in the vessel. "Heads" gives the total number of persons in each family group. Sons aged 15 and over appeared under their own names. For two vessels - the *Betty* and the *Speedwell* - people were listed as they were taken on board the vessel at Rotterdam. In the case of the *Pearl* and the *Sally* the people were listed according to the number of "heads" from single people up to the larger family groups. Forty-nine Montbéliardais, a total of 136 people, were shown in the *Betty*. The *Pearl* transported seven families or 28 Montbéliardais. *Sally* had 28 and 76, respectively. The largest number - 185 souls - formed 49 families in the *Speedwell*. In all, we have143 families, consisting of 425 people. The order below is name, age, occupation: man, woman, half fares, free fares, and *heads*.

(A) BETTY

Pierre Amêt, 56, farmer: 1.1.0.0.2
Jacques Begin, 25, farmer: 1.1.0.0.2
Jacques Bejet, 43, farmer: 1.1.2.1.5
Jean George Bejet, 17, farmer: 1.0.0.0.1
Jacques Biguenet, 22, farmer: 1.0.0.0.1
Mark Bourgogne, 33, farmer: 1.1.3.1.6
Jean Bouteillier, 29, joiner: 1.1.0.0.2
George Boutilier, 23, mason: 1.0.0.0.1
Urbain Certier, 34, farmer: 1.1.2.0.4
Frederick Clemenson, 18, farmer: 1.0.0.0.1
Pierre Coulon, 46, joiner: 1.1.3.1.6
Pierre Coulon fils, 19, joiner: 1.0.0.0.1
David Coulon, 17, joiner: 1.0.0.0.1

Nicolaas Daré, 42, farmer: 1.1.2.2.6
Pierre Demay, 26, farmer: 1.1.0.0.2
Pierre Fevre, 24, mason: 1.1.1.1.4
Jean Pierre Fevre, 17, mason: 1.0.0.0.1
Frederik Gogel, 28, miller: 1.1.1.0.3
Jacques Frederick Grandjean, 21, farmer: 1.0.0.0.1
Jacob Jacot, 30, shoemaker: 1.2.1.1.5
Jonas Jacot, 38, stonecutter: 1.1.0.0.2
Abraham Jacque, 48, farmer: 1.1.2.1.5
Jaques Frederick Jacquin, 45, schoolmaster: 2.1.2.1.6
Jacque Jaudry, 27, farmer: 1.0.0.0.1
Jean Jaudry, 54, farmer: 1.3.1.0.5
Jean George Jaudry, 24, farmer: 1.0.0.0.1
Mark Elie Jaudry, 26, shoemaker: 1.0.0.0.1
Jean Jacques Jeanbas, 25, weaver: 1.1.0.0.2
David Jeanbas, 18, cutter: 1.0.0.0.1
Pierre Jolimoy, 50, farmer: 1.0.2.0.3
Nicolaas LaGarce, 23, farmer: 1.0.0.1.2
Jean LaGarce, 33, farmer: 1.1.0.1.3
David Langile, 31, joiner: 1.0.0.0.1
Leopold Langille, 24, joiner: 1.1.0.1.3
Mathieu Langile, 26, farmer: 1.0.0.0.1
Jean L'eau, 27, mason: 1.1.0.0.2
Daniel Mallbon, 40, farmer: 1.2.3.0.6
Frederick Maliard, 45, farmer: 1.4.3.0.8
Pierre Maliard, 15, farmer: 1.0.0.0.1
Jean Mathieu. 21, farmer: 1.2.1.0.4
Jean Petterquin, 28, joiner: 1.1.0.0.2
Jean Pettrequin, 21, farmer: 1.0.0.0.1
David Robert, 18, farmer: 1.1.2.0.4
Pierre Ubray, 18, farmer: 1.0.0.0.1
Jacques Tisseran, 29, farmer: 1.1.1.2.5
Isaac Veuilamie, 36, farmer: 1.2.0.1.4
Leonard Veuilamêt, 17, farmer: 1.0.0.0.1
Leopold Vienot, 48, farmer: 1.1.2.0.4
Jacques Vienot, 15, farmer: 1.0.0.0.1

(B) PEARL

Jean Pierre Islan, 40, smith: 1.2.2.1.6
Pierre LaGarce, 42, farmer: 1.1.1.0.3
Jean George Lods, 18, farmer: 1.0.0.0.1
Jean Jacques Lods, 38, mason: 1.1.3.1.6
Pierre Mariett, 16, farmer: 1.0.0.0.1
Étienne Marriett, 40, farmer: 1.1.3.1.6
Jacques Nardin, 40, farmer: 1.1.1.2.5

(C) SALLY

George Frederick Baillie, 25, farmer: 1.1.0.1.3
Jean Nicollas Bouteillier, 21, farmer: 1.0.0.0.1
Jacques Bouttelier, 17, farmer: 1.0.0.0.1
Jacques Boutellier, 33, weaver: 1.3.1.1.6
Jean George Bouteillier, 50, joiner: 1.2.2.0.5
Daniel Clemenson, 36, smith: 1.1.0.0.2
Jean George Datterai, 30, farmer: 1.2.0.0.3
Samuel Duré, 24, taylor: 1.0.0.0.1
George Frederik Fenaut: 24, gunsmith 1.0.0.0.1
Jean George Gretaux, 35, joiner: 1.1.3.1.6
Jean George Grosrenaud, 36, farmer: 1.2.1.1.5
Pierre Hugenot, 19, farmer: 1.0.0.0.1
Jean Jacques Langile, 16, farmer: 1.0.0.0.1
David Langile, 34, farmer: 1.1.1.2.5
Jean L'Eau, 40, miller: 1.0.0.0.1
François Louis, 27, smith: 1.0.0.0.1
André Macé, 20, baker: 1.0.0.0.1
Jean Christoph Megnerai, 17, farmer: 1.0.0.0.1
Jean Nicolaus Metin, 17, farmer: 1.0.0.0.1
Abram Monnier, 38, farmer: 1.1.3.1.6
Isaac Monnier, 16, farmer: 1.0.0.0.1
Pierre Surl'Eau, 28, farmer: 1.0.0.0.1
Jean George Veutilot, 36, thatcher: 1.2.1.1.5
Pierre Vurpeillot, 40, sawyer: 1.1.1.1.4

To these we may add,
from Grunstadt:
Jean Christoph Malliardt, 22, farmer: 1.0.0.0.1
from "Württemberg":
Pierre Vallet, 36, farmer: 1.1.0.2.4
Jean Minegare, 43, farmer: 1.1.2.0.4
"Swiss":
André Jaillier, 26, skinner: 2.1.1.2.6, of whom 2 were born in
    Switzerland and 4 were of Montbéliard.

(D) SPEEDWELL

George Frederik Allisçon, 40, wagoner: 2.1.2.0.5
Pierre Banvard, 50, weaver: 1.2.0.0.3
David Banvard, 23, weaver: 1.1.0.0.2
Jean George Besançon, 44, farmer: 1.2.3.1.7
Adam Boullion, 31, joiner: 1.0.0.0.1
Jacques Bourgois, 40, miller: 1.1.2.1.5
George Bouttelier, 26, weaver: 1.0.0.0.1
Abram Calame & Son, 52, masons: 2.3.2.0.7
Jean Carlin, 38, joiner: 1.1.2.0.4
Jean Carling, 38, joiner: 1.1.0.2.4
Etienne Certier, 18, weaver: 1.0.0.0.1
Jean Nicolaas Coulon, 66, & Sons, farmers: 3.1.0.0.4
Guiliaume Cugné, 48, mason: 1.3.3.0.7
Jacques Curié, 27, wagoner: 1.1.0.0.2
David Dauphiné, 25, taylor: 1.2.0.1.4
Jean Dauphiné, 26, shoemaker: 1.0.0.0.1
George Donzell, 40, farmer: 1.1.0.0.2
Pierre Duperrin, 46, taylor: 1.2.2.1.6
Jean Nicolaas Dupuis, 27, mason: 1.1.1.0.3
Jean Durand, 24, stonecutter: 1.0.0.0.1
Frederick Emonaud, 24, farmer: 1.1.0.0.2
Samuel Emonaud, 50, farmer: 1.1.2.0.4
Jean Abraham Greignaud, 46, farmer: 1.1.1.0.3
Pierre Humbert, 24, weaver: 1.0.0.0.1
Jean Christoph Jaudry, 44, farmer: 2.2.3.1.8
Pierre Jaunné, 32, farmer: 2.1.2.2.7

Jean Urban Jeanperrain, 32, stonecutter: 1.0.0.0.1
Jean George Leau, 20, farmer: 1.0.0.0.1
George Leau, 30, joiner: 1.1.0.2.4
David L'eau, 46, farmer: 1.1.0.0.2
Jacques Mallmaveu, 36, thatcher: 1.1.0.0.2
*Frederick Mason, 31, farmer: 1.1.2.2.6
*François Mason, 26, farmer: 1.0.0.0.1
*Jean Jacques Roland, 60,farmer: 1.2.1.1.5
*these three are bracketed on the list.
Jean George Menegau, 44, weaver: 2.2.3.0.7
Jean Frederick Menegau, 38, farmer: 1.2.4.1.8
Jacques Christoph Metatall, 50, tanner: 1.3.1.0.5
Jean Nicolaas Metadall, 30, farmer: 1.1.2.1.5
Jean George Metadall, 20, mason: 1.0.0.0.1
Abraham Milliet, 31, gardener: 1.2.0.0.3
Jean Pierre Mourleaux, 48, farmer: 1.1.3.0.5
Jacques Nardin, 56, & Sons, farmers: 3.1.2.0.6
Jean Jacques Nardin, 36, farmer: 1.1.0.2.4
Jean George Quidore, 36, thatcher: 1.1.2.1.5
Vernier Rigoulett, 40, farmer: 1.1.3.1.6
Abraham Robert, 30, mason: 1.1.0.1.3
Daniel Thom, 31, mason: 1.1.0.0.2
Jean Vuilquie, 36, farmer: 1.1.4.1.7
Pierre Vuielquie, 50, farmer: 1.0.0.0.1

An analysis of the 133 heads of family reveals rural occupations: 73 farmers (54.8%), 13 joiners (9.8%), 11 masons and 3 stonecutters (10.5%), 8 weavers (6%), 3 each of millers, smiths, shoemakers, tailors and thatchers, two wagoners, and one apiece of baker, cutter, gardener, gunsmith, sawyer, skinner and tanner. The one educated man, a schoolmaster, left immediately.

Forty-four were single men, about half of them being the son (14), stepson (1) or younger brother (6) of other immigrants. Though such youths were obligated to work off a full fare there was the compensation that by so doing they were entitled to a full-sized land grant at Lunenburg.

The average age of the 133 men was 32.225 years, which is about 32 years, 2 months and 3 weeks. Jean Nicolas Coulon, 66, was the eldest man, while there was a pair of 15 year-olds at the other extremity of the age spectrum: Pierre Maillard and Jacques Veinot. Two tendencies should be noted regarding the stated ages of the immigrants. Some men, for fear of being turned away by the Rotterdam agent, reduced their age to bring it more into line with what they imagined the recruiting officials sought. Rounding off was another feature of the declared ages: no men were aged 39 or 41, but ten were 40; none were 49 or 51, but six were 50. Rather than duplicate the explanations, I shall deal with age differences between primary documentation and the ships' lists, *passim*, in the genealogical section.

One further observation is that the Montbéliardais in the *Betty* had a significantly younger average age than had those in the *Speedwell*. In the former, the average male head of family was 29 years and 4 months old, whereas in the latter vessel, this age was 36 years and 5 months. The *Sally*, at 32 years and 4 months, and the *Pearl*, at 33 years and 5 months, fall between. Mortality in the last pair of vessels was high, at 15.5%, due to taking three and four months to cross the Atlantic. *Betty* and *Speedwell* crossed in between 68 and 82 days, with mortality rates of 4.3% and 6%, respectively. Because of this variable we cannot draw an inference that mortality related to the age of the passengers.

2) UNIDENTIFIED PASSENGERS

The passenger lists contain references to 25 individuals who cannot be identified with confidence from the available records. Four persons surnamed Curier or Curié, and two women surnamed Richard, appear later in records, and were of Montbéliard origins. These individuals presumably account for six of the twenty-five, although we cannot confidently tell with which household or family, if any, they came to Nova Scotia. The 25 who cannot be explained travelled with the following men:
A) In the *Betty* - Jean-Nicolaas Daré: a child below age 4 (died at sea)
B) In the *Pearl* - Étienne Mariette: a child (died at sea)

C) In the *Sally* - Jacques Bouteillier: 2 women
   Jean-George Gretteau: 2 children aged 4-14
   André Jaillet: 1 child 4-14, 1 child below age 4
   David Langille: 2 children below age 4 (stepsons?)
   Jean-George Tetteray: 1 woman (died at sea; wife?)
   Pierre Virpillot: 1 child 4-14 (died at sea)
D) In the *Speedwell* -
   Pierre-Jacques Bourgeois: 1 child below age 4
   Jean Carlin 1st: 1 child below age 4 (died at sea)
   David Dauphiné: 2 women and 1 child below age 4
   Jean-Abraham Greignaud: 1 child 4-14 (died at sea)
   Jean-Frédéric Ménégaux: 1 woman or 1 child 4-14
   (died at sea)
   Jacques-Christoph Mettetal:1 woman (died at sea)
   Jean-Nicolaas Mettetal: 1 child 4-14 (died at sea)
   Jean-George Quidore: 1 woman (died at sea) and 1 child 4-14
   Pierre Vuilquet: 1 child

*Montbéliardais farmstead of the type built in
the later eighteenth-century*

3) MONTBÉLIARDAIS DEATHS AT SEA, 1752

Age/Sex	Betty	Speed -well	Sally	Pearl	Total	Comments
Male 14 +	1	2	5	1	9	
Female 14 +	1	3	6	1	11	20 adults
Male 4/14	0	0	0	0	0	
Female 4/14	0	0	0	2	2	
Unknown 4/14	0	1	0	0	1	3 ages 4-14
Male 0/4	0	2	1	0	3	
Female 0/4	1	1	5	2	9	
Unknown 0/4	1	3	0	2	6	18 not yet 4
Total	4	12	17	8	41	
Male	1	4	6	1	12	
Female	2	4	11	4	21	
Unknown	1	4	0	3	8	

BETTY (4):
1 man - Frédéric Clemençon; 1 woman - Catherine-Marguerite Jeaudry; 1 female 0/4 - Anne-Elisabeth Lagarce; 1 unknown 0/4 - ... Daré

SPEEDWELL (12):
2 men - David Leau, Jacques Nardin; 3 women - Françoise Banvard, Catherine Ménégaux, Mrs. ... Quidore; 1 unknown age 4/14 - ... Greignaud; 2 male 0/4 - Jean-Jacques Jeaudry, Frédéric Leau; 1 female 0/4 - Marie-Maguerite Mettetal; 3 unknown 0/4 - ... Carlin, ... Carlin, ... Mettetal.

SALLY (17):
5 men - Jean-George Bouteiller, Daniel Clemençon, Jean Migneré.
Abraham Monnier, Jean-George Veutilot; 6 women - Sara Bouteiller,
Anne-Catherine Gretteau, Marguerite Grosrenault, Anne-Françoise
Monnier, Mrs. ... Tetterai, Elise Veutilot; 1 male 0/4 - Daniel-Frédéric
Jaillet; 5 female 0/4 - Jeanne-Marguerite Bouteiller, Anne-Catherine
Monnier, Jeanne Monnier, Catherine-Elisabeth Veutilot, ... Virpillot.

PEARL (8):
1 man - Pierre Mariette; 1 woman - Frédérique-Sybille Leau; 2 female
4/14 - Judith-Marguerite Leau, Marie-Madeleine Nardin; 2 female 0/4 -
Anne Nardin, Susanne Nardin; 2 unknown 0/4 - ... Iselin, ... Mariette.

4) FATE OF THE MONTBÉLIARD IMMIGRANTS OF 1752

	Betty	Speed-well	Sally	Pearl	Total	%
Boarded ship	135	184	75	28	422	-
Died at sea	4	12	17	8	41	9.7
Landed at Halifax	131	172	58	20	381	90.3
1752/3 died Halifax	30	50	11	5	96	22.7
Survived ...	101	122	47	15	285	67.5
in Nova Scotia	60	64	23	8	155	36.7
in United States	22	13	0	0	35	8.3
in New Brunswick	0	1	0	1	2	0.4
location unknown*	19	44	24	6	93	22.0

* between 15 and 20 young men born 1725/44 might have enlisted
and not returned to live in Nova Scotia thereafter. Three reputed
passengers, Mrs. Carlin (*Speedwell*), Daniel Malbon (*Betty*), and Mrs. D.
Clemençon (*Sally*) did not, in fact, take passage. The women remained
in Montbéliard, and Malbon had gone to Boston in 1751 in the *Priscilla*.

5) DISTRIBUTION WITHIN NOVA SCOTIA

	Betty	Speed-well	Sally	Pearl	Total	%
Lunenburg	44	49	13	4	110	71
Halifax	8	4	4	3	19	12
Strait	7	7	5	1	20	13
Cape Breton	1	2	1	0	4	2.6
Hants County	0	2	0	0	2	1.3
Total	60	64	23	8	155	100

6) HALIFAX ORPHANAGE, 1752-53, ADMISSIONS OF MONTBÉLIARDAIS

The information is presented in the order: child's name, age, date of admission, ship on which arrived; to whom put out, date. Those marked with an asterisk (*) were placed in the Orphanage immediately upon landing in Halifax; parents dead.

Bouteillier, George-Frédéric, 8, 16 Dec 1752, Sally; to Spry, carpenter, 23 May 1753.

Bouteillier, Jeanne, 12, 16 Dec 1752, Sally; to Green, labourer, 2 May 1753.

*Clemençon, Jacques-Christoph, 12, 25 Sep 1752, Sally; to [John] Jones, sailmaker, 3 March 1753.

Fevre, Jacques 1st, 12, 27 Dec 1752, Betty; to George Gerrish, blacksmith, 28 March 1753.

Fevre, Jacques 2nd, 2, 17 Mar 1753, Betty; died 10 Apr 1753.

Goguel, Frédéric, 3, 29 Mar 1753, Betty; to Richard Wenman, 31 Aug 1758.

Leau, Claudine, 5, 26 Oct 1752, Pearl; to Walter Manning, 31 July 1758.

Leau, Étienne, 1¾, 26 Oct 1752, Pearl; to James Monck,
    Esq., 17 Nov 1752.
Leau, Jeanne-Catherine, 10, 26 Oct 1752, Pearl; to
    Sharringburg, butcher [J. Martin Scherrenberg, a foreign
    Protestant from Hamburg], 16 March 1753.
Migneré, Jacques, 8, 27 Oct 1752, Sally; to Mrs. Winsent,
    2 June 1753; re-admitted on 23 July 1753, and put
    out to Dr. Bagster [Baxter], 16 April 1754.
Migneré, Jean-Pierre, 13, 27 Oct 1752, Sally; to Richard
    Wenman, 8 Nov 1752.
*Monnier, Isaac, 14, 25 Sep 1752, Sally; to William Best,
    mason, 19 Oct 1752.
*Monnier, Jean-Jacques, 10, 25 Sep 1752, Sally; to John Coddman,
    shopkeeper, 18 Jan 1753.
*Monnier, Susanne, 5, 25 Sep 1752, Sally; to Mrs. Farland,
    5 March 1756.
Nardin, Jean-Christoph, 2, 20 Mar 1753, Speedwell; died
    20 March 1753.
Nardin, Jean-François, 5, 19 Mar 1753, Speedwell; still there, 3 Nov
    1761.
Nardin, Jean-Pierre, 4, 20 Mar 1753, Speedwell; to Dr. John
    Grant, 29 June 1753.
Nardin, Susanne, 10, 20 Mar 1753, Speedwell; to Lieut. Middleton,
    21 Oct 1755.
*Veutilot, Catherine-Elisabeth, 12, 25 Sep 1752, Sally; to
    Richard Wenman, 14 Oct 1752.
*Veutilot, Éléanore, 9, 25 Sep 1752, Sally; to Capt. John
    Gallant, 19 June 1753.

Apart from Frédéric Goguel none of the others appear, at least
recognizably, in Halifax or Lunenburg vital records afterwards, nor do
any appear to have taken the names of those to whom they were
put out.

7) DEATHS OF MONTBÉLIARD IMMIGRANTS AT HALIFAX, 1752/53

Between the arrival of the immigrant ships at Halifax in summer 1752 and the removal of the settlers to Lunenburg in spring 1753, death carried off 22.6% of the newcomers from Montbéliard. With one exception, all the deaths seem to be attributable to natural causes, whether individual illness, contagion or the cumulative effects of a sea voyage, privation and an unfamiliar environment. We possess three major sources of information about this high mortality:

1. The Burial Registers of St. Paul's Church in Halifax and those of St. John's in Lunenburg. These frequently overlap or contradict one another or other sources. An error by an unknown transcriber further reduces their reliability by placing many deaths in the wrong year, as well as erring in reading the earlier record. There are 69 burial records available to us from these rather imperfect sources, of which 32 are the unique record of a death/burial. That the person died is corroborated by their disappearance from other records at or after the burial entry.

2. The Victualling Lists which indicated the delisting of a deceased person by the entry of "DD" by the names of such people. This source is more accurate than the church burials, if only because the originals can still be consulted. There are 37 DD records available to us, 15 of them the sole record of a death. Again, the absence of such parties from later records attests to the fact that they had, indeed, died.

3. Steinfort's monthly musters of the Foreign Protestants in February, March and April 1753. They thus cover only three months or about one-third of the period in question. Nonetheless they account for a further 32 records of mortality, though just two are unique records. Since Steinfort appears the most accurate of the three major sources, his particular value is as a corrective or corroborative one.

There are reports of two deaths from the Halifax Orphan House, one being the sole record of that death. A further six deaths may be inferred by the disappearance of an individual from a family group between the end of one victualling period and the opening of the next victualling list. In all, then, we possess 146 records in support of 96 deaths among the Montbéliard arrivals of 1752. Of these deaths, 56 are reported uniquely, 10 appear in all three main sources, and 30 figure in two sources, thus: 18 appear in the church burial registers and in Steinfort's musters, 9 turn up in the church burials and the victualling lists, 2 can be seen in Steinfort's and the victualling lists, and one in the Orphan House and victualling.

A final caution is in order. As we have seen, there are 93 persons whose fate we do not know. Eleven unnamed individuals landed in Halifax with these families. Two Richard women and four Curié individuals *may* account for six of the eleven. Assuming that to be the case, there remain five people who reached Halifax and whose deaths are not found, or at least recognized, in any extant record.

Name of Person	Burial Date	Steinfort's Muster	Victualling List
Alison, George-Frédéric	2. 5.1753		
Amet, Catherine Langille	21.3.1753	13.4.1753	
Amet, Pierre	16. 3.1753	16.3.1753	
Banvard, Eve	13.3.1753	16.3.1753	
Besançon, Jeanne			DD Aug/Oct 1752
Besançon, Marie-Elisabeth			Gone Oct 52/Feb 53
Bizés, Claudine	13.3.1753	16.3.1753	DD Feb/Apr 1753
Bizés, Éléanore	2/3.1.1753		DD Dec 52/Feb 1753
Calame, Jeanette	17.11.1752		DD Oct/Dec 1752
Calame, Susanne			DD Aug/Oct 1752
Carlin, Catherine	1.4.1753	13.4.1753	
Carlin, Jean	17.3.1753	13.4.1753	
Carlin, Judith-Marguerite	28.9.1752		
Coulon, David	16.4.1753		

Name of Person	Burial Date	Steinfort's Muster	Victualling List
Coulon, Jean-Jacques	20.2.1753	16.2.1753	[delayed burial?]
Coulon, Nicolas			DD Aug/Oct 1752
Coulon, Susanne	7.11.1752		
Demet, Marie	28/30.3.1753	13.4.1753	
Duperrin, Anne-Marie	25/6.12.1752		DD Dec 52/Feb 1753
Duperrin, Marguerite Cath.	30.1.1753		
Duperrin, Pierre-Isaac	19.1.1753		DD Dec 52/Feb 1753
Dupuis, Jean-Nicolas	24.11.1752		
Duré, Samuel	20.2.1753	16.2.1753	[delayed burial?]
Emoneau, Anne-Elisabeth	28/31.3.1753	13.4.1753	
Emoneau, Samuel-Frédéric.			DD Aug/Oct 1752
Euvrai, Pierre	15.3.1753	13.4.1753	
Fevre, Catherine	12.1.1753		
Fevre, Jacques	+10.4.1753		[Orphan House]
Fevre, Pierre	14.3.1753	16.3.1753	
Goguel, Frédéric-Charles		13.4.1753	DD Feb/Apr 1753
Goguel, Marguerite	31.10.1752		
Greignaud, Jean-Abraham			DD Feb/Apr 1753
Gretteau, Louis-Nicolas	19.4.1753		
Grosrenauld, Anne-Marg'te			DD Aug/Oct 1752
Grosrenauld, Pierre			DD Feb/Apr 1753
Jacot, Catherine	20.10.1752		
Jacot, Madeleine	27.12.1752		

Name of Person	Burial Date	Steinfort's Muster	Victualling List
Jacque, Abraham	14.11.1752		
Jacque, Elisabeth		16.2.1753	
Jaillet, Marie-Madeleine			Gone Oct 52/Feb 53
Jeaudry, Anne-Catherine	28.12.1752		DD Dec52/Feb 1753
Jeaudry, Catherine	9.3.1753	16.3.1753	DD Feb/Apr 1753
Jeaudry, Jean-George	22.2.1753	16.3.1753	DD Feb/Apr 1753
Jeaudry, Jean-Jacques			DD Aug/Oct 1752
Jeaudry, Joseph	26.10.1752		
Jeaudry, Pierre	24.2.1753	16.3.1753	DD Feb/Apr 1753
Jeauné, Samuel			DD Aug/Oct 1752
Jolimois, Jean-Nicolas	9.5.1753		
Jolimois, Pierre	10.3.1753	16.3.1753	
Lagarce, Elisabeth	14.4.1753		
Lagarce, Pierre	12.3.1753	16.3.1753	DD Feb/Apr 1753
Langille, Marie-Catherine	29.9.1752		
Leau, Jean-Jacques			DD Aug/Oct 1752
Leau, Marie-Madeleine	8.2.1753		
Malbon, Anne-Marie	5.4.1753		
Malbon, Susanne-Elisabeth	17.3.1753		DD Feb/Apr 1753
Malmahu, Nanette-Catherine	16.4.1753		
Mariette, Marie	3.3.1753	16.3.1753	
Mariette, Michel	28.11.1752		
Masson, Nanette			Gone Oct 52/Feb53

Name of Person	Burial Date	Steinfort's Muster	Victualling List
Ménégaux, Anne			DD Aug/Oct 1752
Ménégaux, Jean-Frédéric	3.12.1752		
Ménégaux, Jean-George	19.10.1752		[accidental death]
Ménégaux, Jean-George	3/30.12.1752		
Ménégaux, Susanne-Margt.			Gone Oct/Dec 1752
Migneré, Jean-Christoph	28.9.1752		
Nardin, Anne-Judith		16.3.1753	DD Feb/Apr 1753
Nardin, Jacques	23.1.1753	16.2.1753	
Nardin, Jean-Christoph	20.3.1753		[Orphan House]
Nardin, Jean-Isaac		16.3.1753	
Nardin, Jean-Jacques	1.1.1753		
Nardin, Madeleine	28.2.1753	16.3.1753	**DD Feb/Apr 1753**
Nardin, Pierre			DD Dec 52/Feb 1753
Quidore, child	2.1.1753		
Quidore, Jean	23.1.1753	16.2.1753	
Quidore, Jean-George	26.2.1753	16.3.1753	DD Feb/Apr 1753
Rigouleau, Jacques	10.3.1753	16.3.1753	DD Feb/Apr 1753
Rigouleau, Jeanne	6.4.1753	13.4.1753	
Rigouleau, Pierre-Nicolas	21.3.1753	13.4.1753	
Rolland, Anne-Catherine	9/12.3.1753	16.3.1753	DD Feb/Apr 1753
Rolland, Catherine	27.10.1752		
Rolland, Jean-Jacques	26.3.1753	13.4.1753	
Surleau, Pierre	26.3.1753	16.4.1753	DD Feb/Apr 1753

Name of Person	Burial Date	Steinfort's Muster	Victualling List
Thom, Françoise	7.5.1753		
Tisserand, George	25.12.1752		DD Dec 52/Feb 1753
Tisserand, Jacques	1.5.1753		
Tisserand, Pierre	27.5.1753		
Valette, Madeleine			Gone Oct 52/Feb 53
Veuilamet. Isaac	2.8.1752		
Vienot, Jean-Christoph (or George)	10.3.1753		DD Feb/Apr 1753
Vienot, Jeanne	20.2.1753		DD Feb/Apr 1753
Virpillot, Marguerite			DD Aug/Oct 1752
Virpillot, Pierre			DD Oct/Dec 1752
Vuilquet, Catherine-Marg'te	27.10.1752		
Vuilquet, Pierre-Anthoine			DD Aug/Oct 1752
Vuilquet, Suzette			Gone Oct 52/Feb 53

Death Dates in 1752: 1 in Aug, 3 in Sep, 6 in Oct, 5 in Nov, 6 in Dec,
12 between Aug and Oct, and 1 between Oct and Dec...........Total 34
Died Dec 52/Feb 53 - 1; gone Oct 52/Feb 53 - 6.....................Total   7
Death Dates in 1753: 8 in Jan, 8 in Feb, 20 in Mar, 8 in Apr, 5 in May,
I in Jan/Feb, 2 in Feb/Mar, and 3 in Feb/Apr...........................Total 55

APPENDIX B: GENEALOGIES

Dr. Winthrop Bell's *Register* of Foreign Protestants covered the years 1749-1770. This genealogical section attempts to bridge the period from 1700 to 1815. Due to the repetition of names and the tendency of English-speaking clerks to confuse Christian names, there will be oversights and mistakes in what is presented here. In the process of going where the records led, I may disagree with or debunk some of the pseudo-history surrounding these people. I make no apology for doing so.

A wide variety of sources has been utilized, many of them only occasionally. Those are explained where they appear. Commonly occurring words and sources have been abbreviated or are represented by symbols. The various churches have been assigned the following shorthand:

Lunenburg Churches

(A) - St. John's Anglican Church, records 1753> (in English)
(C) - Dutch Reformed (Calvinist) Church, records 1770> (in German)
(L) - Zion Lutheran Church, records 1772> (in German)

Halifax Churches

(B) - Brunswick Street Methodist, Halifax, records 1784>
(G) - St. George's Anglican, formerly Dutch Church, Halifax, 1784>
(M) - St. Matthew's Presbyterian, formerly Mathers Meeting, 1768>
(P) - St. Paul's Anglican, Halifax, records 1749>
(RC) - Roman Catholic (St. Peter's until 1833), records 1800>

Symbols represent the five frequently noted events in life:
* Birth, or born
~ Baptism, or baptised
= Marriage, or married
+ Death, or died
■ Burial

Dates are written as figures, in the sequence day.month.year, e.g.:
25.11.1770 is 25 November 1770.

The names shown in **bold face** in the genealogies are those of the Montbéliardais immigrants to Nova Scotia. When one of two or more given names is presented in *italics,* it indicates which of those names was commonly used by or for that individual.

The eighty-six surnames treated in the genealogical section are listed here, together with *some* of the anglicizations that arose for them. Families known to have male-line descendants in North America 250 years later are *italicized.* There are several instances where the family left Nova Scotia and male-line descendants could exist elsewhere unknown to me. Such families are indicated by an asterisk (*) following their name. I can find no basis in contemporary records for believing that modern families surnamed Coolen and Wilkie are of Montbéliardais origin, from Coulon and Vuilquet. The former are English Cowlings, the latter were Loyalists of Scots origins.

Alison *
Amêt
Bailly
Banvard
Begin
Besançon (Bezanson)
Biguenet (Bigney)
Bizés (Bissett)
Bouillon
Bourgeois
Bourgogne (Burgoine)
Bouteillier
Calame
Carlin *
Certier (Sarty)
Clemençon
Coulon *
Curié *
Daré (Dares, Dorey)
Dauphiné (Dauphinee)

Demet
Donzel
Dupuis
Duperrin
Durand
Duré
Duvoisin (Davison) *
Emonot (Emoneau)
Euvrai
Fainôt
Fevre
Goguel
Grandjean *
Greignaud
Gretteau (Gratto)
Grosrenauld (Grono)
Guigné *
Huguenot
Humbert
Iselin *

Jacot

Jacques

Jacquin (Jackins)

Jaillet (Sawyer)

Jeanbas (Chambers)

Jeanperrin (Perrin)

Jeaudry (Jodry,Jodrie)

Jeauné (Jonah)

Jolimois (Jollimore)

Lagarce

Langille

Laurillard

Leau (Lowe)

Louis

Macé

Maillard (Millard)

Maillardet *

Malbon *

Malmahu

Mariette (Marriott, Marryatt)

Masson (Mason)

Mathieu (Matthews) *

Ménégaux (Mingo)

Mettetal (Mattatall)

Mettin *

Migneré *

Miliet

Monnier *

Morleau *

Nardin *

Petrequin (Patriquin)

Quidore

Richard

Rigouleau

Robert (Robar)

Rolland

Sertie (Sarty)

Surleau

Tetteray (Tattrie)

Thom

Tisserand

Valette

Veuilamet *

Veutilot

Vienot

Virpillot

Vuilquet *

Old Montbéliardais Peasants

(From Renard's *Nouvelle Histoire*)

ALISON

Antoine ALIZON and Evotte PERRENOT of Allenjoie had issue:

1. Jean * 1675 ■ 24.10.1736 age 61; lived at Bart; = (I) 25.1.1701 at
   Allenjoie, Françoise-Marguerite + 16.3.1710 at Allenjoie, dau of
   Laurent and Marie-Catherine (Ferrand) PROH/PROST of Bart. Six
   children. He = (II) 11.11.1710 at Allenjoie, Anne-Marie FALLOT
   * ca. 1673 + 13.8.1744, and had a daughter. His issue:
   1) Pierre-Joseph ~ 5.11.1701 at Bart, witness to marriage in 1734.
   2) Françoise-Marguerite ~ 23.1.1703 at Bart.
   3) Catherine ~ 11.1.1705 at Allenjoie.
   4) **George-Frédéric** ~ 17.1.1706 at Allenjoie. He was a wagoner
      and in 1752 came to Nova Scotia in the *Speedwell* at the stated
      age of 40 [he was 46] in a household of 2.1.2.0, ■ at Halifax,
      2.5.1753; = 15.6.1734 at Allenjoie, **Catherine-Elisabeth**, dau. of
      Jean George and Elisabeth (Depoutot) GOL of Brognard * ca.
      1703/4, widow of Gaspard PERRENOT.[1] She was scalped
      26.4.1759. By her, Alison had four children:
      1a) Charles-Christophe * 26.7.1735 + 21.12.1738 at Allenjoie.
      2a) **Michel-Gabriel** * 14.3.1738 at Allenjoie; living in 1760.
      3a) **Marie-Elisabeth** * 11.1.1741 at Allenjoie; living in 1784/5;
          = 8.6.1756 (A), David Josué **ROBERT** ~ 21.9.1733 at Étobon,
          and moved his family to Cape Breton Island in1784/5. Issue.
      4a) **Anne-Charlotte** ~ 17.12.1744 at Allenjoie, scalped
          26.4.1759 with her mother and step-father, near Lunenburg.
   5) Susanne-Catherine ~ 16.4.1708 at Allenjoie.
   6) Jean-George ~ 21.12.1709 at Allenjoie; youngest by first wife.
   7) Jean-Pierre ~ 11.1.1713 at Allenjoie; = 14.9.1734 at Allenjoie,
      Catherine-Marguerite, dau. of Jean-Christophe CUENOT. Issue.
2. Jean-Christophle * 1680; = 18.7.1701, Catherine GOL of Brognard.

---

[1] Catherine-Elisabeth GOL = (I) 1.5.1727, Gaspard ~ 29.10.1701
■ 13.1.1730, son of Jean-Nicolas and Catherine (Maîtrot) PERRENOT of
Brognard and had one child, Jean Perrenot ~ 22.9.1729 ■ 2.7.1730. She
= (III) 20.5.1753 at Halifax, Jonas TRIPPEAU * 1714 in Switzerland, who
came to Nova Scotia in the *Betty* in 1752. She and Jonas were scalped
26.4.1759 near Lunenburg, NS. They had no children.

AMET

Pierre Amêt, a farmer from Courcelles, age 56 according to the passenger list, and 50 according to his burial record, came to Nova Scotia in the *Betty* in 1752 in a household of 1.1.0.0, and ■ at Halifax, 16.3.1753. He = Judith BOILLEY, but was a widower when he emigrated from Dampierre-les-Bois, with his daughter

1. **Catherine** * 12.4.1733 at Courcelles ■ 21.3.1753 at Halifax, where she = 31.8.1752 (P), David LANGILLE. No issue.

BAILLY

Pierre BAILLY, mason * 1628 + 9.5.1703 age 75; = (I) 20.2.1655 at Héricourt, Judith CHEVALLIER + ca. 1680. Three children. He = (II) 28.2.1682 at Héricourt, Anne + 15.10.1715 age 72, dau. of Abraham OTTENIN, a miller from the manor of Arquet near Yverdon, Canton Vaud, Switzerland. His widow Anne lived at the *Lion d'Or*, an inn kept by Nicolas Monnier at Héricourt.[2] Issue:

1. Étienne, mason at Héricourt * 1656 ■ 17.8.1716 age 60 at
   Héricourt; = ca. 1684, Judith RECEVEUR * 1658, living 1704 (État spéc.). Three children.
2. Elisabeth * 1664 ■ 10.8.1682 at Héricourt, unmarried.
3. Charles, mason at Héricourt * 1666, living 1704 (État spéc.);
   = 24.1.1688 at Héricourt, Françoise * 1664 (État spéc.)
   + 27.3.1737 age 80 (Héricourt), dau of the late Emer CLERC from Morges, Canton Vaud, Switzerland.[3] They had four children:
   1) Anne-Judith * 1688 + 2.1.1727 in childbed; = 29.12.1722 at
      Héricourt, Gaspard, weaver at Héricourt * 1697 + 27.2. 1755, son of George and Catherine (Rayot) PICCARD of Héricourt. Three children.

---

[2] "État spécifique du nombre des personnes de la ville d'Héricourt de leurs nom, âge, vocation et religion (1704)". Archives de la Haute-Saône, E446. Hereafter (État spéc.).

[3] *Familiennamenbuch der Schweiz* (Zürich, 1989), I, 358, states that the Clerc family held citizenship in Colombier and Ecublens, both near Morges and Lausanne in Canton Vaud.

2) Pierre, mason at Héricourt * 1692 + 8.9.1741; = 16.1.1720 at Héricourt, Elisabeth * 1694 + 1.8.1762, dau. of the late Adam BIDAUD of Échenans- sous-Mont-Vaudois. Four children.

3) Jean, shoemaker at Héricourt * 1696 + 5.1.1780 age 84, at Héricourt; = (I) 11.2.1719, Henriette-Marguerite * 1695 + 1740, dau. of the late Étienne NARDIN, shoemaker, and his wife Claudine GEORGE * 13.12.1668 at Brevilliers. Bailly had nine children by the first marriage and four by his second, contracted at Héricourt on 23.9.1742 with Claudine BOUTEILLIER who + 17.12.1768, all baptised at Héricourt:

1a) Clémence-Marguerite ~ 19.12.1719.

2a) Adam ~ 10.6.1721 + in childhood.

3a) Jean, shoemaker at Héricourt ~ 2.3.1723 + 2.2.1778.

4a) **George-Frédéric** ~ 28.6.1725 at Héricourt ■ 24.3.1807 (C), stocking weaver by trade, a farmer and French schoolmaster in Nova Scotia. He came to Nova Scotia in the *Sally* in 1752 with a household of 1.1.0.1. He = 31.10.1746 at Héricourt, **Frédérique-Sybille** ~ 16.11.1721 ■ 12.3.1803 (C), dau. of Jean-Henry and Elisabeth-Catherine (Mellezal) RICHARDOT of Héricourt. They had six children:

1b) Jean-Frédéric ~ 22.8.1747 at Héricourt + in infancy.

2b) **Jean** ~ 28.10.1749 at Héricourt + ca. 1756 Lunenburg.

3b) Jeanne-Marguerite * 22.10.1753 at Lunenburg + there, 25.4.1836[4]; = 13.7.1783 (A), Romkes COMINGO ~ 13.8.1754 + 24.9.1825, and had issue.

4b) Catherine-Marguerite * 24.1.1756 at Lunenburg + 21.7.1835; = 27.4.1783 (L), Rev. Bruin Romkes COMINGO, father of her elder sister's husband, * 21.10.1723 at Leeuwarden, Friesland, Netherlands

---

[4] Mather Byles DesBrisay, *History of the County of Lunenburg*, 2nd ed.(Toronto, 1895), 30, states that hers was "the first birth in the new community'. Her literate father recorded her birth as 22 October, several months *after* Lunenburg's founding and *after* a dozen or so other children had been born there. DesBrisay's informant was mistaken.

+ 6.1.1820 at Lunenburg.[5] They had six children.
5b) Barbara-Elisabeth * 20.11.1758 + 8.7.1837 (C);
   = 18.8.1805 (C), Johannes KNIESE, a former gunner in the
   Hessian forces during the American Revolution * 1751/53
   at either Römersburg or adjacent Bischhausen in Hesse,
   and + 19.10.1827 at Lunenburg.[6] No issue.
6b) Joseph, shoemaker * 2.3.1761 at Lunenburg + 13.3.1842
   at Lunenburg; = 20.2.1806 (A), Elizabeth * 14.3.1782
   + 2.2.1882, dau. of Leonard Christopher and Magdalena
   (Kneller) SCHWARTZ of Garden Lots, Lunenburg. They
   had nine children.[7]
5a) Jean ~ 1.4.1727.
6a) Marie-Marguerite ~ 21.3.1729.
7a) Pierre, a surgeon + 17.1.1733 + 21.6.1790 at Héricourt.
8a) Jeanne-Marguerite ~ 26.2.1735.
9a) Adam ~ 15.2.1740 + 28.6.1740, youngest by first marriage.
10a) Pierre ~ 1.8.1743.

---

[5] Comingo had the trade of a wool comber when he first came to Nova Scotia. His career as a Calvinist pastor began in mid-life when a special consistory was held at Halifax on 3.7.1770 to ordain him "to the office of the Holy Ministry over the Dutch Calvinistic Presbyterian Congregation of Lunenburg." Cf., Winthrop P. Bell, The 'Foreign Protestants' and the Settlement of Nova Scotia (Toronto, 1961), 599-600.

[6] It is possible, with the help of the estate papers at Marburg, to ascertain that this man was Johann Adam Kniese, a member of the Grenadier-Battalion Köhler, Kompanie von Wissenbach, and not the Konrad Kneise speculated about in Johannes Helmut Mertz. The Hessians of Nova Scotia (Hamilton, 1997), 130. Adam Kneise may be found in HETRINA (Hessische Truppen in Amerikanischen Unabhängigigkeitskrieg), I (Marburg, 1984), 42, nos. 1395-7.

[7] His children are given in Terrence M. Punch, "A Genealogy: George-Frédéric Bailly," in Journal of the Royal Nova Scotia Historical Society, 5 (2002), 160-161. The same article gives the background of the Richardot and Nardin families as well.

11a) Elisabeth-Marguerite ~ 15.11.1745.

12a) François ~ 7.12.1747.

13a) Pierre-Jacques ~ 3.6.1750 + 14.11.1756 at Héricourt.

4) Adam, mason at Héricourt * 1698, living in 1771 when his wife
died; = 6.4.1723 at Héricourt, Henriette-Marguerite ~ 9.1.1701
+ 31.8.1771 at Héricourt, dau. of the late Jacques SURLEAU, of
Héricourt employed at the forges at Chagey, and his wife Anne
BOILLOU. They had seven children, all baptised at Héricourt.

4. Elisabeth * 1685, living with her mother in 1704 (État spéc.).

BANVARD

This surname appeared in Montbéliard, at Brognard, about 1634, having
come from either Canton Bern or Canton Lucerne in Switzerland.
Banvard represents the approximate pronunciation of a Swiss name
Bannwart, indicating a field ranger. Three children of a Swiss father lived
in Brognard in the 1690s: Judith * 1668, and Anne * 1679, and their elder
brother, Jean BANVARD, bailiff at Brognard * 1658, living 1723; =
Marguerite BRAN(D) * 1663, and had six children:

1. Jeanne * 1690; = Pierre LODS.

2. Françoise * 1692; = Jacques FALLOT.

3. Catherine * 1694.

4. Jean-Jacques * 1698; = 26.11.1726, Elisabeth VURPILLOT (age
42 in 1728), widow of Jean JEAND'HEUR of Champey.

5. Elisabeth * 1700; = 5.12.1724, Friderich FRANÇOIS, Brevilliers.

6. **Pierre** * 1702 at Brognard; a weaver, he came to Nova Scotia in the
Speedwell in 1752, with a household of 1.2.0.0, ■ 19.8.1754 at
Lunenburg; = 3.9.1726 at Brognard = **Françoise** * ca. 1704
+ summer 1752 at sea, dau. of Daniel JEANPERRIN of Allenjoie.
They had issue:

1) George * ca. 1727 + before 1752 at Brognard.

2) **David** * 2.5.1729 + 13.8.1770 at New York City; a weaver, he
emigrated to Nova Scotia in 1752 in the *Speedwell*, with a
household of 1.1.0.0., and moved from Nova Scotia to New
York after 10.10.1763, when he sold land at Lunenburg
(Lunenburg Co. Deeds, I, ƒ 166 #382). He = (I) 9.10.1751 at
Dambenois = **Eve PETREQUIN** * ca. 1727 ■ 13.3.1753 at

Halifax. He = (II) 20.5.1753 at Halifax, Catherine-Elisabeth
* 5.5.1722 at Allondans + 12.12.1791 at New York, dau. of Simon
and Henriette (Marçonnet) LOVY, and widow of Jean CARLIN.
David had six children by her:

1a) David ~ 18.12.1753 ■ 18.9.1754 (A).

2a) Catherine-Elisabeth ~ 1.8.1755 (A), living 1778 in New York.

3a) Mary Catherine ~ 29.10.1757 (A) + 15.2.1841 age 84 at New
    York. She had a child by Robert TOWNSEND alias Samuel
    CULPERS, Jr., an American agent during the Revolutionary
    War. She = (I)1784/85, Marmaduke Van BUSKIRK + 1792/3
    and had a daughter. She = (II) 3.6.1793 at New York, William
    DERRY.[8]

4a) Mary Margaret ~ 21.10.1759 (A).

5a) Jane ~ 20.12.1761 (A), alive in 1774.

6a) Daniel * 20.12.1767 at New York (Moravian Church) + 1831
    at New York; = Elizabeth MEAD, and had eleven children.

3) **Marguerite-Elisabeth** * 11.4.1732 at Brognard, ■ 19.1.1799 (A);
    = 20.5.1753 at Halifax, Jean DAUPHINÉ and had issue.

BEGIN

David Nicolas BECHIN, weaver from Montbéliard Town + 4.4.1740; =
23.9.1721, Susanne ROUGE had a son **Jacques BEGIN** * 27.3.1725 at
Magny Danigon. He came to Nova Scotia in 1752 in the *Betty*, in a
household of 1.1.0.0, and was living at North West Range, near Mahone
Bay, NS, in 1794.[9] For part of the years 1756-64 he served in the 45th
Regiment. He = (I) 20.4.1751 at Magny Danigon, **Marie-Madeleine** ■
1.8.1753 at Lunenburg, dau of Jacques JAQUE, a roofer, and his wife

---

[8] *Cf.*, Harry Macy, Jr., "Robert Townsend of New York City,"in
The New York Genealogical and Biographical Record (January 1995), 25-34.
Macy believed that the Banvard woman associated with Townsend was 4a)
Mary Margaret, but I believe that the death record in 1841 stating that she
was in her "85th year" is decisive in the reference being to Mary Catherine.

[9] In the Magny Danigon register we read of this man, "*Celui-ci
est sorti avec sa femme pour aller s'etablir dans l'ille de l'Écosse, le
courant du mois d'avril dans l'anné 1752.*"

Marie MATTHEY of Magny Danigon. He = (II) 18.12.1766 (A), Jeanne
* 1743, dau. of George- Frédéric MAILLARD, who + at Tatamagouche.
Begin = (III) 22.10.1776 (A), Mary Margaret, dau. of Guillaume GUIGNÉ
or GUENON of Colombier-Châtelot, and widow of Jean-Frédéric
MASSON. There were three children of the third marriage:

1. Catherine-Elisabeth * 18.6.1777 (A), living 1831; = 18.11.1798 (A),
   John-George GRONO ~ 29.5.1768 (A), living 1843. Issue.
2. James Christopher * 30.9.1778 (A) ▪ 17.12.1831 (A). He was master
   of a coastal vessel at Mahone Bay. He = (I) Elizabeth - - - - + 1817/18,
   and had three children. He = (II) 31.12.1818 (A), Elizabeth MARTIN
   of Prospect, near Halifax, widow of William MARLOW, RN. Issue:
   1) Elizabeth * ca. 1812; = 19.4.1834, Nicholas EISENHAUER.
   2) James * 29.1.1816 (A) ▪ 28.3.1845. He died due to falling over a
      bank into the LaHave River and drowning (A); = 4.12.1834 (A),
      Mary, dau. of Adam MADER. Five children.
   3) Benjamin * 14.3.1817 (A) ▪ 13.9.1826 (A).
3. David Nicholas * 16.4.1784 ~ 25.4.1784 (A).

BESANÇON

Christofle BESANÇON of Brognard = Catherine GAGNEBIEN and had an
eldest son,

1. **Jean-George**, a farmer, 44, who came to Nova Scotia in 1752 in the
   Speedwell, with a household of 1.2.3.1. The État des pauvres, 6.2.1750,
   lists him as *"n'ayant rien d'autre que sa femme et 4 enfants don't le plus
   âgé a 12 ans"*.[10] He + at Lunenburg between July and Dec 1755; = (I)
   = **Jeanne** - - who + at Halifax between Aug. and Oct. 1752, age about
   40. Five children. He = (II) 20.5.1753 (P), Anne-Catherine ~ 25.8.1718
   ▪ 27.10.1796 (C), dau. of Pierre & Elisabeth (Vautherin) BOUTEILLIER
   of Chagey, and widow of Jacques TISSERAND. Two children. She =
   (III) 1.1.1756 (A), Étienne MARRIETTE and had issue. Besançon's
   issue were:
   1) **Marie-Catherine** * ca. 1735, living 1775; = 3.12.1753 (A), David
      LANGILLE * 19.1.1715 at Étobon + -.7.1804. Issue.
   2) **Nicolas** * ca. 1738; had license, 28.10.1761, to marry Mary
      RICHARDS.

---

[10]   Archives Doubs, EPM 446 list of 1750; census of 1723, *ibid.*

3) **David** + 1755/56 at Lunenburg.

4) **Marie**, living 1756.

5) **Marie-Elisabeth** + Aug 1752/May 1753 at Halifax.

6) Jean-Jacques [known variously in records as James or Jacob], grist miller ~ 17.6.1754 (A) + between 1802 and 1804; = 29.10.1776 (C), Ann Mary ~ 27.8.1758 (A), dau. of Joseph LOY. They had thirteen children:

1a) Joseph ~ 28.11.1777 (C) + 26.1.1849 at Chester, NS.; = 16.4.1799 at Chester, Sarah, * 7.1.1781 at Chester + 1865, dau. of John PULSIFER. Issue.

2a) Alexander * 10.7.1779 (C) + 1825; = (I) 17.5.1803 (A), Catharine SWINAMER. Issue. He = (II) 8.11.1808 at Chester, Ann Barbary * 2.3.1786, dau. of John Frederick LANTZ. Issue.

3a) John George * 16.5.1781 (C); = 4.4.1805, Mary, dau. of George MILLETT, and widow of James J. VAUGHAN. Issue.

4a) Gideon * 4.2.1783 (C) + 1818; = 10.11.1805 at Chester, Mary + 23.11.1854 (Chester), dau. of John PULSIFER. Issue.

5a) Ann *Mary* ~ 2.3.1785 (C), living 1808.

6a) John * 22.12.1786 (C) + 4.9.1872; = (I) 31.1.1813 at Chester, Sophia HEMMEON + 15.7.1815. He = (II) 28.7.1816 at Chester = Ann + 6.1.1858 at Chester, dau. of James ANDERSON, a Loyalist from Baltimore, MD. Issue by both marriages.

7a) John Caspar * 1.3.1789 (C); = 29.12.1813 at Chester, Hannah * 8.7.1793 at Chester, dau. of Patrick CLINTON. Issue.

8a) George Bernard * 23.5.1791 (C) + young.

9a) John *William*, St. Marys River, NS * 1.7.1793 (C); = 21.11.1815 (Rev. Dimock), Lydia * 1795, dau. of Elijah MELVIN. Issue.

10a) Barbary * 2.9.1795 at Chester; = 17.3.1816, John QUILTY.

11a) Peter * 15.2.1798 at Chester + 17.11.1875 at Isaacs Harbour, NS; = Martha . . . . . * 1804, living 1871. Issue.

12a) Benjamin ~ 2.12.1799 at Chester; = 24.7.1830 (A), Mary DUGGAN * 1811 + 6.12.1835 at Country Harbour, NS. Issue.

13a) James * 9.11.1802 at Chester + 16.4.1872 at Hammonds Plains; = 1.5.1827 (G), Dorothy * 1809 + 1866, dau. of Amos MELVIN. Issue.

7) Susanne-Catherine ~ 5.4.1756 (A); = (I) 16.3.1784 (A), Peter ROBERT/ROBAR and had issue. She = (II) 11.3.1802 (A), Joseph BOUTEILLIER.

BIGUENET

Jacques Biguenet * ca. 1729 at Blamont + 1805 at Lower Wentworth, NS, and known as James BIGNEY. He was a farmer and came to Nova Scotia in 1752 in the *Betty* as a single man. He = 7.5.1754 (A), Marie, dau. of Abraham and Elisabeth (Bourquin) CALAME. Issue:
1. Jacques ~ 12.10.1756 (A); = Nancy McCALLUM and had issue.
2. John Nicholas ~ 28.4.1760 (A) + young.
3. John George ~ 26.6.1761 (A) + in 1845; = Agnes, dau. of Mathieu LANGILLE, and had issue.
4. Catherine ~ 5.2.1765 (A); = John Frederick PETREQUIN. Issue.
5. Peter ~ 19.1.1768 (A) + in 1828; = Althea Mira STEVENS and had issue.
6. Mary Catherine * 28.4.1771 (A); = Peter METTETAL and had issue.
7. Mark * ca. 1774 at Tatamagouche + in 1846; = Ann STEVENS and had issue.

BIZÉS[11]

Jacques-George Bizés, known in Nova Scotia as BISSETT, of Sainte-Marie * 24.3.1709, living 1777, came to Nova Scotia in the *Betty* in 1752, in a household of 1.1.2.1. He was a weaver by trade and moved as a young man from Sainte-Marie to Brevilliers, where he = 5.2.1737, **Anne-Catherine** ~ 2.1.1704, living 1770, dau. of Jean-Jacques and Jeanne (VALITON) METTEY of Brevilliers and widow of Jean-Nicolas GUYON.[12] They had four children:

---

[11] The surname Bize or Bizés was found in Sainte-Marie in the 18th century, and came to Montbéliard from Villarzel, near Moudon, Canton Vaud, Switzerland. In Nova Scotia the name became Bissett. Jacques-George was a son of Jean-Antoine Bizé the elder and Catherine JEAIN.

[12] Guillaume + by 1726, and Anne (BONNIER) GUYON of Brevilliers had a son Nicolas who + by 1737; = 17.2.1726, Anne-Catherine * 1704, dau. of the late Jean-Jacques METTEY of Brevilliers, and had five children who either died before their step-father emigrated or who remained in Montbéliard: George-Frédéric * 1728 - 1733, Anne-Clémence * 1729, Anne-Catherine * 1731, Anne-Catherine * 1733, Catherine-Elisabeth * 1734.

1. **Jean-George** ~ 8.11.1737 at Brevilliers, who follows.
2. Jacques ~ 9.11.1739 at Brevilliers + 12.9.1741 at Brevilliers.
3. **Claudine-Catherine** * 15.12.1741 at Brevilliers, ■ 13.3.1753 at Halifax.
4. **Éléanore** * 27.4.1744 at Brevilliers, ■ 3.1.1753 at Halifax.

Jean-George Bizés, farmer age 17 [sic] appears in his own right on the passenger list of the *Betty* in 1752; ~ 8.11.1737 at Brevilliers, son of the foregoing couple. His estate was probated in Halifax County, 15.10.1808, and he is given as late of Cole Harbour, NS; = 2.4.1754 (A), Anne-Judith * ca. 1738, dau. of Hugues and Elisabeth (Bouffay) METTIN of Bethoncourt. They had twelve children:

1) George * 1755 + 1757/62.
2) Anne-*Catherine* ~ 12.12.1756 (A), living 1770.
3) Margaret ~ 31.5.1759 (A); = 18.1.1780 (P), Isaac MARTIN, weaver.
4) John George ~ 7.2.1762 (A) + 30.1.1847 at Cole Harbour; = 16.2.1795 (P), Anne Jane, dau. of Alexander HAWTHORN. Issue.
5) *James* Frederick ~ 5.8.1764 (A), living 1844; = 18.9.1814 (RC), Catherine Anne * 1791 + 15.1.1844, dau. of Richard YOUNG. Issue.
6) Catherine Louisa ~ 2.11.1766 (A); = - - - - HARRIS.
7) George Frederick ~ 26.2.1769 (A) + 24.3.1834 at Cole Harbour; = 18.11.1816 (P), Mary Ann MURPHY, widow of James MADDOX, Newfoundland.
8) Joseph Frederick * 28.6.1771 (A) + 23.12.1854 at Cole Harbour; = 22.2.1799 (P), Anne Catharine MILLER * 1780 + 25.3.1853. Issue.
9) Mary Anne * 1773 + 8.10.1857 at Lawrencetown, Halifax Co.; = 8.7.1791 (P), John GAMMON * 1767 + 8.10.1861. Issue.
10) Samuel * ca. 1775, living 1850; = (I) 18.3.1806 (P), Catherine * 3.9.1787 + 11.11.1820, dau. of Joseph GLASGOW. Issue. He = (II) 9.3.1823 (B), Rachel LANEGAN * 1787 + 31.1.1850. Issue.
11) Anne * ca. 1778; = 4.8.1805 (M), John COGELL of Eastern Passage, NS * 1777 + 6.10.1841. Issue.
12) Benjamin * ca. 1781 ~ 31.5.1786 at Halifax + 1838/42; = 16.7.1809 (P), Louisa ~ 24.8.1793 at Halifax + 12.11.1854, dau. of Joseph and Catherine GILES of Cole Harbour. Issue.

BOUILLON

Adam Bouillon was a son of Jean-Nicolas and Marguerite (Bran) Bouillon of Fesches-le-Châtel[13] * ca. 1721, living 1773. He was a joiner and came to Nova Scotia in the *Speedwell* in 1752, as a single man. He = (I) 20.9.1757 (A), Lucy-Judith MONNIER ▪ 9.3.1763 (A), widow of Jean-Nicolas MATTATALL. He = (II) 16.8.1763 (A), Marie-Marguerite LANDE * ca. 1713, widow of Samuel METTIN and of Jacques BOUTEILLLIER. Bouillon had two daughters by his first marriage:
1. Mary Margaret ~ 26.3.1758 (A), living 1770.
2. Anne-Judith ~ 10.3.1763 (A) + infancy.

BOURGEOIS

Pierre-*Jacques* Bourgeois, a miller by trade * ca. 1712 at Valentigney, and came to Nova Scotia in 1752 in the *Speedwell*, in a household of 1.1.2.1., and + ca. 1787 at Newport, NS.[14] He = 26.5.1739 in Montbéliard Town, **Anne-Catherine** ▪ 10.11.1755 (A), dau. of Jean-Jacques CHERTON of Montecheroux. Issue:
1. ***Pierre*-David** ~ 11.3.1740 at Montbéliard Town, living at Lunenburg in 1755.
2. **Marguerite** * ca. 1742 + in 1818 at Windsor, NS; = (I) 17.4.1757 at Halifax [as Margaret BUTLER], William HE<u>AL</u>Y and had a son, John HA<u>LE</u>Y. She = (II) 25.9.1781, apparently at Halifax, William BROTHERS + 1819 at Windsor, and had further issue.

With Bourgeois came a young woman, probably his daughter by a previous marriage:

---

[13] Adam and Marguerite Bouillon sold half of lot A13, Northwest, to Judith Bisset for £1, on 2.6.1766 (Lunenburg Co. Deeds, I, *f* 278 #667). The low price and the fact both parties had Mettin links suggest kinship. Adam had four older siblings who did not come to Nova Scotia, namely Anne-Marie (* 1711), Marguerite (* 1712), Jean-George (* 1714), and David (* 1717). Adam's wife Marguerite was a dau. of David BRAN, age 86 in 1717 (Archives Doubs, 25 - EPM 698 - dénombrement population).

[14] The reader will note that the child below the age of 4 on the passenger list cannot be identified. The most likely explanation is that this was a child born in the late 1740s and who died in the crossing in summer of 1752.

3. **Susanne-Thérèse**; = (I) 23.4.1753 at Halifax, Louis GOURBON. Issue. She = (II) 3.8.1762 at Halifax, William TURNER ■ 6.7.1767 at Halifax.

BOURGOGNE[15]

Jean-Georges BOURGOGNE, workman at Étupes * 1690 + 1719/22; = Jeanne VIÉNOT * 1692 + 3.12.1757 at Blamont. Their only son was
1. **Marc Bourgogne**, a farmer * 30.9.1718 at Étupes; emigrated to Nova Scotia in the *Betty* in 1752, in a household of 1.1.3.1; ■ 26.4.1804 at Lunenburg (L); = 30.10.1741 at Étupes, **Anne-Elisabeth** ■ 27.12.1776 (L), dau. of Jean-Henri FRITSCH + by 1741, who came from Lorenthal, Bailliage of Lontzburg[16] in Canton Bern, Switzerland. Eight children:
   1) **Jean-Georges** * 8.1.1742 at Étupes + 1753/54 in NS.
   2) **Catherine-Elisabeth** * 17.3.1745 at Étupes, living 1809; = 19.11.1765 (A), Christopher OBERSTAHL/HABERSTROH, a.k.a. HAVERSTOCK + 18.11.1809 at Sackville, NS. Issue.
   3) **Jacques** * 13.3.1748 at Étupes, living 1757.
   4) **Jean-David** * 3.10.1750 at Étupes + 12.2.1825 at Oakland, NS; = 2.11.1773 (L), *Anna* Barbara, ~ 4.11.1754 (A) + 5.12.1843 (L), dau. of Peter CLATTENBURG. Issue:
      1a) Jo*anna* Barbara * 3.4.1777 (L), alive 1825; = 14.1.1796 (L), Peter HIRTLE or HARTLING. Issue.
      2a) *Catherine* Barbara * 19.10.1778 (L), living 1825; = 24.9.1805 (L), John Frederick HARTLING of Necum Teuch, NS. Issue.
      3a) John Jacob, twin * 6.6.1781 (L), ■ 19.4.1784 (L).
      4a) *John* David, twin * 6.6.1781 (L) + 16.8.1846 (L); = 8.10.1811 (L), Mary Ursula * 23.2.1794 (C), dau. of Wilhelm HEISON. Issue.

---

[15] In Nova Scotia this surname was anglicized as Burgoyne and Burgoine. Archives Doubs, 25-EPM 698 (dénombrement 1719, 1723).

[16] Neither Lorenthal nor Lontzburg have been located, but the surname Fritschi is found in Aargau canton, at Spreitenbach and Teufenthal, on either side of Lenzburg, which was probably "Lontzburg". (*Familiennamenbuch der Schweiz*, I, 598).

5a) John *George* * 9.1.1784 (L) + 23.9.1867; = 16.1.1810 (L),
   Catharine Barbara, dau. of John Adam WEINACHT. Issue.
6a) Anne Mary *Elizabeth* * 23.9.1786 (L), living 1825; = (1)
   22.10.1807 (C), John HEISON, ■ 21.7.1811 (C), and had
   two daughters. She = 10.4.1814(L), Philip ERNST
   ~ 20.4.1790 (L) + 29.6.1831 (C). Issue.
7a) John *Jacob*, of Aaldersville * 10.8.1789 (L) + 10.8.1873;
   = 29.12.1812 (L), Catharine Elizabeth, dau. of George
   Peter MOSER. Issue.
8a) Susanna *Christina* * 14.3.1792 (L), drowned 26.1.1815
   (L), unm.
9a) George *Frederick* * 28.12.1794 (L) + -.10.1870 at Mahone
   Bay; = 7.11.1820 (L), Anna Elizabeth ~ 1.8.1797 (L), dau.
   of Jacob Michael ACKER. Issue.
10a) Mary Magdalen * 18.2.1798 (L), ■ 24.1.1801 (L), died of
   smallpox.
5) Jean-George ~ 13.7.1754 (A), living 1796.
6) Marie-Catherine ~ 10.5.1757 (A) + young.
7) John *Jacob* [James] ~ 13.2.1759 (A) + Sep./Oct. 1822 at
   Oakland; = 18.6.1782 (L), Anne Barbara ~ 28.6.1762 (A)
   ■ 8.3.1840, at French Village, dau. of John Conrad
   KNICKEL. Eleven children:
1a) John David * 23.5.1783 (L), ■ 26.9.1783 (L).
2a) John David * 3.9.1784 (L) + 25.9.1784 (L).
3a) Catharine Barbara * 27.8.1785 (L), ■ 11.10.1785 (L).
4a) *Mary* Catharine * 14.2.1788 (L), living 1822; = 13.5.1809
   (bond date), John Peter BOUTILIER, Southwest Cove. Issue.
5a) *Susan* Elizabeth * 20.11.1790 ~ 11.12.1790 (L) + 7.6.1846
   at Chester; = 12.1.1814 (P), James DAUPHINEE * 15.12.1788
   (A) + 21.1.1862 at St. Margarets Bay, and had issue.
6a) John *Jacob* * 11.7.1793 ■ 9.8.1829 (P), age 40 [sic].
7a) Joanna Catharine * 25.2.1796 (L) + by 1822;
   = 25.10.1814 (P), James LEWIS.
8a) Christian * 17.10.1798 (L).■ 20.2.1801 (L), died of smallpox.
9a) John George * 19.12.1800 (L) + August/September 1826,
   unm.

10a) John * 1.3.1803 (L), ■ 5.2.1885 at French Village;
   = 7.5.1824 (P), Catherine BOUTILIER.
11a) Ann Sophia * 24.6.1805 (L); = 5.4.1825 (P),
   William KEDDY, fisherman, and had issue.
8) Susanne-Elizabeth ~ 4.7.1762 (A) ■ 29.1.1794 (L); =
   27.12.1781 (L), John Philip HIRTLE ~ 10.7.1760 (A). Issue.

BOUTEILLIER-I

Jean-George Bouteillier * ca. 1726 in Montbéliard, a weaver, came
to NS in 1752 in the *Speedwell* as a single man; ■ 10.5.1757 (A);
= 17.12.1754 (A), Madeleine, dau. of Abraham CALAME. She = (II)
28.3.1758 (A), Pierre COULON. Child:
1. Susanna Catherine ~ 23.11.1757 (A) ■ 18.6.1758 (A).

BOUTEILLIER-II

Jean Bouteillier * ca. 1723 in Montbéliard, and was a joiner by trade. He
came to Nova Scotia in 1752 in the *Betty*, with a household of 1.1.0.0,
and was living in 1772; = (I) ca. 1750, **Françoise - - - -**, who + 1769/71
and had seven children. He = (II) 25.8.1771 (A), Marie PETITPAS[17] and
had a pair of twins. His nine children were:
1. Marie-Elisabeth ~ 2.9.1753 (A) + 24.10.1849 at St. Margarets Bay;
   = 29.12.1776 (A), Jean-Christopher DAUPHINEE and had issue.
2. Pierre *Jacques* ~ 7.1.1755 (A) + young.
3. Daniel Nicholas ~ 29.3.1757 (A), living 1770.
4. Peter ~ 6.1.1760 at Halifax, living 1770.
5. Margaret ~1.3.1762 at Halifax.
6. Susanne Catherine ~ 28.1.1765 (A).
7. George ~ 11.9.1767 (A), living 1770; youngest child by Françoise.

---

[17] From her name, she may have been Acadienne or Métisse.
One of Margaret and Susanne Catherine was alive for the township return
in 1770. Present information does not identify which girl died prior to that
date.

8. Joseph, twin * 11.4.1772 (A).
9. Mary Catherine, twin * 11.4.1772 (A) ■ 27.4.1772 (A).

BOUTEILLIER-III

Jacques BOUTEILLIER, "regent d'école" at Vernoy, had a son:
1. **Jacques**, a weaver * ca. 1718 at Lougres, ■ 2.3.1762 (A); he came to Nova Scotia in the *Sally* in 1752, with a household of 1.3.1.1.[18] He = 4.7.1747 at Aibre, **Marie-Marguerite** * ca. 1713, dau. of Pierre LANDE and Marguerite Surleau and widow of Samuel METTIN of Laire. She = (III) 16.8.1763 (A), Adam BOUILLON. Issue:
   1) Henriette * 24.9.1747 at Aibre, ■ 13.8.1751 at Lougres.
   2) **Jeanne-Marguerite** * 25.12.1750 at Aibre + summer 1752 at sea.
   3) James-Louis ~ 15.5.1755 (A), living 1757.

BOUTEILLIER-IV[19]

---

[18] There are two women aged above 14 with him on the passenger list. They are not identified, nor have I sufficient information to do so. The person aged 4-14 was his step-daughter, **Anne-Judith METTIN**, see page 145.

[19] Four members of this family appear separately in the passenger lists of 1752, a father and three of his sons. Jean-George, age 50, had a household of 1.2.2.0, one of the women being unidentified in Nova Scotian records. He traveled in the *Sallly*, as did his sons Jean-Nicolas, age 21, and Jacques, age 17, each entered as a farmer, single man. The eldest son, Jean-George, age 26, a weaver, made the voyage in the *Betty*, the ship on which traveled the family of the woman he married within a month of reaching Halifax, and his sister Catherine with her husband Jonas Jacot. As usual, the names of those who actually emigrated appear in **bold** print.

Jehan Guillaume BOUTHEILLER of Chagey had a son Nicolas who =
(I) Ursule BREUCHOT * ca. 1600,■ 30.3.1670 at Étobon. Nicolas
= (II) 24.1.1671 at Étobon, Madeleine-Jeanne * 1609 + 11.4.1679,
dau. of Nicolas MIGNERÉ. His son by Ursule:
1. Guillaume * 1642 + 17.6.1712 at Étobon; = 23.8.1670 at Étobon,
   Jeanne * ca. 1648 + 29.11.1723 at Étobon, dau. of Gratien
   MIGNERÉ. Eleven children:
   1) Jeanne * 13.8.1671 at Étobon + young.
   2) Isaac ~ 30.9.1672 at Étobon + 19.10.1672 at Étobon.
   3) Pierre ~ 19.9.1673 at Étobon + young.
   4) Catherine ~ 4.4.1675 at Étobon + young.
   5) Jeanne-Marie ~ 9.8.1678 + suddenly 26.4.1755 at Étobon;
      = 22.2.1719 at Étobon, Jean-Louis, labourer ~ 18.8.1678
      + 25.3.1729 at Étobon, son of François & Jeanne (Pochard)
      CHAMOT. Issue.
   6) Pierre ~ 27.1.1680 at Étobon.
   7) Jean, a carpenter ~ 22.11.1682 + 24.2.1750 at Étobon; = (I)
      25.2.1707 at Étobon, Marie ~ 24.5.1685 + 16.7.1716 at
      Étobon, dau. of Esaüe & Clémence (Petit) AUBERT, and had
      issue. Jean = (II) 13.10.1716 at Étobon, Catherine * 1691
      + 27.6.1717 at Étobon, dau. of Claude & Marguerite (Pourchot)
      BOILLOUD, and had a daughter. He = (III) ca. 1720, Jeanne
      ~ 14.10.1680 + 1.10.1761 at Étobon, dau. of Jean & Claudine
      (Lecrisle) RACINE, and had two sons.
   8) Catherine * 16.8.1685 or * 16.12.1685 at Étobon + young.
   9) Marguerite * 1687 + 16.4.1762 age 76 at Étobon; = 14.5.1709
      at Étobon, Daniel~ 18.11.1687 + 24.11.1751 at Étobon, son of
      Jérémie & Françoise (Rebillard) PLANÇON. Fourteen children.
   10) Catherine ~ 16.9.1689 at Étobon; = 9.11.1728 at Étobon, as
       his second wife = David LeCRILE, labourer ~ 2.4.1665
       + 8.7.1743 at Échavanne, and had one son.
   11) Jean-George ~ 19.8.1691, who was the progenitor of the
       Nova Scotia Boutillier families. See next page.

11) Jean-George Bouteiller, carpenter, ~ 19.8.1691 at Étobon, emigrated to Nova Scotia in the *Sally* in 1752, claiming to be 50, though in fact being 60,[20] with a household of 1.2.2.0; = 29.1.1723 at Étobon, **Sara** * ca. 1702, dau. of Pierre GRANGE. Both George and his wife Sara perished during the voyage from Rotterdam to Halifax during the summer of 1752.They had nine children:
1a) Catherine * 7.1.1724 at Étobon + in infancy.
2a) Catherine ~ 13.1.1726 at Étobon, ■ 20.10.1752 at Halifax; = 16.2.1751 at Étobon, Jonas JACOT * 1714 ■ 12.10.1755 (A). Issue.
3a) Nicolas ~ 26.2.1728 ■ 11.3.1728 at Étobon.
4a) **Jean-George**, mason ~ 30.6.1729 at Étobon, emigrated in 1752 in the *Betty* as a single man, d. 12.3.1784 ■ 14.3.1784 (A); = 31.8.1752 (P), Anne-Catherine ~ 6.12.1733 at Chenebier, dau. of Jean-Frédéric and Anne-Judith (Gugné) MAILLARD. Thirteen children:
 1b) *Frederick* Nicholas ~ 17.7.1754 (A), living at Little Bras d'Or, Cape Breton, in 1809; = 27.7.1779 (L), Anna Barbara ~ 1.10.1758 (A), dau. of Jacob HIRTLE. Eleven children.
 2b) John *George* ~ 11.3.1756 (A) + 3.1.1831 at St. Margarets Bay= 4.4.1780 (A), Elizabeth-Catherine ~ 7.10.1759 (A), living 1806, dau. of Jean LEAU. Thirteen children.
 3b) John Frederick ~ 13.2.1759 (A) + 1823/24 at St. Margarets Bay; = 5.1.1779 (A), (H)anna ~ 16.11.1756 (A), dau. of Johann Conrad KNICKEL. Twelve children.
 4b) James ~ 23.11.1760 (A) ■ 9.9.1840 at South West Cove; = 24.10.1780 (A), Susan Barbara ~ 6.6.1762 (A) + 6.4.1838, dau. of Étienne MARIETTE. Fourteen children.
 5b) Catherine ~ 24.7.1763 (A) + 1822/1826; = 28.9.1783 (C), John Conrad WESTHAVER ~ 31.10.1758 (A). Issue.

---

[20] Bell, 155-6,201, 206, 291, 296-7, discusses the reliability of the ages stated in the passenger lists. The presence of the senior Boutillier couple would appear to be an instance of younger people being unwilling or unable to leave their ageing parents behind.

6b) John James ~ 17.2.1765 (A); convicted and hanged, with his
    younger brother, George-Frédéric, for the Emeneau murders,
    9.5.1791, unm.[21]
7b) Susanne ~ 20.7.1766 (A); = (I) 1782, Henry SHUBLEY
    + 2.2.1786, age 66 (C). Issue. She = (II) 30.4.1786 (C), Pvte.
    William CHINEY or CHEANEY, living in 1792 at LaHave
    Islands. She = (III) 17.12.1805 (A), John Frederick JEAUDRY.
8b) James *David,* schooner master, ~ 8.11.1767 (A), sometime
    resident of Tatamagouche, + -.10.1847 at St. Margarets Bay;
    = 11.11.1797 (A), Mary Catherine BOUTEILLIER.[22] Issue.
9b) George Frederick ~ 13.8.1769 (A); convicted and hanged, with
    his older brother, for the Emeneau murders, 9.5.1791, unm.
10b) Joseph * 10.11.1771 (A) ■ 9.8.1847 at St. Margarets Bay;
    = 31.1.1797 (A), Mary Elizabeth SLAUNWHITE. They had
    fifteen children.
11b) Joan *Margaret* * 30.12.1772 (A) + 1810/1815; = 19.12.1790
    (P), George Melchior WEINACHT ~ 22.9.1771 (C). Issue.
12b) John George * 31.3.1774 ■ 10.4.1774 (A).
13b) John Peter * 17.9.1775 (A) ■ 3.12.1848 in Queens County;
    = 9.1.1798 (A), Mary Gertrude * 12.1.1774 (A) + -.1.1841,
    dau. of George MINGO, and had nine children.
5a) **Jean-Nicolas** ~ 22.10.1731 at Étobon, ■ 17.12.1799 (L);
    = 3.5.1757 (A), Anne-Judith * 6.5.1739 at Aibre, dau. of Samuel
    and Marie-Marguerite (Lande) METTIN, and stepdau. of Jacques
    BOUTEILLIER. Issue:
1b) John George ~ 27.4.1758 (A) + young.
2b) Catherine ~ 3.7.1761 (A) + 21.8.1814; = 20.5.1786 (P),
    Leopold-Frederick LANGILLE + 17.9.1819, age 89 (A). Issue.

---

[21] Kenneth S. Paulsen, "The Emoneau Family of the Principality
of Montbéliard and Lunenburg Township, N.S.," in *NEXUS*, XII, 147 - 149.

[22] The only tenable explanation for her identity is that Mary
Catherine was a first cousin of David Bouteillier. His uncle, Jacques
Bouteillier, had a dau., Mary Catherine, born in 1781 (*infra*).

3b) Mary Elizabeth ~ 2.10.1763 (A) + 23.8.1863; = 29.8.1784
  (A), John OICKLE ■ 13.9.1830 age 75 (A). Issue.
4b) John George ~ 7.9.1765 (A), living 1807; nicknamed
  Coolah; = 30.12.1788 (A), Anna Barbara ~ 16.7.1769 (A),
  dau. of Peter CLATTENBURG and had issue.[23]
5b) George *Frederick* ~ 26.8.1767 (A) ■ 13.1.1863 at St.
  Margarets Bay; nicknamed *Coolah;* = 29.11.1791 (L), Mary
  Catharine * 6.8.1774 (A) ■ 20.7.1845, dau. of Conrad
  KNICKLE . Issue.
6b) Peter ~ 29.10.1769 (A).
7b) John James* 14.2.1772 (A), living 1815 at Aspotogan;
  = 7.4.1798 (P), *Mary* Elizabeth * 9.11.1778 (A), dau. of
  John Christopher DAUPHINÉ. Issue.
8b) John Christopher * 20.3.1774 (A), ■ 27.4.1839 at French
  Village = 4.5.1799 (P), Mary Catherine, dau. of his cousin,
  John Frederick BOUTEILLIER. Issue.
9b) Elizabeth * 21.6.1776 (A); = 23.5.1803 (P), John Peter
  BOUTEILLIER, son of her uncle Jacques (p. 68) Issue.
10b) James * 29.7.1779 (A).
11b) Ann Catherine * 27.6.1782 (A).
12b) George * 10.10.1785 (A).
13b) John * 17.3.1788 (A).
6a) Pierre ~ 12.6.1734 + 24.6.1734 at Étobon.
7a) **Jacques** ~ 11.8.1735 at Étobon + in May 1827[24]; = 27.12.1765
  (A), Susanne * ca. 1745, dau. of Vernier RIGOULEAU. Issue:
1b) James Frederick * 20.2.1766 (A), living 1815; =11.3.1794 (P),
  Susan Elizabeth * 13.7.1771 (A), dau. of Jacob
  SLAUNWHITE. Issue.

---

[23] There is no connexion to the later Coolen family found on the
western shore of St. Margarets Bay. The epithet or nickname "Coolah" was a
local reference to their father having been Nicholas, a dialect form of which
it was.

[24] His death at Sydney River, Cape Breton, was reported in the
Acadian Recorder, 9.6.1827. He moved to Coxheath, Cape Breton, in 1811.

2b) John James * 26.5.1768 (A).

3b) Catherine Elizabeth * 9.2.1770 (A), living 1803; = 16.10.1788 (P), Henry LEWIS, St. Margarets Bay, and had issue.

4b) George Jacob * 28.10.1772 ■ 6.12.1772 (A).

5b) John Peter * 18.10.1773 (A), living 1809; = 23.4.1803 (P), Elizabeth, daughter of his uncle Nicolas BOUTILIER [page 67], and had issue.

6b) *John* George * 16.9.1777 (A); = Anne Catherine, dau. of James BOUTEILLIER, his cousin.

7b) Ann Catherine * 1.5.1780 (A).

8b) Mary Catherine * 9.8.1781 (A) + 6.7.1875 at St. Margarets Bay; = 11.11.1797 (A), James *David* BOUTEILLIER, her cousin.[25]

9b) John David * 13.8.1784 (A); = Elizabeth BARKHOUSE and had issue. They lived at St. Margarets Bay.

10b) Susan Margaret * 28.10.1786 (A) + 1879/80; = 18.4.1802 (P), John *Jacob* ANDREWS ~ 4.1.1778 (C) + 11.12.1835, and had issue.

11b) Henry Joseph * 29.7.1789 (A) + 1880/81; married with issue.

8a) **Jeanne** ~ 15.7.1739 at Étobon; in orphanage at Halifax in 1753.

9a) **George-Frédéric** ~ 3.11.1742 at Étobon; in orphanage at Halifax in 1753 and was apparently still alive in 1784.

CALAME

Abraham Calame * 16.1.1695 at Beutal[26]; a mason, he came to Nova Scotia in 1752 in the *Speedwell*, with a household of 2.3.2.0, and ■ 21.3.1758 (A). He = (I) 27.1.1728 at Beutal, Susanne-Marguerite HUMBERT + ca. 1730. He = (II) Elisabeth BOURQUIN + ca. 1746 and had issue. He= (III) 29.10.1748 at Beutal, **Susanne Catherine** ~ 18.4.1704 at Ste-Suzanne + in Halifax ca. 1.10. 1752, dau of Henri FROMONT and widow of Pierre BOUVIER. The children were:

---

[25] This identification is based on a process of eliminating all the other reasonable possibilities.

[26] Son of David CALAME of Beutal and his first wife Françoise MOUHOT + 1697. David Calame + 1.6.1701 at Beutal at the age of 40.

1. **Marie**, living 1774 at Tatamagouche, NS; = 7.5.1754 (A), Jacques BIGUENET, and had issue.
2. **Jeanette** or Thiennet ~ 29.4.1733 at Beutal ▪ 17.11.1752 at Halifax.
3. **Jacques** * 2.9.1736 at Beutal, who lived in New York from 1762 to 1771, when they moved to Philadelphia; = 24.3.1758 (A), Susanne-Judith, dau. of Jacques-Christophe METTETALL, and had issue:
   1) Judith-Margaret ~ 17.2.1759 (A).
   2) Susanna Margaret "Calland" ~ 13.6.1762 at Halifax.
4. **Abraham** * 9.10.1738 + 25.10.1738 at Beutal.
5. **Marie-Madeleine** * 19.11.1739 at Beutal, living 1762; = (I) 17.12.1754 (A), Jean-George BOUTEILLIER, ▪ 10.5.1757 (A). She = (II) 28.3.1758 (A), Pierre COULON. Issue.
6. **Catherine** * 8.5.1742 at Beutal ▪ 1.10.1778 at Halifax; = 18.5.1762 (A), Jacques COULON. Issue.

Jacques sold his lands to Sebastian Zouberbuhler, 27.8.1761 (Lunenburg Co. Deeds, I, *f* 52 # 110), presumably in preparation for leaving the province.

CARLIN -I

Jean Carlin, joiner, * ca. 1714 at Colombier-Châtelot, living in 1753, came to Nova Scotia in the *Speedwell* in 1752, in a household 1.1.0.2. He = 8.2.1735 at Longevelle, Suzanne CHARLES (did not come). Issue:
1. **Catherine** ~24.1.1736 at Longevelle ▪ Halifax 1.4.1753, age 15 [?].
2. George ~ 31.10.1737 at Beutal.
3. Étienne ~ 8.1.1740 ▪ 18.1.1742 at Beutal.
4. Suzanne ~ 19.12.1742 at Beutal; = 1.11.1768 at Beutal, Jean-George LAGARCE, and had seven children.
5, 6. **(Two unnamed children aged 0-4)** + at sea, summer 1752.[27]

---

[27] I am not satisfied with either my own or Dr. Bell's interpretation of the record of this family. One would expect that 1.1.0.2 meant a male and a female above the age of 14, and two children below the age of 4. If the age of the female given in the April 1753 return is correctly recorded, she would have to be the *adult* female of the passenger list. A quite different explanation appears from the Beutal record. Suzanne CHARLES, wife of Jean CARLIN, was buried 2.4.1778 age 70, leaving one daughter. It appears that she and her daughter Suzanne (born 1742) did not emigrate

CARLIN-II

Pierre + by 1745, son of Pierre CARLIN of Dung; = 20.1.1705 at Bavans, Catherine, dau of Pierre GOUX of Étobon. Issue:
1. Catherine ~ 18.7.1705 at Bavans.
2. Anne-Judith ~ 3.7.1707 at Bavans.
3. Pierre ~ 28.7.1709 at Bavans; = 12.4.1746, Marguerite MOUHOT.
4. Joseph ~ 1.11.1711 at Bavans.
5. **Jean,** a house joiner ~ 18.12.1715 at Dung; came to Nova Scotia in 1752 in the *Speedwell*, with a household of 1.1.2.0, ■ 17.1.1753 (P); = ca. 1743, **Catherine-Elisabeth** * 5.5.1722 at Allondans + 12.12.1794 at New York, dau. of Simon LOVY.[28] Issue:
   1) **Judith-Marguerite** * 17.8.1745 at Ste.-Susanne ■ 28.9.1753 (P).
   2) **Jeanne** * 6.10.1747 at Ste.-Susanne; moved to New York ca. 1765/66.
   3) Pierre-Joseph * 8.3.1751 at Dung + in infancy.
   4) Jean-Pierre ~ 13.10.1752 (P); moved to New York ca. 1765/66.
6. Jeanne * ca. 1717; = 15.4.1749, Jean-George VILLE dit Blle. Issue.

CERTIER[29]

Pierre CERTIER dit Mareschal * ca. 1600 + 14.4 + 14.4. 1649 at Longevelle; = 30.1.1621 at Longevelle, Claude, dau. of Pierre MIGAINE of Colombier-Châtelot, and had issue, including a son:
1. Pierre * 11.11.1627 at Longevelle; = 4.2.1651 at Longevelle, Anne * 9.11.1628 + 18.9.1662 at Longevelle, dau. of Pierre CERTIER dit Filand (+ 11.3.1634 at Longevelle; = 27.6.1625 at Longevelle, Jacquotte, dau. of Toussaine PARROT dit Thourot) and had a son:

---

[28] Nicolas LOVY * 1645 + 26.1.1698 of Allondans was father of Simon LOVY * 1679 + 2.3.1740; = 29.8.1702 at Issans = Henriette * 1679, dau. of Jean MARÇONNET of Allondans. They had eight children, including Catherine-Elisabeth (*supra*), wife of Jean CARLIN and then of David BANVARD. Her second marriage, to Banvard, on 20.5.1753, makes it clear *which* of the two Jean Carlins had been buried in January 1753.

[29] In Nova Scotia this name was anglicized to Sarty. A second Sarty family derives from the Sertier family (*infra*). Pierre Certier dit Mareschal was a son of another Pierre, mayor of Longevelle + 28.6.1635 of the Plague.

1) Antoine~ 24.4.1664 at Longevelle + 24.2.1726 at Héricourt;
   = 9.1.1683 at Longevelle, Claudine HUMBERT of Colombier-Châtelot. Eleven children:
   1a) Pierre ~ 10.8.1684 at Longevelle + young.
   2a) Jean ~ 13.9.1685 at Longevelle + 1733/34; = 22.11.1712, Anne-Marie-Madeleine DUFORT of St.-Maurice, and had eight children:
      1b) Susanne ~ 12.10.1713 at Longevelle + young.
      2b) Anne-Catherine ~ 9.8.1715 at Longevelle; = 25.10.1738 at Montbéliard Town, Pierre-Joseph MORLOT, weaver. Issue.
      3b) Louise ~ 26.5.1718 at Longevelle.
      4b) Jacques-Christophle ~ 6.3.1721 at Longevelle.
      5b) Marguerite ~ 6.3.1724 at Longevelle.
      6b) Jean-Léonard ~ 24.3.1727 at Longevelle.
      7b) Susanne ~ 19.3.1730 at Longevelle.
      8b) **Étienne**, weaver. born posthumously, ~ 29.4.1734 at Longevelle; emigrated to Nova Scotia in 1752 in the *Speedwell*, as a single man. He was ■ 26.2.1782 (A); = 26.3.1769 (A), Catherine * 1737, dau. of Jean-Christoph JOUDRY, widow of Jean PATRIQUIN and had a son. She = (III) 12.5.1783 (L), Peter WAMBOLT. Issue:
         1c) John * 6.8.1771 (A), ■ 27.11.1830 at Martins River (A); = 24.2.1795 (A), Catherine-Elizabeth ~ 28.6.1779, dau. of Christophe-Jacques VEINOT. Twelve children:
            1d) Catherine Elizabeth * 16.10.1795 (A), living 1830; = 16.2.1819 (A), Henry HILTZ, Indian Point * 30.9.1797 (L).
            2d) James Frederick * 3.9.1797 (A).
            3d) John George * 3.12.1799 (A).
            4d) John * 14.4.1802 (A).
            5d) Ann Catherine * 15.6.1804 (C).
            6d) Catherine Regina 'Rachel' * 107.1807(C), living 1830.
            7d) Catherine Lucy, living 1830.
            8d) Sarah, living 1830.
            9d) George Lewis * 12.2.1810 (A) ■ 8.10.1828 (A).
            10d) Susan * 5.8.1812 (A).
            11d) Mary Ann * 5.4.1815 (A), living 1830.
            12d) Jacob * 27.2.1820 (C), living 1830.
            13d) Eliza * 24.12.1823 (A) ■ 3.1.1828 at Martins River.

3a) Marguerite ~ 28.12.1687 at Longevelle + 1730/32;
= 23.7.1709 at Longevelle, Jean-Joseph DAUPHINÉ, tailor
and had issue.[30]

4a) Antoine ~ 15.1.1689 at Longevelle; = 3.8.1717 at Longevelle,
Madeleine TATTEREI of Chagey. Issue.

5a) Nicolas ~ 21.2.1692 at Longevelle; = 30.3.1728 at Héricourt,
Anne-Rosine, dau. of the late Étienne DeFRANCE. Issue.

6a) Anne ~ 1.2.1694 at Longevelle.

7a) Pierre ~ 30.10.1695 at Longevelle.

8a) Antoinette; = 21.11.1724 at Héricourt, Gabriel JUILLARD.
Issue.

9a) **Catherine-Marguerite** ~ 26.12.1698 at Longevelle + summer
1752 at sea en route to Nova Scotia; = 8.7.1721 at Longevelle,
Jean JODRI of Bavans, and had issue.

10a) Louise ~ 25.3.1701 at Longevelle.

11a) Judith ~ 2.3.1704 at Longevelle.

C L E M E N Ç O N - I

Claude CLEMENÇON ■ 30.12.1694 at Clairegoutte age 50 and his
wife Suzanne DUPUIS had issue, including a twin son, Claude-Pierre
~ 18.4.1678 at Clairegoutte; = 9.6.1705 in Montbéliard Town, Jeanne
CHARLEMAGNE. Their sixth child and fifth son was:

1. **Daniel**, a smith by trade ~ 6.1.1715 at Temple St.-Martin,
Montbéliard Town + summer 1752 at sea en route to Nova Scotia in
the *Sally*; = 27.12.1734 at Clairegoutte, Anne * 29.5.1708 (did not
emigrate), dau. of Abraham and Madeleine (DONZEY) HORY of
Clairegoutte, and had a son,

   1) **Jacques-Christophe** * ca. 1738/40; orphan at Halifax in 1752/3.
   Put out to Jones, sailmaker, 3.3.1753.

---

[30] Through this marriage to Dauphiné and that of her younger
sister to Jodri, the three Nova Scotian Montbéliard families of Dauphinee,
Jodrey (part) and Sarty (part) are related.

CLEMENÇON-II

Frédéric Clemençon, farmer * 1733/34 in Montbéliard, possibly at Dasle. He was a farmer and set out for Nova Scotia in the *Betty* in 1752, but died at sea en route, summer 1752.

COULON-I

Jean-Nicolas Coulon was a farmer aged 66, travelling to Nova Scotia in 1752 in the *Speedwell* with a household of 3.1.0.0. There is some reason to believe that he was born in Les Verrières, Canton Neuchâtel, Switzerland ca. 1686. He + at Halifax between August and October 1752, shortly after landing in Nova Scotia; = **Susanne** - - - -,
■ 7.11.1752 (P). They brought with them two sons:
1. **Jean-George** * ca. 1735/36, living in 1755.
2. **Jean-Jacques** * ca. 1738, ■ 20.2.1753 at Halifax. [Steinfort reported him dead by 16.2.1753, age 16. The burial register may have recorded the date incorrectly.]

Traditional Costume:

the girls were 'diaichottes'

and the men were 'bouebes'

C O U L O N - II[31]

Jean-Jacques COULON dit Martin, carpenter * 1666 at Les Verrières, Canton Neuchâtel, Switzerland + 1.6.1746 at Étobon; = (I) 16.8.1701 at Étobon, Françoise * 1666 + 23.6.1726, dau. of Nicolas and Marguerite (Jeanmaire) REBILLARD, and had issue. He = (II) 16.9.1727 at Étobon, Jeanne MONNIER, widow of Étienne FERTÉ of Chenebier. The four Coulon children were:

1. **Pierre** * 28.4.1702 at Étobon, living 1762, a joiner, 46 years old [sic] when he embarked for Nova Scotia in 1752 in the *Betty*, with a household of 1.1.3.1.[32] He = (I) 8.1.1726 at Étobon, Elisabeth RACINE + 26.12.1730 at Étobon. Three children. He = (II) 21.8.1730 at Étobon, **Marie-Magdalen** * 1710, dau. of David & Catherine (Valliton) JACOT and had nine children. His issue were:

   1) Marie ~ 27.3.1727 at Étobon; sponsored brother's baptism in 1743.
   2) Jean-Pierre ~ 21.12.1728 + 16.1.1729 at Étobon.
   3) Anne-Marguerite ~ 30.6.1730 + 6.11.1730 at Étobon; youngest by Elisabeth.
   4) **Pierre** ~ 17.4.1733 at Étobon; a joiner, listed as single man age 19 in 1752 on the passenger list of the *Betty*; = 28.3.1758 (A), Marie-Magdalen, dau. of Abraham CALAME, and widow of Jean-George BOUTEILLIER. Two daughters:

---

[31] Despite this family's numbers in 1752, there seems to be no incontrovertible evidence for its continuation in Nova Scotia much beyond 1763. The family seems to have moved *en masse* to another jurisdiction. It is likely, even probable, that they removed to New York. At least one piece of evidence suggests that destination. A man named Jonas COULON married Elizabeth TELLER on 7.4.1780 at the French Church in New York.

Subsequent Coolen families in Nova Scotia seem to have divided origins. The largely Catholic family in the Prospect area claim Irish derivation, whilst those in the Fox Point and Mill Cove neighbourhood appear to originate with a Joseph or William Cooling. Research connects neither man to those coming from Montbéliard.

[32] The business with his age is probably another instance of the emigrants betraying fear of being turned away because they were deemed "too old" to go to Nova Scotia.

1a) Catherine ~ 22.10.1759 (A).
2a) Catherine-Marguerite ~ 17.2.1762 (A).
Pierre Coulon sold his lands at Lunenburg and Northwest Range on 29.7.1762 and 25.10.1762 (Lunenburg Co. Deeds, I, ƒ 88 #191 and ƒ 90 #196.)
5) **David** ~ 19.2.1735 at Étobon; a joiner, listed as single man age 17 in 1752 on the passenger list of the *Betty*, ■ 16.4.1753 at Halifax. Confirmed at Étobon, 28.3.1751.
6) Catherine-Elisabeth ~ 17.6.1737 + 28.2.1747 at Étobon.
7) Jean-George ~ 10.3.1739 at Étobon + young.
8) **Jacques** ~ 10.4.1740 at Étobon ■ 9.6.1784 (P); = 18.5.1762 (A), Catherine, ■ 1.10.1778 (P), dau. of Abraham CALAME. Issue:
1a) John Peter ~26.3.1763 (A).
9) **Jean-George** ~ 17.4.1743 at Étobon + 1757 at Lunenburg.
10) **Catherine** ~ 11.4.1745 at Étobon, living 1757.
11) Marguerite ~ 2.3.1747 + 11.4.1747 at Étobon.
12) **Jonas** ~ 21.3.1748 at Étobon, living 1757, and New York 1780.
2. Jeanne-Elisabeth * 20.12.1703 + 27.9.1729 at Étobon, unm.
3. Josué * 6.8.1705 at Étobon + 1706.
4. Marie * 7.2.1707 + 12.8.1748 at Étobon; = 3.5.1729 at Étobon, Daniel * 1702, son of Pierre GOUX, and had eight children.

CURIÉ

Jacques Curier or **Curié** * ca. 1725; a wheelwright at Ste.-Suzanne, he and his wife emigrated to Nova Scotia in 1752 in the *Speedwell*. He, a son of Jean Curie of Lougres = 7.9.1751 at Bavans, **Marguerite-Julienne**, living at New York in 1775, dau of Joseph and Marguerite MORLOT of Bart. On 19.4.1762 he sold his lot at First Peninsula (Lunenburg Co. Deeds, I, ƒ 81 # 175) and removed to New York where he died late in 1767 or early 1768. Issue:
1. Jean-George * 9.1.1752 at Lougres + in infancy.
2. Susanne-*Catherine* ~ 20.3.1754 (A); = ca. 1770 at New York, Jean-Pierre, son of Pierre VAUTIER, and had issue, baptised in the French Church at New York:
1) Pierre * 27.7.1771 at New York.
2) Jacques * 30.8.1773 at New York.
3) Susanne * 16.8.1775 at New York.

3. *Marie*-Marguerite ~ 4.1.1757 (A), sponsored Jacques Vautier's baptism in 1773 at New York.
4. Susanne-Catherine ~ 29.12.1758 (A).
5. Barbara ~ 17.12.1761 (A).
6. Marguerite * 9.8.1764 ~ 12.8.1764 at the French Church, New York.
7. Jacques, posthumous * 15.3.1768 ~ 20.3.1768 at the French Church, New York.

Miscellaneous Curier or Curié individuals in records of the 1750s:[33]

a) Susanne CURIER = 2.1.1753 (P), André JAILLET (*q.v.*). It is worth noting that Jaillet crossed with a wife and one child in a household listed as 2.1.1.2. That leaves a man over 14, a girl 4-14 and a child 0-4 unaccounted for. Possibly one or more of the Curiers made up some or all of those three persons.

b) Anne CURIER = (I) 26.5.1753 (P), Jean-George L'EAU/LODS, and (II) 21.3.1766 (A), Jean-Joseph RENAUD [REYNO], by whom she had five children. She + July 1816, allegedly 96. An age of about 80 seems more likely, given her first marriage in 1753 and last child in 1778.

c) Susanne CURIER = 20.5.1755 (A), Jacques JEANBAS and had a child.

d) Henry CURIER = 9.10.1759 (A), Maria Barbara MÜLLER.

D A R É

Martin DAREL ~ 12.2.1660, son of Anthoine and Jeanne (Muhot) Darel; = Marguerite MAIRE. Their eldest child (of eight) was:
1. Louis DAREY ~ 12.5.1682 at Coisevaux + 25.4.1720 at Coisevaux; = 15.6.1706 at Trémoins, Catherine VEUILLAMIE of Échenans-sous-Mont-Vaudois. Issue:
   1) Jean ~ 27.2.1707 at Trémoins; = 12.10.1734 at Coisevaux, Sibylle, dau. of Jean-Guillaume and Jeanne (Marage) LODS of Tremoins. Issue.

---

[33] Four other persons surnamed Curier or Curié appear in Nova Scotian records during the 1750s. Since Jacques Curié came with only his wife, the others (if they came with Dick's recruits) must have traveled with persons of other surnames. Possibly one or two arrived later on their own and not as part of the settlement scheme.

2) **Jean-Nicolas** ~ 2.6.1709 at Trémoins, ■ 14.3.1767 (A). A farmer, he emigrated to Nova Scotia in the *Betty* in 1752, with a household of 1.1.2.2; = 12.11.1743 at Trémoins, **Susanne** ~ 30.1.1721 at Champey + 19.4.1786 (A), dau. of Jean-Jacques and Susanne JACOT. Susanne Daré = (II) 27.8.1775 (A), Léopold VIENOT. Daré had twelve children:

1a) **Jeanne** ~ 30.4.1744 at Trémoins + 26.1.1787 (A); = 8.4.1762 (A), Jaques-Christophe VIENOT* 23.12.1747 at Blamont ■ 25.11.1802, age 65 (A). Issue.

2a) **Jacques** DARES ~ 1.5.1746 at Trémoins, living 1795 at Northwest Range; = 20.10.1772 (A), Catherine * 28.5.1752, living 1812, dau. of Léopold LANGILLE. Issue:

1b) James Frederick * 16.8.1774 + 30.1.1783 (A).

2b) Susan Catherine * 1.1.1777 (A); = (I) 14.11.1799 (C), Samuel ALLEN ■ 3.3.1801 (C). Issue. She = (II) 20.11.1814 (A), Alexander REID, widower, and had a son, David.

3b) George Frederick * 1.3.1779 (A); = 8.5.1804 (C), Elizabeth * 27.12.1780 (C), dau. of John Peter KNOCK. Issue.

4b) John Nicholas * 5.1.1782 (A); = 5.11.1805 (C), Philippina ~ 11.4.1784 (A), dau. of John BACKMAN. Seven children.

5b) Catherine Elizabeth * 25.10.1784 (A).

6b) Sarah Barbara * 3.12.1786 (A).

7b) James Frederick * 7.5.1789 (A); = 30.9.1813 (A), Ann Elizabeth * 7.9.1792 (A), dau. of John Peter LOWE.

8b) a child * 7.2.1792 ~ 18.3.1792 (A) [no name recorded]

3a) **Catherine** * ca. 1748 + 28.10.1842 (A); = 15.3.1768 (A), Jules-*Frederick* JOUDREY ~ 20.4.1743 at Allondans + 29.12.1812. Issue.

4a) **a child** * ca. 1750/1 + summer 1752 during the ocean passage.

5a) **Jean-Urban** ~ 7.7.1753 ■ 14.8.1753 (A).

6a) **Mary Margaret** ~ 16.1.1755 (A).

7a) **John Peter** ~ 12.4.1756 (A) + infant.

8a) **John George** DOREY ~ 15.3.1758 (A) ■ 13.9.1831 at Hubbards; = 27.11.1792 (A), Frances Catherine * 29.1.1774 (L), dau. of John Jacob SLAUNWHITE. Issue:

1b) James Frederick DAURIE, St. Margarets Bay * 17.8.1793
(A); = 28.11.1814 at Chester, Sophia Elizabeth * 12.4.1797
(A), dau. of John Conrad WESTHAVER. Issue.

2b) John *George* DAURIE * 17.9.1794 (A) + 12.4.1880 at
Hubbards; = 28.12.1814 at Chester, Elizabeth
~ 15.12.1797 (C), dau. of John Adam WHYNOT. Issue.

3b) Mary Catherine * 29.1.1796 ■ 22.3.1801 (A).

4b) Hannah Catherine * 3.8.1797 (A) + by 1826; = 1.12.1818
(Chester), Jacob HARNISH * -.6.1798, living 1871. Issue.

5b) Elizabeth * 2.6.1799 (A).

6b) George Henry * 27.12.1800 (A).

7b) *John* George, Hubbards * 20.8.1802 (A); = 19.11.1826 (G),
Hannah Elizabeth * 15.8.1806, living 1849, dau. of John
George HARNISH. Issue.

8b) Susan Elizabeth * 24.4.1805 (A).

9b) *William* Alexander * 12.12.1807 (A) + 16.5.1892 Hubbards;
= 4.12.1831 (P), Elizabeth * 21.6.1814 + 22.6.1886, dau.
of John Frederick DAUPHINÉ. Issue.

10b) Casper Edward, Hubbards * 7.11.1809 (A); = 15.4.1833
at Chester, Elizabeth Sarah, dau. of Joseph COOLEN.
Issue.

9a) Elizabeth Margaret ~ 30.8.1760 (A);[34] = 27.4.1779 (A), John
George ROBERT ~ 30.4.1756 (A) + 1801. Issue.

10a) Mary Catherine ~ 2.5.1762 (A); = 16.10.1781 (A), John
CROUSE ~ 3.4.1757 (A) + 22.1.1847 (L). Issue.

11a) John Christian ~ 3.7.1763 (A) + young.

12a) Catherine Margaret ~ 4.5.1766 (A); = 14.8.1783 (A), William
LEGGE, Martins River ■ 3.5.1825, age 60 (A). Issue.

3) Pierre ~ 18.11.1711 at Trémoins + 19.11.1774 at Coisevaux;
= 31.12.1743 at Brevilliers, Elizabeth, dau. of Anthoine GUION of
Brevilliers. Issue.

4) Catherine ~ 5.12.1714 at Trémoins.

5) Magdeleine ~15.4.1718 at Trémoins.

---

[34] This listing of the Dares/Dorey family is incomplete. The
branch at Blandford appears to originate with Elizabeth Margaret Darez,
who married Robar in 1779.

DAUPHINÉ[35]

Jean-Joseph DAUPHINÉ, of Longevelle-sur-Doubs * 1686; = (I) 23.7.1709 at Longevelle, Marguerite ~ 28.12.1687 + 1730/32, dau. of Antoine and Claudine (Humbert) CERTIER dit Simonet of Longevelle. He = (II) 11.11.1732 at Longevelle, Marguerite GEIN of Sainte.-Marie, who + 1735/36, and he = (III) 27.11.1736, Marie DUCOMUN, who + 1737. He = (IV) 28.1.1738 at Longevelle, Marguerite PARROT dit Thourot. His three children, all by the first marriage, were:

1. **Jean** ~ 4.2.1724 at Longevelle; a shoemaker by trade, he came to Nova Scotia in 1752 in the *Speedwell* as a single man, and was
   ■ 1.1.1799 (A); = 20.5.1753 (P) , Marguerite-Elisabeth ~ 11.4.1732 at Brognard, ■ 19.1.1799 (A), dau. of Pierre and Françoise (Jeanperrin) BANVARD. Eleven children:
   1) Mary Elizabeth ~ 11.7.1754 (A); = (I) 29.9.1772 (A), George EMONEAU and = (II) 11.11.1783 (L), John Adam WAMBOLT ~ 2.11.1755 (A). Living 1794. She had issue by both marriages.
   2) James *Christopher* ~ 23.4.1756 (A) + 17.8.1841 at St. Margarets Bay; = 16.5.1790 (C), Sarah Philipps ~ 6.4.1766 (A) + -.3.1846, dau. of James Christopher VIENOT. Issue:
      1a) Mary Catherine *22.2.1791 (A); = John Just BOUTEILLIER.
      2a) Mary Elizabeth * 23.12.1792 (A).
      3a) *John* George * 10.4.1794 (A); = Margaret BOUTEILLIER. Issue.
      4a) *Frederick* Christopher * 7.2.1796 (A).
      5a) John *Christopher* * 10.1.1798 (A).
      6a) *Joseph* Frederick * 1.11.1800 (A) + 19.1.1828 at French Village.
      7a) Catherine * 27.12.1801 (A).
      8a) John * 1.11.1803 (A).
      9a) *James* Frederick * 2.1.1806 (A) + 12.1.1828 at French Village.
      10a) Susan Elizabeth * 25.9.1808 (A).
      11a) *Peter* Christopher * -.11.1809 + 22.1.1828 at French Village.

---

[35] This family was related to the Certiers and one of the Jodrey families who also came to Nova Scotia in 1752. Some of James Dauphinee's family (p. 81) settled in western Newfoundland and were known as Duffeny.

3) *John* Christopher ~ 27.10.1757 (A) + 31.5.1835; = 29.12.1776 (A),
  Mary Elizabeth, dau. of John BOUTEILLIER. Issue:
  1a) James Nicholas * 7.12.1777 ■ 14.12.1777 (A).
  2a) *Mary* Elizabeth * 9.11.1778 (A), living 1821; = 7.4.1798 (P),
    John Joseph BOUTILLIER. Issue.
  3a) John Joseph * 31.10.1780 (A).
  4a) *Sarah* Elizabeth * 11.11.1782 (A),■ 18.8.1859; = 6.2.1803 (P),
    Michael REUTHER [Rhuda] ■ 14.4.1853 age 77. Issue.
  5a) John George * 6.10.1784 (A) + 1785/89.
  6a) George Frederick * 17.3.1786 (C) + in infancy.
  7a) George Frederick * 11.7.1787 (A). Issue.
  8a) *John* Frederick * 2.3.1789 (A) + 21.3.1846 at Hubbards;
    = 1.6.1814 at Chester, Mary Elizabeth BOUTILIER. Issue.
  9a) John *George,* of Boutiliers Point * 22.10.1791 (A). Issue.
  10a) Ann Catherine ~ 25.6.1794 (P)
  11a) Susan Catherine * 2.7.1796 (A) + 16.2.1841; = 30.12.1815 (P),
    John CROUCHER of St. Margaret's Bay * 1794 + 1819/20. Issue.
  12a) John * 1.6.1798 (A) ■ 18.2.1801 (A).
  13a) John Frederick * 7.5.1800 (C).
  14a) John, a twin ~ 31.10.1801 (P).
  15a) Margaret *Elizabeth,* twin ~ 31.10.1801 (P); = 28.12.1818 (P),
    John JOHNSON ~ 29.8.1796 (L), and had at least ten children.
4) Joseph ~ 26.8.1759 (A), living 1796.
5) Mary Catherine ~ 14.3.1761 + -.12.1837; = 26 or 29.10.1779 (A),
  John Christopher PERRIN ~ 22.8.1756 (A). Issue.
6) George-*Frederick* ~ 22.5.1763 (A) + 11.12.1831 at First Peninsula;
  = 11.12.1787 (A), Mary Barbara * 2.6.1771, dau. of Jacques-
  Frédéric SERTIE. Issue:
  1a) Mary Catherine * 9.2.1789 ■ 11.4.1789 (A).
  2a) *Ann* Judith * 24.5.1790 (C); = Leopold *Paulus* LANGILLE. Issue.
  3a) *John* Frederick * 21.8.1791 (A) + 28.7.1827 (A). Issue.
  4a) James * 4.10.1794 ■ 2.2.1801 (A).
  5a) *Mary* Catherine * 28.9.1796 (A); = John SPIEDEL. Issue.
  6a) Mary Anne * 25.10.1798 ■ 4.11.1798 (A).
  7a) Mary *Elizabeth* * 1.7.1800 (A); = Nicholas SPIEDEL. Issue.
  8a) *George* Louis * 25.12.1802 (A); = 31.5.1824 (L), Catharine Ann ~
    19.9.1802 (L), dau. of John Nicholas WENTZEL.

9a) James Joseph * 26.3.1805 (A). Issue.

10a) Lucy * 9.6.1807 ■ 5.3.1827 (A).

11a) Francis * 12.3.1810 (A); = Anne ALLEN. Issue.

12a) Jacob * 21.3.1813 ■ 5.3.1827 (A).

7) John-*George* ~ 28.10.1764 (A) + -.10.1811 at St. Margarets Bay; = 18.11.1783 (A), Sarah Phillips ~ 24.3.1765 (A), living 1813, dau. of Christopher-James VIENOT. Issue:

1a) Mary Catherine * 26.8.1784 (A).

2a) George Christopher * 24.12.1786 (A).

3a) James * 15.12.1788 (A) + 21.1.1852 at St. Margaret's Bay; = 12.1.1814 (P), *Susanne* Elizabeth BOURGOGNE. Issue.

4a) *John* Frederick * 15.12.1790 (A). Issue.

5a) Catherine *Elizabeth* * 27.10.1792 (A); = James BOUTEILLIER.

6a) Hannah Elizabeth * 16.11.1794 (A); = Jacob BOUTEILLIER.

7a) John *Frederick,* Hubbards * 18.3.1797 (A). Issue.

8a) Elizabeth * 22.2.1799 (A); = George BOUTEILLIER.

9a) *Sarah* Catherine * 11.5.1801 (A) ■ 24.3.1878; = John Valentine WESTHAVER, French Village ~ 29.7.1801 (A). Issue.

10a) *Anne* Sarah * 1803.

11a) *Susannah* Elizabeth * 30.10.1805 (A); = Henry GARRISON.

8) James ~ 8.11.1767 (A), living 1812 at St. Ann's Bay, Cape Breton; = 25.4.1791 (A), Susan Catherine ~ 2.11.1766 (A), dau. of Peter JOLLIMOIS. Issue:

1a) John Frederick, Boularderie Island * 11.9.1791 (A), living 1838.

2a) Susan Elizabeth * 11.3.1793 (A).

3a) John ~ 1.2.1795 (A).

4a) Mary Elizabeth * 5.3.1796 (A).

5a) Mary Catherine * 12.8.1797 (A).

6a) John George * 15.1.1799 (A).

7a) *John* James * 5.4.1800 (A) + in childhood.

8a) Peter * ca. 1803, living at Ingonish in 1838.

9a) *John* James * 18.5.1805 (A), living 1829.

9) Ann-Judith ~ 29.4.1770 (A) ■ 26.2.1811 (A); = 8.11.1791 (A), Peter James VIENOT ~ -.10.1770 (A) ■ 21.9.1834 of cholera. Issue.

10) Barbara ■ 27.1.1772, age 4 days (A).

11) John *Peter* * 9.2.1773 (A); = 3.7.1797 (C), Mary Elizabeth ~ 22.9.1776 (C), dau. of John EISENHAUER. Issue:

1a) John Frederick * 25.3.1800 (A).
2a) Mary Elizabeth * 1.6.1802 (A).
3a) Mary Anne * 30.7.1804 (C).
4a) John * 10.3.1806 (A). Issue.
5a) Arthur * 12.2.1809 ▪ 3.4.1809 (A).
6a) Paulus * 20.3.1811 (A).
7a) Isaac * 28.10.1813 (A).
8a) Sophia * 1.9.1817 (A).
2. **David** ~ 7.10.1726 at Longevelle; a tailor by trade, he emigrated to Nova Scotia in the *Speedwell* in 1752, with a household of 1.2.0.1. No further record.[36]
3. Éléanore ~ 21.5.1730 at Longevelle + 17 Nov 1786 at Lougres; = 17.2.1756 at Bavans, Jacques CURIÉ. No issue.

DEMET

Pierre DEMET, weaver and innkeeper at St.-Valbert = Catherine, dau. of Pierre-Anthoine DORMOY, and had issue:
1. **Pierre** ~ 11.10.1726 at Héricourt; a farmer, he emigrated to Nova Scotia in the *Betty* in 1752, with a household of 1.1.0.0, and + 1754/55 at Lunenburg; = (I) **Marie - - - -**, ▪ 28.3.1753, age 26 at Halifax. He = (II) 13.11.1753 (A), Mary Elizabeth, ▪ 30.11.1808, age 75 (C), dau. of Johann Bernhard HERMAN, having = (II) 3.2.1756 (A), John EISENHAUER + 26.11.1818 (C) and having had issue of her second marriage.
2. Elisabeth-Madeleine ~ 30.9.1731 at Héricourt.
3. Elisabeth-Catherine ~ 17.6.1733 at Héricourt.
4. Frédéricke-Sybille ~ 31.1.1736 at Héricourt.

---

[36] The two women over 14 and the child 0-4 who travelled with him were among those Montbéliardais who appear in Nova Scotia seemingly out of thin air. There were the Curiés (*q.v.*, p. 24), and two women named Richard whose arrival in Nova Scotia needs to be explained by their inclusion with someone such as David Dauphiné. Indeed, for the Richards, this looks the likeliest person with whom they may have traveled.

DONZEL

George DONZEL of Montbéliard Town; = - - - - BRETENIER. His son,
1. **George**, farmer, ~ 4.9.1712 at Montbéliard; emigrated to Nova Scotia
in the *Speedwell* in 1752, age 40, with a household of 1.1.0.0, and
- 17.9.1794 (L), age 86 [sic]; = **Anne-Barbara** - - - - , who died at
Petite Rivère, NS, ■ -.7.1775 (L), age ca. 60. Their only known child
was Pierre * 1754 + 1756/57.

DUPUIS

Jean-Nicolas Dupuis (confirmed at Étobon, 31.3.1743, a son of Jean
Dupuis of Belverne) * 1724/25, a mason by trade who emigrated to Nova
Scotia in the *Speedwell* in 1752, with a household of 1.1.1.0, and was ■
at Halifax, 24.11.1752; = 12.10.1745 at Bavans, **Anne-Catherine** ■
26.8.1772 (A), dau. of Jean-George RICHARD of Ste.-Suzanne. She =
(II) 23.1.1753 at Halifax, Jean VUILQUET, a widower. Dupuis had issue
1. **Pierre** * ca. 1747/48, living 1753, being about 5-6 years old.

DUPERRIN[37]

Pierre DUPERÉ of Courcelles-les-Montbéliard = 22.9.1705 at Allenjoie,
Susanne-Judith GROSBETY and had issue:
1. **Pierre-Isaac** ~ 20.8.1706 at Allenjoie; a tailor by trade, he emigrated
to Nova Scotia in the *Speedwell* in 1752 with a household of 1.2.2.1;[38]
- 19.1.1753 (P); = ca. 1731, **Marguerite-Catherine** FROMONT,
- 30.1.1753 (P). Issue:

---

[37] Halifax records render this DuPaivette, a name from Vaud,
just north of Lausanne, either from Montpreveyres or Le Mont-sur-Lausanne.
In Rougemont, Switzerland, one finds Duperret, Duperrex, Duperrez.

[38] The distribution of the family on the passenger list was 1 man,
2 women, 2 children aged 4-14, and one 0-4, Pierre-Nicolas born in 1732
had likely died and his name given another, younger, child, who came here in
1752. Anne-Marie born July 1737, just fell into the half-fare category of 4 to
14 year-olds in spring 1752, but there is little chance that Pierre-Nicolas, then
20, could have passed as being below 14. Marguerite or Pierre was evidently
the child below the age of 4 in spring 1752, though which is an open
question for want of conclusive evidence.

1. **Pierre-Nicolas** ~ 3.2.1732 at Allenjoie, living Lunenburg, 1755.
2. **Catherine**; = 27.2.1753 (P), Jean-Christophe MAILLARD
   ~ 1.12.1729 at Chenebier, ■ 30.1.1758 (A), having had issue.
3. Susanne-Catherine, twin * 5.7.1737 ■ 16.5.1738 at Allenjoie.
4. **Anne-Marie**, twin * 5.7.1737 ■ 25.12.1752 (P).
5. **Marguerite**, living 1755 at Lunenburg.
2. Jean-George ~ 9.10.1707 at Allenjoie.
3. Eve ~ 1.3.1709 at Allenjoie.
4. Michel ~ 22.1.1711 at Allenjoie.

DURAND

Louis DURAND, schoolmaster at Belverne, came from Renan, Canton Bern, Switzerland; = 25.4.1721 at Étobon, Anne-Barbe, dau. of Louis GRISIER. They had issue, including:
1. Louis * 31.12.1721 at Étobon.
2. Jacques Christophle * 30 Sep 1723 + 12 June 1724 at Étobon.
3. *Jean*-Nicolas * 29.5.1725 at Étobon; a stonecutter, he emigrated to Nova Scotia in 1752 in the *Speedwell*, at a stated age of 24, and was at Lunenburg in 1753.[39]
4. Pierre-Friderich ~ 2.2.1728 at Étobon.
5. Jean ~ 6.7.1732 at Étobon. [possibly this is the "Jean Durand" who came to Nova Scotia.]

DURÉ

Samuel Duré, a tailor, emigrated to Nova Scotia in 1752 in the *Sally*. He was 24, single, and came from the Principality of Montbéliard. He was ■ at Halifax, 20.2.1753, unmarried. [Steinfort reported him dead by 16.2.1753.]

DUVOISIN

Jean-Harry Duvoisin from Montbéliard Principality came to Nova Scotia in the *Ann* in 1750, with a household that was 1.1.1.2, if calculations based on his indebtedness are correct. He was naturalized at Halifax, 10.7.1758 (NSA, RG 1, Vol. 382). He died between 1758 and 1765 = (1)

---

[39] Can this be the 'Durand' listed with the "Mortgagors & Debtors" to the estate of Catharina Barbara Zouberbuhler on 2 July 1778?

—**NN**—, who apparently + 1750 at sea, having had issue:
1. **Marguerite** * ca. 1745 + 1753/55.
2. **Daniel** * 1747, living in Halifax in 1763, by 1768 a wigmaker in Philadelphia, and known as *Daniel DAVISON*. [Lunenburg Co. Deeds, I ƒ 320 #816.]
3. **a child** + at sea in 1750, as an infant.
Duvoisin = (II) 28.4.1753 (A), Marianne GRIFFIE.⁴⁰

E M O N O T - I⁴¹

George Esmonnot dir Girard = 1.2.1701 at Bethoncourt, Suzanne GUILLERMOT + 13.4.1729. Their son was **Samuel-Friderich Emonot** ~ 29.1.1702 at Bethoncourt, who came to Nova Scotia in 1752 in the *Speedwell*, with a household of 1.1.2.0. He + Aug/ Oct 1752 at Halifax, age 50/51; = (1) 9.10.1731 at Bethoncourt, Elisabeth ~ 18.2.1706, dau. of Pierre FLEURDELYS of Montbéliard, and had a daughter,
1. **Elisabeth** + 1755; = 4.1.1752 at Bethoncourt, **Frédérich-Melchior EMMENOT** [page 86].
Samuel-Frédéric = (II) ca. 1746 **Elisabeth-Marguerite** BOVET or BOUFFAY,⁴² widow of Hugues METTIN, and had issue:
2. **Anne-Elisabeth** ~ 17.10.1747 at Bethoncourt, ■ 31.3.1753 at Halifax.
Elisabeth-Marguerite = (III) 21.11.1752 (P), Jean-George GRETTEAU and had three children. Elisabeth-Marguerite BOVET had a daughter by Mettin, who also came to Nova Scotia, namely **Anne-Judith METTIN** * ca. 1738, living 1776; = 2.4.1754 (A), Jean-George BIZÉS and had issue.

---

⁴⁰ Quite possibly this was Marie, widow of Jean-Abraham GREIGNAUD.

⁴¹ See Kenneth S. Paulsen, "The Emoneau Family of the Principality of Montbéliard and Lunenburg Township, N.S., " in *NEXUS*, XII, 146 - 152.

⁴² The only other person surnamed BOVET in Nova Scotia was a Swiss, Elias BOVET, * ca. 1718, who = 8.9.1760 (P), Sophia, widow HARMER. He came to Nova Scotia in 1752 in the *Betty*.

EMONOT-II

Jean Esmonnot dit Serré + 26.6.1736 at Bethoncourt, son of Jean and Catherine (Colin) Esmonnot; = Jeanne * 6.5.1689, dau. of Jean-Estienne and Evotte (HANDEY) FIDELE of Brevillers. Their son **Frédéric-Melchior Emoneau** ~ 18.2. 1728 at or near Bethoncourt; came to Nova Scotia in 1752 in the *Speedwell*. He was a farmer, and was murdered with his second wife and a granddaughter on 19.3.1791 by the Boutilier brothers;[43] = (I) 4.1.1752 at Bethoncourt, **Elisabeth** + late 1755, dau. of Samuel EMONNOT (p. 85). He = (II) 3.2.1756 (A), Julianne Elizabeth FRANK [?] * ca. 1728, murdered with her husband 19.3.1791, widow of George Jacob FEINDEL. They had three children:

1. John *George* ~ 29.3.1756 (A) + 28.2.1778, age 22 (A) [sic; all here is almost certainly not as it seems in the records]; = 29.9.1772 (A), Mary-Elizabeth, dau. of Jean DAUPHINÉ. She = (II)11.11.1783 (L), John Adam WAMBOLT ~ 2.11.1755 (A). George's issue:
   1) Catherine Margaret * 8.11.1773 + 12.12.1775 of smallpox (A).
   2) Jane Catherine * 14.2.1775 + 9.12.1775 of smallpox (A).
   3) Catherine Elizabeth * 28.12.1776 (A), murdered 19.3.1791, with her grandparents.
   4) Mary Margaret * posthumously, 10.6.1778 (A) + 1868 at Mahone Bay; = 10.6.1794 (C), John Nicholas EISENHAUER, Second Peninsula, ~ 7.12.1765 (A), + 20.4.1826 (C), with a large family.
2. Susan Catherine ~ 9.11.1757 (A) + by drowning, 14.8.1767 (A).
3. Frederick, First Peninsula ~ 3.5.1759 (A) ■ 13.2.1816 (A); = 26.11.1777 (A), Mary Elizabeth ~ 28.3.1761 (A) ■ 16.2.1833 (A), dau. of John Adam WAMBOLT. Twelve children, eleven of whom married:
   1) Mary Elizabeth Barbara * 12.5.1779 (A); = 12.7.1795 (L), John Caspar YOUNG, of Peter Miller's Island, Mahone Bay, ~ 5.7.1769 (A), ■ 23.12.1842 at Chester. Issue.
   2) *George* Frederick, First Peninsula * 5.11.1781 (A) + 18.5.1823 (C); = 12.12.1805, Ann Catharine, dau. of George M. ZWICKER. Issue.

---

[43] For an account of this event, *cf.*, DesBrisay, 501 - 506. The proceedings of the Boutilier trial in May 1791 were published as a contemporary pamphlet. No Montbéliardais served on the jury. A modern account appears in Paulsen, "The Emoneau Family . . .," *NEXUS*, xii, 147 - 149.

3) Mary Catherine * 28.11.1783 (A) + 16.8.1852 (L); = 16.4.1799 (L), John Peter ZINCK * 28.6.1776 (L). Issue.
4) Mary Eva * 2.4.1786 (A); = 17.2.1807(C), Lawrence WENTZEL * 8.8.1784 (L). Issue.
5) *Ann* Mary * 19.3.1789(A); = 23.4.1807 (C), Rudolph WAGNER, Upper LaHave, * 2.10.1781 (L). Issue.
6) *Catherine* Elizabeth * 10.6.1792 ■ 28.6.1793 (A).
7) John *Henry,* First Peninsula * 17.5.1794 (A) + 24.6.1855; = 3.8.1823(L), Mary Regina (*Rachel*), * 19.4.1805 (L), dau. of Peter YOUNG. Issue.
8) Ann Barbara * 6.12.1796 (A); = 10.2.1820 (L), Andrew RHODENIZER * 5.4.1794 (L) + 1882. Issue.
9) John *Joseph* * 6.3.1798 (A).
10) John Daniel * 17.3.1800 (A); = 19.3.1823 (C), Mary Anne * 17.9.1801 + 20.10.1878, dau. of Melchior SILVER. Issue.
11) Catherine *Elizabeth* * 23.2.1802 (A); = 6.2.1823 (L), John Jacob SILVER * 14.11.1796 (L) + 22.1.1832 (C). Issue.
12) *Frederick* Frank * 13.1.1807 (A) ■ 2.1.1847 (A); = 6.12.1827 (L), Sophia Catharine * 2.12.1808, dau. of Jacob HIRTLE. Issue.

EUVRAI

Louis OUVRARD or EUVRAI + 19.1.1711, age ca. 80, and his wife Marie, née FLAMMAND, converted from Catholicism at Étobon. Issue:
1. Charles, sabot maker at Belverne * 1664 + 15.3.1738 at Belverne; = 3.1.1690 at Étobon, Marie DELILE of Étobon * 1660 + 22.3.1724. They had five sons:
1) Noë * 15.10.1691 at Étobon.
2) Abraham * 10.12.1692 at Étobon.
3) Jean-Pierre * 26.9.1695 at Étobon; married with children at Étobon.
4) Jean-Nicolas, labourer at Étobon * 10.4.1698 + 8.9.1747 at Étobon; = (I) 1.3.1718, Marie Rose + 25.8.1724, dau. of Abraham PLANSON and had four children. He = (II) 6.5.1727 at Étobon, Julianne * 18.9.1705, living 1747, dau. of Jean RACINE, and had eleven further children, the fourth of whom was

8a) **Pierre Euvrai**, farmer ~ 9.7.1732 at Étobon; came to Nova
Scotia in the *Betty* in 1752 as a single man; ■ 15.3.1753 (P),
unmarried. Confirmed at Étobon, 30.3.1749.
5) Jean-George * 1.11.1703 at Étobon; married with children at
Étobon.
2. Marie * ca. 1671; = 14.1.1710 at Étobon, Claude BOILLOUD, church
elder, and died in 1714, leaving issue.
3. Louise.

FAINÔT[44]

George-Frédéric Fainôt * ca. 1727 in Montbéliard, either at Allenjoie or
Blamont; a gunsmith, he emigrated to Nova Scotia in 1752 in the *Sally*,
as a single man. He was ■ 18.2.1765 (A); = 13.11.1753 (A), Françoise
* 1732, dau. of Jean-George MÉNÉGAUX. Issue:
1. Susan Catherine ~ 5.10.1754 (A), living 1757.
2. John George ~ 11.6.1757 (A).
3. John Frederick ~ 11.12.1759 (A).

FEVRE

Jean-Pierre Fevre, mason * ca. 1735 in Montbéliard, probably at
Clairegoutte, living 1754. He emigrated to Nova Scotia in the *Betty* in
1752, alone.

Pierre Fevre or Faivre, mason * ca. 1725 in Montbéliard, perhaps at
Clairegoutte, ■ 14.3.1753 at Halifax; emigrated to Nova Scotia in the
Betty in 1752 with a household of 1.1.1.1; = **Catherine - - - -**,
■ 12.1.1753 at Halifax. One son,
1. **Jacques** * ca. 1750 + 10.4.1753 at Halifax.

With Pierre came **Jacques Fevre** * 1739; admitted to the Halifax
Orphan House in December 1752, and put out to George Gerrish,
blacksmith, 28.3.1753.

---

[44] Fainôt had a grist mill at Northwest Range, on lot B11 (300
acres), which he sold on 20.6.1764 to Joseph Pernette for £135 (Lunenburg
Co. Deeds, I, *f* 194 #440).His widow and the surviving children apparently
left the province soon after Fainôt's death.

Just how these several people were related must be speculative, though they clearly were. Pierre and Jacques travelled as one household. Jean-Pierre and Pierre were masons by trade and they sailed in the same ship. Jean-Pierre * 20.3.1738, and Jacques-Christophe * 11.10.1739 were sons of Pierre and Suzanne (Mignerey) of Clairegoutte, and are likely the two younger men of the name who came to Nova Scotia.

G O G U E L

Jean-Nicolas BOILLOU ~ 20.10.1691 at Chagey + by 1752, son of Jacques Boillou of Luze, a weaver, and of Jeanne Nochier; = 6.11.1714 at Héricourt, Elisabeth * 1689 + 11.11.1752 at Héricourt, dau. of Jehan and Evotte (Carpet) RICHARDOT of Héricourt. They had eight children, of whom the fourth:

4. **Marguerite** ~ 20.9.1722 at Héricourt, ■ 30/31.10.1752 at Halifax;[45]
  = 26.7.1746 at Héricourt, **Frédéric-Charles Goguel**, a miller
  * ca. 1723 ■ Feb/Mar. 1753 at Halifax; emigrated to Nova Scotia in the *Betty* in 1752 with a household of 1.1.1.0. Issue:
  1) **Frédéric** * ca. 1747; = (I) 25.7.1773 (P), Juliana Sophia
     ~ 1.5.1755 (A) + 1773/74, dau. of Paul Heinrich ANSCHUTZ.
     Frédéric = (II) 26.5.1774 (P), Mary WEBBER. As an orphan,
     Frédéric was put out to Richard Wenman, 31.8.1758.
  2) Elisabeth ~ 28.9.1752 at Halifax + infancy.

G R A N D J E A N

Daniel GRANDJEAN, mason, of LeLocle, Canton Neuchâtel, Switzerland + 14.3.1695 at Clairegoutte; = 22.8.1665 at Clairegoutte, Catherine de CHEZJEAN of that place. Issue:
1. Claudine ~ 7.7.1667; = (I) 3.11.1691 at Héricourt, Nicolas CACUN
   + 1710. Issue. She = (II) 1.11.1712 at Héricourt, Pierre WETZEL,
   Montbéliard Town.
2. Judith ~ 14.2.1672 + 16.2.1672 at Étobon.

----

[45] Through her mother, Marguerite Boillou was a first cousin of Jean-Henri Richardot, whose dau., Frédérique-Sibylle, was the wife of the emigrant, George-Frédéric BAILLY. This is one more pre-emigration link among the Montbéliardais who came to Nova Scotia. Not for nothing did its people refer to Montbéliard as "*le pays de cousins*".

3. Pierre ~ 26.6.1673 + 26.6.1673 at Étobon.
4. Pierre ~ 16.11.1674 at Étobon.
5. Marguerite ~ 4.1.1678 + 12.6.1678 at Étobon.
6. Jean-Jacques ~ 14.1.1681 at Étobon.
7. Elisabeth-Alexandrine ~ 19.2.1683 at Étobon.
8. Daniel ~ 1.2.1685 at Étobon; = (I) 1.9.1709 at Héricourt, Catherine
   + 15.1.1730, dau. of David CARMIEN and had a child,
   1) Sybille-Catherine * 18.8.1711 at Étobon, living 1727.
   Daniel Grandjean = (II) 1.8.1730 at Étobon, Marguerite
   * 12.5.1693 + 7.12.1758 at Étobon, dau. of Adam and Claudine
   (Plançon) GOUD. Two children:
   2) Jean-George ~ 25.11.1730 at Étobon; = 8.6.1756 at Étobon,
      Elisabeth * 19.6.1712 at Étobon, dau. of Josué METTEY, and
      widow of Pierre MIGNERÉ.
   3) **Jacques-Frédéric**, farmer ~ 29.3.1732 at Étobon; emigrated to
      Nova Scotia in 1752 in the *Betty*, single man living in 1753 at
      Halifax.
9. Catherine ~ 1.7.1688 at Étobon.
10. Julius-Frederich * 19.9.1692 at Étobon.

GREIGNAUD[46]

Jean-Abraham Greignaud * 1705 in Montbéliard + spring 1753 in
Halifax. He was a farmer who emigrated to Nova Scotia in the
Speedwell in 1752, with a household of 1.1.1.0; = **Marie** - - - -, living
1753,[47] and had issue:
1. **a child** * 1738/47 + at sea in the summer of 1752.

---

[46] If Greignaud is correct, the most likely birthplace of Jean-
Abraham would be Roches-lès-Blamont. However, the name may properly
have been Guignaud, or even a mistaken attempt to spell Grosrenaud.

[47] Possibly the Marianne GRIFFIE who = 28.4.1753 (P),
Jean-Henry DUVOISIN.

GRETTEAU

Daniel GRATTOZ, carpenter, of Tramelan, Erguel Lordship, Bern, Switzerland = 15.6.1717 at Ste.-Suzanne, Françoise BATAILLARD. Their son:
1. **Jean-George Gretteau**, a joiner * ca. 1717; emigrated to Nova Scotia
   in the *Sally* in 1752, with a household of 1.1.3.1,[48] + by 1795 at
   Frederick River, River John, NS; = (I) 15.6.1745 in Montbéliard Town,
   Anne-Catherine BARTHOLET, who + during the crossing in the
   summer of 1752. Issue:
   1) **Marguerite-*Elisabeth*** ~ 30.7.1746 at Montbéliard Town;
      = 2.5.1769 (A), Pierre-Christophe MAILLARD, living 1786
      at Tatamagouche.
   2) **Louis-Nicolas**, twin * 18.11.1748 at Montbéliard ■ 19.4.1753 (P)
   3) **Anne-Catherine**, twin * 18.11.1748 at Montbéliard Town.
   Jean-George = (II) 21.10.1752 at Halifax, Elisabeth-Marguerite
   BOUFFAY, widow of Samuel EMONOT, and had further issue:
   4) Susan-*Catherine* ~ 23.9.1756 (A), living 1796; = 6.4.1776 (A),
      John Peter RUDOLPH, a widower, * 1711 in the Palatinate
      + 1790, as his will was proved at Chester on 15.6.1790. They
      had five children, all of whom survived their father.
   5) Catherine-Elizabeth ~ 12.6.1758 (A), living 1770.[49]

---

[48] One of the children aged 4-14 who traveled with Gretteau was
evidently not his child. Possibly they were his wife's issue by a first marriage.
A George *MENIGO*, born in Europe, appears in the 1770 township return of
Lunenburg, while George *GRETTOT* had a household of man and wife, three
girls (all accounted for *supra*), and *two* boys. Given that a George and a John
MINGO turn up at Tatamagouche area in the 1770s near the Gratto family, it
is possible that this is one explanation of their appearance. Another possibility
is that discussed on the Ménégaux pages (pp. 142-3).

[49] She *just may* have been the wife of John MINGO and had
children born 1782-1793. The lack of any number of substantial records for
the families along Northumberland Strait for the late eighteenth century renders
it difficult to do more than speculate about many of the relationships. Tales
about some of the families amount more to folklore than to history. The
unsourced tale printed in Frank H. Patterson's *History of Tatamagouche, Nova
Scotia* (Halifax, 1917), 23, concerning a religious affray in Montbéliard, is an
instance of this. See page 9, *supra*.

6) John *James* ~ 3.7.1761 (A) + by 1801, when land at River John, NS, was granted to 'the heirs of James Gratto; = Mary Catherine, dau. of Matthew LANGILLE. Four children, living in 1809 at Northumberland Strait, including George, Matthew and Elizabeth, wife of John Peter JEANPERRIN.

GROSRENAULD

Jean GROSRENAULD of Bussurel + 25.1.1698, son of Pierre, = 8.9.1657 at Vyans, Sabine ~ 20,12.1635, dau. of Pierre and Evotte (Ballué) CABURET of Vyans, had issue, including:

1. Pierre, a blacksmith * 1669 + 4.3.1748 at Héricourt; = 8.5.1700 at Héricourt, Elisabeth *Margueritte* * 1678 + 12.12.1735 at Héricourt, dau. of Jacques and Anne (Petithorry) NARDIN.[50] They had issue:
   1) Pierre ~ 17.7.1702 + young at Héricourt.
   2) Jean ~ 17.1.1704 at Héricourt.
   3) Frédéric, a blacksmith, ~ 21.8.1705 at Héricourt; = 27.8.1726 at Héricourt, Elisabeth, dau. of Étienne FAIVRE, church elder at Clairegoutte. Issue:
      1a) Jean-George ~ 12.7.1727 at Héricourt.
      2a) Elisabeth-Marguerite ~ 26.12.1728 at Héricourt.
   4) Marguerite ~ 6.10.1707 + young at Héricourt.
   5) Jean-George ~ 2.12.1710 at Héricourt.
   6) Pierre ~ 17.11.1712 at Héricourt.
   7) **Jean-Jacques** ~ 6.3.1714 at Héricourt; a carpenter, emigrated to Nova Scotia in the *Sally* in 1752, with a household of 1.2.1.1,[51] and + ca. 1755; = (I) ca. 1737, **Marguerite JACQUES**, who + 1752 during the crossing, having had five children:

---

[50] Elisabeth Margueritte was the dau. of Jacques NARDIN *le vieux* * 1628 + 16.1.1715 at Héricourt, by his second wife, Anne * 1633 + 6.3.1691, dau. of François * 1595 + 26.9.1675, son of Pierre PETITHORRY of Magny Danigon. Anne's mother was Barbe, ■ 4.1.1675, age 73, dau. of Jean ROSSEL. Barbe Rossel = 3.6.1623 at Héricourt, François Petithorry, shoemaker.

[51] The passenger list seems mistaken here; a distribution of 1.1.2.1. would be accurate.

1a) a son */+ 1738 at Héricourt.

2a) **Anne-Marguerite** ~ 30.10.1740 at Héricourt + Sep/Oct 1752 at Halifax.

3a) **Jean-Christophe** ~ 21.5.1743 at Héricourt, living at Oakland in 1792; = 30.12.1766 (A), Mary Catherine, dau. of John George MÉNÉGAUX. Five children:

1b) John *George* ~ 29.5.1768 (A), living 1843 at Gays River; = 18.11.1798 (A), Catherine Elizabeth * 18.6.1777 (A), living 1831, dau. of James BEGIN. Issue:

1c) Mary Ann *Barbara* * 4.3.1800 (A).

2c) Catherine Elizabeth * 3.8.1801 (A).

3c) Elizabeth * 24.1.1804 (A).

4c) *James* Christopher * 8.3.1805 (A).

5c) John *Frederick* * 20.4.1806 (A).

6c) Martin * 11.12.1813 (G).

7c) Barbara * 25.5.1816 (A).

8c) Jenny * 10.12.1819 (P).

2b) Mary Catherine * 10.9.1770 (A); = 28.11.1799 (A), John WARD.

3b) Catherine Elizabeth * 12.4.1773 (A).

4b) George *Christopher* * 17.4.1775 (A) ■ 30.8.1859 at St. Margarets Bay; = 18.11.1798 (A), Barbara Elizabeth BOUTILIER, ■ 10.9.1862 age 88 years, 5 months, at St. Margarets Bay. Issue:

1c) Catherine Elizabeth * 3.8.1801 (A) + young.

2c) George Frederick * 19.2.1804 (C).

3c) Catherine Elizabeth * 8.12.1805 (A).

4c) Amelia Sophia ~ 25.9.1810 (P).

5c) William ~ 7.11.1811 (P); = 1.12.1834 at French Village, Isabella, dau. of George Frederick DAUPHINEE.

6c) Hannah ~ 27.9.1813 (P).

7c) James Frederick * 27.5.1819 (P).

8c) John Christopher * 16.11.1822 (P).

5b) John *Frederick* * 29.12.1777 (A); = 20.3.1803 (P), Ann-Catherine BOUTILIER. Issue:

1c) Catherine * 30.1.1804 (C).

2c) John James ~ 1.4.1806 (P).

4a) Jean-George ~ 10.3.1746 + in infancy at Héricourt.

5a) **Pierre** ~ 26.12.1750 at Héricourt + Feb/Apr 1753 at Halifax.
Jean-Jacques = (II) 5.12.1752 (P), Anne-Marie GERMAIN * ca. 1708
+ 3.6.1778 (A), widow of Jean MATHIEU of Échavanne and of Jean-
Jacques COULERUS. She = (IV) 6.7.1756 (A), John Michael
KAYSER

8) Jean-Nicolas ~ 3.11.1716 at Héricourt.

9) Marguerite ~ 27.5.1720 at Héricourt.

2. Marguerite * 1673 + 15.10.1743; = 30.12.1704, Jacques MINAL.

GUIGNÉ[52]

Jean CUGNEI of Colombier-Châtelot = Simonne GUILLOT of
Longevelle. Issue:

1. **Guillaume** ~ 25.10.1703 at Longevelle; a mason, he emigrated to
   Nova Scotia in1752 in the *Speedwell*, with a household of
   1.3.3.0, and was living at Lunenburg in 1761;[53] = 25.8.1725 at
   Longevelle = **Madeleine-Marguerite** QUESLET of Vandoncourt,
   living 1763 at Lunenburg. Issue:
   1) **Marie-Marguerite** ~ 28.6.1726 at Longevelle, living 1780; = (I)
      17.12.1754 (A), Jean-Frédéric MASSON, who + 6.8.1776 (A).
      Issue. She = (II) 22.10.1776 (A), Jacques BEGIN, and had
      three children.[54]
   2) Jean-Christophle ~ 6.10.1728 + young at Longevelle.

---

[52] Pastor Mathiot's writings about Montbéliard surnames were
serialized in the Lutheran weekly, **L'Ami Chrétien**. In May 1981, we read,
"Cunier: Cugney, Cuney. peut-être la forme Cunier, diversement ortho-
graphiée, dérive-t-elle aussi de Cuenin." Of Cuenin, Mathiot writes, "Cuenin
Cuenot. Formes dérivées de Huguenin, avec les variantes Guenin, Guenot."

[53] The complete disappearance of the parents and all but their
eldest, married, daughter from the local records after 1763 strongly suggests
that they removed from Nova Scotia to some other part of British America
about that time.

[54] If she was actually born in 1726 and had three children born
between 1777 and 1780, she is a remarkable instance of a woman child-
bearing into her fifties.

3) David, twin ~ 19.2.1730 + young at Longevelle.
4) Pierre, twin ~ 19.2.1730 + young at Longevelle.
5) **Susanne** ~ 2.6.1732 at Longevelle, living 1752.
6) Anne ~ 7.11.1735 + young at Longevelle.
7) **Pierre** ~ 31.8.1738 at Longevelle, living 1756.
8) **Susanne** ~ 12.6.1741 at Longevelle, living 1755.
9) **Catherine** * ca. 1743, living 1760.
2. Pierre ~ 18.7.1706 at Longevelle; = 16.10.1731 at Longevelle,
   Marguerite CARLIN of Blussangeaux, and had issue:
   1) Pierre ~ 14.12.1731 at Longevelle.
   2) Urbain ~ 15.5.1739 at Longevelle.
3. Madeleine ~ 10.8.1710 at Longevelle.

HUGUENOT

Pierre-Esaie HUGUENOT dit la Lance = 18.2.1727 in Montbéliard
Town, Marie-Marguerite MEYER. Their son **Pierre-David** * 10.9.1733
in Montbéliard Town; a farmer, he emigrated to Nova Scotia in the
Sally in 1752 as a single man. He was living in Halifax in late 1752.

HUMBERT

Jacques HUMBERT of Grand Charmont = 9.7.1727 in Montbéliard Town,
Marie VUILLAMIN-BEDERVILLE. Their son was
1. **Pierre-Christophe** * 3.3.1731 in Montbéliard Town; a weaver age 24
   [sic], he emigrated to Nova Scotia in 1752 in the *Speedwell*, a single
   man. He was living in Halifax in spring 1753.

ISELIN[55]

Pierre ISELIN, nailmaker and church elder at Clairegoutte ~ 28.11.1651
+ 9.6.1694, son of Jean and Anne (ROSSOL) HINZELIN; = 12.9.1673,
Catherine LEHAUT and had issue:
1. Jean, nailmaker ~ 24.12.1678 + 13.1.1756 at St.-Valbert; = 22.4.1704
   at Héricourt, Marie, dau. of Jean & Jeannette (Dupond) PECHIN, and
   had six children:

---

[55] The Iselin family descends from a Huguenot nailmaker from
Pont-du-Bois, France, Nicolas HENZELIN + 1595 at Frédéric-Fontaine. He
left three sons, one of them Jean, father of Pierre (*supra*).

1) Madeleine ~ 3.1.1706 at Héricourt.
2) Marguerite ~ 16.1.1707 + 5.8.1769 at Héricourt; = 16.9.1727,
   Jean-George L'HÔTE + 5.10.1733 of a fall. Three children.
3) Jacques-Christoffle ~ 27.6.1709 at Héricourt.
4) Henriette-Marguerite ~ 12.5.1711 at Héricourt.
5) Jean-George, nailmaker * 1713 + 11.1.1792 at Héricourt;
   = 17.9.1737 at Héricourt, Catherine DEMET. Seven children. at
6) Catherine ~ 3.3.1715 at Héricourt.
2. Pierre, nailmaker at St.-Valbert ~ 10.12.1676, living 1738; = (I)
   19.6.1703 at Héricourt, Elisabeth * 1684 + 19.6.1736 at Héricourt,
   dau. of Jean PECHIN[56] They had seven children:
   1) Jean ~ 21.3.1704 at Héricourt.
   2) Pierre, nailmaker ~ 16.8.1705 at Héricourt, living 1741;
      = 4.12. 1725 at Héricourt, Elizabeth * 1691 + 6.12.1741 at St.-
      Valbert, dau. of Étienne & Catherine (Tournier) DeFRANCE.
      One child:
      1a) Catherine-Elisabeth ~ 16.7.1731 at Héricourt.
   3) George, nailmaker ~ 29.2.1708 at Héricourt.
   4) **Jean-Pierre** ~ 25.11.1711 at Héricourt; a nailmaker, he emigrated
      to Nova Scotia in the *Pearl* in 1752, with a household of 1.2.2.1,
      and + Apr/Aug.1753;[57] = 22.9.1733 at Héricourt, **Elisabeth**
      * 1713, dau. of Jean and Marie (Vernier) JEAND'HEUR, tailor at
      Héricourt. She = (II) 16.10.1753 (A), Jacques MALMEHU. Issue:
      1a) Elisabeth-Catherine ~ 12.5.1735 at Héricourt + young at St.-
          Valbert.

---

[56] Jean PECHIN, a gardener at St.-Valbert + 15.12.1725, age ca.
85; = Jeannette DUPOND, who + 19.4.1701 at St.-Valbert, age 55. Their two
daughters, Marie and Elisabeth, married the Iselin brothers, Jean and Pierre,
respectively.

[57] One wonders whether the burial, at St. Paul's, Halifax, on
19 July 1753, of John "WINSTON" - a surname otherwise not found in 18th-
century Halifax - could possibly be that of Jean-Pierre Iselin. Given the
erratic spellings of the name Iselin in Halifax records, it is not as unlikely as
might at first appear; e.g.,Eysley, Easely, Eizland, Easling, Einsley.

2a) **Alexandrine-Marguerite** ~ 30.7.1736 at Héricourt, living 1772; = 30.3.1756 (A), Pierre JEAUNNÉ. Issue.

3a) Pierre ~ 24.7.1739 at Héricourt + young at St.-Valbert.

4a) **Catherine** ~ 26.10.1743 at Héricourt, living 1771; = 26.6.1759 (A), George METTETAL, and had issue.

5a) **Pierre-Étienne** ~ 21.4.1746 at Héricourt + 8.3.1815 in Halifax as *Peter Easling*, and had lived at Tatamagouche for several years; = 8.3.1768 (A), Susanne, dau. of Pierre-Frédéric MAILLARD. They had eight children:

1b) Catherine ~ 12.11.1769 (A) ■ 9.1.1776 (A).

2b) *Mary* Elizabeth * 11.1.1774 at Tatamagouche ~ 5.6.1775 (A), living 1812; = (I) 24.9.1797 (P), John TOWNSHEND and had four children. She = (II) Hannibal MURRAY.

3b) Catherine * 14.8.1776 (A), living 1836; = 2.12.1793 (P), Elias NAUGLE + 1836, and had issue.

4b) Margaret * 19.1.1778 (A), living 1804; = 28.9.1795 (P), Thomas YOUNG, and had issue.

5b) Mary Magdalen * 28.11.1779 (A) + 7.12.1815 at Halifax; = 26.11.1798 (P), Thomas HUNNEWELL ■ 24.11.1835, age 58, and had nine children.

6b) Sarah LaCour ~ 10.8.1782 (P).

7b) Eleanor ~ 1.2.1784 (P) ■ 12.12.1800 (P).

8b) John Easelin/Einsley * 7.1.1786 (P), out of Nova Scotia in 1812; = 23.9.1817 (P), Jane or Jean ~ 9.7.1800 (M), dau. of Robert and Catherine LOWDEN.

6a) Jacques ~ 31.8.1749 at Héricourt.[58]

7a) Elisabeth-Madeleine ~ 17.9.1751 at Héricourt.

5) Jean-George,[59] nailmaker ~ 28.1.1715 at Héricourt; = 20.10.1739 at Héricourt, Elisabeth * 12.1.1719, dau. of Jean JOLYMOIS of

---

[58] One of Jacques and Elisabeth-Madeleine had died before the family emigrated in spring 1752, while the other died on the transatlantic voyage that summer. Neither lived in Nova Scotia.

[59] Jean-George Iselin with his wife and family emigrated to Massachusetts in 1752/53.

Belverne.[60] They had issue:
  1a) Elisabeth-Marguerite ~ 20.8.1740 at Héricourt.
  2a) a son * 1744.
  3a) a dau. * 1746.
  4a) Pierre-Étienne ~ 4.1.1749.
 6) Jeanne ~ 9.5.1718 at Héricourt.
 7) Jean-George ~ 21.6.1721 at Héricourt.
Pierre = (II) 18.2.1738 at Héricourt, Alexandrine RICHARDOT.

| Lordship of | Town of | Lordship of |
| Blamont | Montbéliard | Héricourt |

JACOT

David JACOT, master miller, * ca. 1682 at LeLocle, Neuchâtel, Switzerland + 7.10.1735 at Étobon; = ca. 1708, **Catherine** VALITON * ca. 1682, living 1753 at Frankfurt, Maine, and had issue:
1. **Marie-Madeleine** * 1710, living 1753; = 21.8.1730 at Étobon, Pierre COULON * 28.4.1702 at Étobon and had issue. They emigrated to Nova Scotia in 1752.
2. Christoffle * 8.6.1712 at Étobon + by 1718.
3. **Jonas**, stonecutter * 24.5.1714 Étobon, ■ 12.10.1755 (A); emigrated to Nova Scotia in the *Betty* in 1752, with a household of 1.1.0.0;
   = 16.2.1751 at Étobon, **Catherine** ~ 13.1.1726 at Étobon,
   ■ 20.10.1752 at Halifax, dau. of Jean-George BOUTEILLIER of Étobon, who also emigrated to Nova Scotia. Issue:
   1) Catherine-Marguerite ~ 14.6.1751 + 13.8.1751 at Étobon.
   2) Catherine ~ 12.8.1752 (P) + in infancy.

---

[60] Elisabeth was a sister of Pierre-Anthoine JOLIMOIS who emigrated to Nova Scotia in 1752.

4. Elisabeth ~ 9.1.1716 at Étobon.
5. David, stonecutter at Échavanne * 26.2.1718 at Étobon; = (I) 8.2.1746 at Étobon, Henriette-Marguerite* 23.8.1720 + 22.11.1749 at Étobon, dau. of Gérard PETREQUIN, and had two children:
   1) Susanne ~ 4.6.1747 + 24.6.1747 at Étobon.
   2) Jacques-Christoph ~ 1.12.1748 at Étobon.
   David = (II) 30.11.1751 at Étobon, Anne-Judith, dau. of Jean-Louis CHAMOT, and widow of Gabriel RACINE. Issue:
   3) Elizabeth * 10.9.1752 at Étobon.
6. **Jacob,** a shoemaker * 31.3.1720 at Étobon, living 1753 at Frankfurt, Maine; emigrated to Nova Scotia in the *Betty* in 1752, with a household of 1.2.1.1;[61] = **Catherine - - - -**. Issue:
   1) **Jacob**, victualed at Halifax Aug/Oct 1752, and to Maine in 1753.
   2) **Madeleine,** ■ 27.12.1752 at Halifax.
7. Jean-Daniel, a mason * 2.11.1722; = 2.5.1756 at the French Church in New York, Marie, dau. of David and Catherine (Martin) VOGIE from Montbéliard. Daniel emigrated directly to New York in 1754.
8. Marie-Marguerite * 2.11.1722 at Étobon; = ca. 1747, Pierre-Abraham PERRET of Étobon * 12.12.1718, and had issue.

JACQUES

David and Anne Marie (Perrenot) JACQUES had a son, Abraham, nailmaker ~ 15.5.1663, living 1717; = 13.1.1685, Evotte * 1664, living 1717, dau. of Daniel PETITHORY. Their elder son:

1. **Abraham** * 2.2.1706 at Magny Danigon; served in the Army; later was a farmer; emigrated to Nova Scotia in the *Betty* in 1752, with a household of 1.1.2.1, and ■ 14.11.1752 (P); = (I) 7.2.1730 at Magny Danigon, Marie-Madeleine GAUTHIER of Cortébert, Bern, Switzerland, who + 20.3.1730 at Magny. He = (II) 28.11.1742 at Magny Danigon = **Eve** * ca. 1706 ■ 29.11.1787 (A), dau. of Abraham and Judith (Bretenier) JACQUE, charcoal burner, widow of Antoine RACINE. She = (III) 20.5.1753 (P), George L'EAU. Issue of Abraham and Eve:

---

[61] The second adult female was his mother, Catherine, née Valiton.

1) Elisabeth * 12.7.1743 + 1.8.1743 at Magny Danigon.
2) Elisabeth * 23.11.1744 + 9.3.1747 at Magny Danigon.
3) **Marguerite** * 15.2.1747 at Magny Danigon, living 1757.
4) Elisabeth * 27.7.1749 + 4.8.1749 at Magny Danigon.
5) **Elisabeth** * 30.12.1750 at Magny Danigon + -.2.1753 at Halifax.
. . . and perhaps:
6) **Jeanne** *1738/1741, living 1752 at Halifax.[62]

JACQUIN[63]

Simon JACQUIN of Colombier-le-Châtelot + 1718; = 23.10.1700 at Clairegoutte = Anne CLEMENÇON * 1675 + 1749 at Montbéliard. Issue:
1. **Jacques-Frédéric** * 15.4.1706 at Clairegoutte; a weaver and schoolmaster, emigrated in the *Betty* in 1752, with a household of 2.1.2.1. He drowned in the Kennebec River, Maine, 8.9.1756; = 19.2.1732 at Clairegoutte, **Marguerite** ISELIN, who = (II) Joshua WHITE. Issue:
   1) Pierre-Christoph * 21.10.1732 + 20.1.1747 at Clairegoutte.
   2) **Jean-George** ~ 1.2.1735 at Clairegoutte + 8.4.1768 at Alford, Maine; = Catherine - - - - and had issue:
      1a) Pierre ~ 17.9.1766 at the French Church in New York.
   3) **Jacques-Frédéric** * 20.10.1739 at Clairegoutte + -.12.1820 at Waterville, Maine. Issue.
   4) **Elisabeth-Marguerite** * 1742, living 1752.
   5) **Christophe** * 8.1.1748 at Clairegoutte + 9.2.1826 at Pittston, Maine. Issue, who went by the name Jackins.
2. Elisabeth-Marguerite, twin * 28.6.1708 at Clairegoutte.
3. Nicolas, twin * 28.6.1708 + 5.3.1743 at Clairegoutte = 16.7.1737 at Clairegoutte, Elisabeth ROY.

---

[62] More likely to have been *Jean* Nicolas Racine ~ 31.1.1737 at Clairegoutte, a child of Mrs. Jacques' first husband, Antoine RACINE of Frédéric-Fontaine, whom she had = 29.8.1730 at Clairegoutte, and had two sons. The elder, Abraham Racine ~ 2.3.1733 + 3.12.1736.

[63] Family "late from Halifax", reported at Frankfort, Maine, by 13 September 1752.

JAILLET

Moÿse JAILLET, nailmaker and hammerer * 1670 at Vallorbe, Canton Vaud, Switzerland + 3.4.1736 at St.-Valbert. He = (1) –NN–. They moved to Héricourt ca. 1722. Issue:

1. Jacob, employed at the forge at Couthenans + 10.12.1745 age ca. 40;= Anne-Marie MATTEI and had issue:
    1) **André**, skinner and tailor ~ 1.1.1726 at Audincourt + by 9.9.1780 at Lunenburg;[64] came to Nova Scotia in the *Sally* in 1752, with a household of 2.1.1.2;[65] = (I) 4.2.1750 at Héricourt, **Marie-Madeleine** + Oct/Dec 1752 at Halifax, widow of André MAIGRET, and dau of the late Jacques DUBOIS, mayor at Trémoins. Issue:
       1a) Jean-George ~ 21.8.1750 + 10.9.1750 at Héricourt.
       2a) **Daniel-Frédéric** ~ 8.12.1751 at Héricourt + 1752 at sea.
    André Jaillet = (II) 2.1.1753 (P), Susanne CURIER, and had issue:
       3a) Jane *Margaret* ~ 29.1.1754 (A), living 1757.
       4a) Susan Catherine ~ 13.3.1756 (A) ■ 29.3.1756 (A).
       5a) Mary *Catherine* ~ 19.2.1757 (A), living 1777.
       6a) George *Frederick* ~ 9.5.1759 (A).
       7a) *George* ~ 23.4.1761 (A).
       8a) James ~ 29.1.1763 (A) + young.

---

[64] His property was sold to settle his estate on 12.3.1781, at which time his heirs were entitled to the 30-acre lot B-8, Clearland (NSA, reel 410, probate papers, Halifax).

[65] We can try to reconcile the information about the family. One man was Jaillet, the woman his wife, and one child below age 4 was his son Daniel. The identity of the other man is uncertain. The child 4-14 and a second below the age of 4 were children of Mme. Jaillet by her late husband Maigret [Pierre Henri Maigret, 14 in 1752, and Jean Gaspard, 9 in 1753. A Jean Magras or Marguerat = 29.1.1761 (P) Maria Elizabeth HAWES and had a dau. Maria Magdalen ~ 15.11.1761 (P), and a Peter MAIGRET and wife Margaret had a son John ~ 15.4.1764 (P). Jaillet's young aunt Sybille, definitely came out in 1752. I suspect that she was mistakenly counted as the second man in the listing; otherwise her means of arrival is unaccounted for.

9a) John Peter ~ 8.4.1765 (A) + 15.11.1837 at Buctouche, NB;[66]
   = ca. 1788, Madeleine LÉGER. Issue.
10a) Mary Anne.
11a) Guillaume/William.
Moÿse = (2) Susanne PICCARD * 1696 + 22.5.1743. Issue:
2. **Sybille-Catherine** ~ 17.2.1726 at Héricourt; = 14.1.1753 (P),
   Theobald WOOLABER, and had issue.
3. Marguerite ~ 29.3.1728 at Héricourt.
4. George ~ 28.6.1732 at Héricourt.
5. Jean-Nicolas ~ 15.8.1734 at Héricourt.

JEANBAS[67]

Jean CHAMBERT, weaver in the town of Montbéliard + 23.5.1701;
= 21.11.1682 (Temple St.-Martin), Martha SURLEAU + 3.10.1724, and
had seven children, the eldest of whom, Jean George, a master weaver
* 1.2.1683 + 8.6.1738; = 8.6.1717 (Temple St.-Martin), Judith Marguerite
DESSERT. Three of their children came to Nova Scotia in the *Betty* in
1752:
6. **Jean-Jacques**, a weaver * 22.1.1725 ■ 9.8.1760 (P) as "John
   Chambers"; = 20.5.1755 (A), Susanne Marie CURIER. Issue:
   1) Anne Catherine ~ 23.11.1756 (A).
   2) William ~ 10.12.1758 (P).
7. **Judith** * 15.9.1727 ■ 8.10.1754 (A); = 23.11.1752 (P), Conrad
   GRASS [Cross] ■ 8.8.1804 (C). Their two children died in infancy.
9. **George *David***, a cutter * 15.10.1731 ■ 16.3.1800 (P). In all records
   after his marriage on 8.6.1759 (P) to Mary TANNER + 13.12.1820
   age 81, he is consistently referred to as "David Chambers". There

---

[66] Several of that name are listed in Buctouche in the 1870/71
directory, the name being written either as Jallais or Jaillet. Some later
anglicized the name as S(h)awyer, which perhaps expressed the way it was
then being pronounced.

[67] The family came to the Principality of Montbéliard by 1680
from Bérolle in the baillage of Morges, Canton Vaud, Switzerland. The name
was recorded, variously, Chambaz, Chambe, Jambe and Chambard. It is
probably a clerical error by a Dutch clerk that accounts for "Jeanbas". The
name as recorded in Halifax reverted more closely to the original spelling.

does not appear to have been issue of the marriage. On 10.12.1763 David Chamber, farmer at Lunenburg, sold his half share in lot C1 Zouberbuhler's Division. This establishes that David Jeanbas and David Chamber(s) were identical.

JEANPERRIN

Jacques JEANPERRIN of Beutal ~ 27.11.1648 at Longevelle, son of Jacques and Thiennon (Mouhot) Jeanperrin = Anne BOUVET. Issue:
1. Antoine ~ 4.7.1680 at Longevelle + 11.4.1756; = (I) 23.11.1706 at Longevelle, Claudine JACQUIN of Lougres, who + ca. 1713/14. Issue:
   1) Jacques ~ 17.11.1707 + young at Longevelle.
   2) Marguerite ~ 18.8.1709 at Longevelle.
   3) David ~ 11.12.1712; = 29.11.1735 at Longevelle, Susanne-Catherine, dau. of Étienne and Suzanne LAIGLE. Issue:
      1a) Marguerite ~ 19.10.1738 at Longevelle.
      2a) David ~ 14.7.1740 at Longevelle.
   Antoine = (II) 12.2.1715 at Longevelle, Claudine JEANPERRIN of Lougres and had thirteen further children:
   4) *Anne*-Catherine ~ 10.11.1715 at Longevelle.
   5) **Jean-Urbain** ~ 3.3.1717 at Longevelle; a stonecutter, he emigrated to Nova Scotia in the *Speedwell* in 1752, as a single man, and was living in 1800 at River John, NS; = (I) 1752/53, Jeanne ~ 18.6.1724 at Chagey, ■ 22.12.1789 (A), dau. of Abraham TATTERE, and had two children. He = (II) 16.5.1790 (C), Judith ~ 14.4.1726 at Longevelle, dau. of Jean-Jacques JEAUDRY, and widow of Pierre JOLIMOIS. Issue by Jeanne:
      1a) John George ~ 6.9.1754 (A), lived at St. Margarets Bay until ca. 1800, when he moved to River John, where he was living in 1815; = 22.10.1782 (A), Catherine Elizabeth ~ 15.5.1758 (A) + 1850 at River John, dau. of Pierre JOLIMOIS. Issue:
      1b) Judith Margaret * 11.9.1783 (A).
      2b) Mary Margaret *23.12.1784 (A) + 1860; = 1800, John Louis* 1775 + 1860, son of David LANGILLE. Issue.
      3b) Susan Catherine * 4.4.1786 (A) + 1870s at Cleveland, Ohio; = George Frederick * 1777 + 1835, son of John James and Eva LANGILLE of Tatamagouche. Issue.
      4b) *John* Urban * 3.10.1788 (A). Issue.

5b) James * 25.9.1790 (A).

6b) Catherine Elizabeth * 23.11.1792 (A).[68]

7b) Catherine Barbara * 27.4.1794 (A).

8b) Louisa Margaret * 1.4.1796 (A).

9b) George * 20.1.1797 (A).[69]

2a) John Christopher ~ 22.8.1756 (A) + 1835 at River John; = 26/29.10.1779 (A), Mary Catherine ~ 14.3.1761 (A), living 1798, dau. of John DAUPHINÉ. Issue:[70]

    1b) Mary *Catherine* * 27/28.12.1780 (A) + 1849; = 1798, John George, son of David LANGILLE, Tatamagouche. Issue.

    2b) Catherine *Louisa* * 21.3.1782 (A); = 1798 = John David, son of David LANGILLE, Tatamagouche. Issue.

    3b) Mary Elizabeth * 5.1.1784 (A).

    4b) John *George* * 29.7.1785 (A).

    5b) George *Frederick* * 30.7.1787 (A), living 1815.

    6b) *James* John * 6.2.1789 (A); = Eleanor BYERS; left for Ohio in 1838. Issue.

    7b) John *Peter* * 13.1.1791 (A); = Elizabeth, dau. of John James GRETTEAU. Issue.

    8b) John Frederick * 13.6.1792 (A); to Ohio in 1838. Issue.

    9b) a daughter * 1794/96 probably at River John.

    10b) a daughter * 1794/96 probably at River John.

    11b) David * 1798 probably at River John, living 1850 at Waynesfield, Ohio, with a wife Elizabeth and five children.

6) Susanne-*Catherine* ~ 10.4.1718 + young at Longevelle.

---

[68] Catherine Elizabeth **or** Catherine Barbara = David PATRIQUIN and had issue.

[69] This George PERRIN was the progenitor of the PELHAM family of Herring Cove, near Halifax, NS - *cf.*, Terrence M. Punch, " Some Surprising 'Foreign Protestants'," *The Nova Scotia Genealogist*, XXX/I (Spring 2012), 5 - 8.

[70] His petition for a land grant in 1815 states that he had eleven children: 6 sons and 5 daughters, and that he had moved to River John ca. 1800.

7) Anne-*Marie* ~ 20.10.1719 at Longevelle.
8) Catherine ~ 23.10.1720 at Longevelle.
9) Marie-*Elisabeth* ~ 28.11.1721 at Longevelle.
10) Susanne ~ 18.4.1723 at Longevelle.
11) George, twin ~ 20.8.1724 at Longevelle.
12) Jacques, twin ~ 20.8.1724 + young at Longevelle.
13) Anne-*Judith* ~ 29.1.1726 at Longevelle.
14) Antoinette ~ 23.3.1727 at Longevelle.
15) Jacques ~ 17.3.1728 + young at Longevelle.
16) Jacques ~ 20.4.1730 at Longevelle.
2. Perrenon [female] ~ 5.4.1683 at Longevelle.

Lordship of
Clémont

Lordship of
Châtelot

J E A U D R Y - I

Grosjean JODRY of Bavans * ca. 1560 + 1.11.1627 had a son:
1. Claude, of Bavans + 13.4.1669; = 8.8.1615 at Bavans, Marguerite,
   dau. of Adam BRUN of Grand-Charmont. Their youngest son,
   1) Claudot JODRY * 9.3.1634 at Bavans + 12.1.1693 at
      Allondans; = 1654, Claudine GOGUEL + 6.3.1707 at Allondans,
      age 75. Issue:
      1a) Madeleine ~ 31.12.1654 at Allondans.
      2a) Pierre ~ 11.10.1657 + young at Allondans.
      3a) Guenin ~ 26.2.1660 + 12.1.1710 at Allondans. Issue.
      4a) Pierre ~ 12.10.1665 at Allondans.

5a) Claudine ~ 31.1.1669 at Allondans; = David BELPOIX. Issue.

6a) Jean-Nicolas ~ 6.4.1671 + 12.10.1708 at Allondans.

7a) Jean-Jacques ~ 21.3.1675 + 7.12.1733 at Allondans; = 6.7.1706 at Allondans, Susanne * 1688 + 27.2.1724, dau. of Samuel MAIGRET. Eight children:

1b) **Jean-Christophe** ~ 16.11.1707 at Allondans; a farmer, he emigrated to Nova Scotia in the *Speedwell* in 1752, with a household of 2.2.3.1, and + 23.7.1777 (A); = (I) 16.2.1734 at Temple St.-Martin in Montbéliard Town, **Anne-Catherine** * 1712/13, ■ 3.3.1753 at Halifax, dau. of Pierre and Anne-Rose (Charpiot)VEUILLEMIN of Grand Charmont. Six children. He = (II)14.8.1753 (A), Jeanne * 4.2.1715, ■ 6.4.1788 (A), dau. of Pierre and Judith (Perretgentil) RACINE of Échavanne, and widow of Josué ROBAR. Two children. His eight children were:

1c) **Jean-George** ~ 20.2.1735 at Allondans ■ 22.2.1753 (P).

2c) **Anne-Catherine** ~ 19.4.1737 at Allondans, living 1788; = (I) 8.5.1753 (P), Jean PETREQUIN, ■ 19.12.1764 (A), having issue. She = (II) 26.3.1769 (A), Étienne CERTIER ■ 26.2.1782 (A), and had one son. She = (III) 12.5.1783 (L), Peter WAMBOLT, farmer, First Peninsula * 29.2.1720 at Zwingenberg, Hessen-Darmstadt + by drowning in a lake, 24.12.1786, widower of Elisabetha STORCK.

3c) **Pierre** ~ 23.12.1739 at Allondans, ■ 24.2.1753 at Halifax. Another version of the record has his date of death as 3.1.1753 at Halifax.

4c) **Jules-Frédéric** ~ 20.4.1743 at Allondans + 29.12. 1812 at Fauxbourg, NS = 15.3.1768 (A), Catherine * 1748 + 28.10.1842 (A), dau. of Nicolas DARÉ. Issue:

1d) Mary *Elizabeth* ~ 11.1.1769 (A), living 1808.

2d) Mary Catherine * 10.7.1770 (A).

3d) *James* Frederick * 6.9.1771 (A). Issue.

4d) John *Peter* * 6.6.1773 (A), living 1818. Issue.

5d) John George * 3.5.1775 + 16.12.1775 (A).

6d) John *George,* Fauxbourg * 17.10.1776 (A); = 30.5.
   1809 (A), Susan Catherine, dau. of John Peter
   LOWE. Issue.
7d) John *Christopher* * 30.11.1777. Issue.
8d) John *Frederick* * 1.2.1780 (A). Issue.
9d) Catherine * 8.12.1781; = 7.7.1805 (A), John Peter
   VIENOT * 23.2.1784 (A). Issue.
10d) *Jane* Elizabeth * 6.3.1783 (A); = 21.12.1803 (L), John
   Nicholas HAMM ~ 1.7.1778 (C) + 9.12.1825. Issue.
11d) Margaret * 4.1.1785 (A); = 10.10.1802 (A),
   George Frederick VIENOT * 3.4.1782 (A). Issue.
12d) Susan * 15.4.1789 (A) + by 1812.
5c) **Jean-Urbain** * 5.1.1748 at Allondans + 28.6.1822 (C)
   = 12.1.1770 (P), Elizabeth-Henriette * -.2.1748 at Kloster
   Lobenfeld, Palatinate + 25.6.1830 (C), dau. of John
   Bernard HERMANN. Issue:
   1d) Elizabeth *"Betsy"* * 1770 + 4.7.1838; = 24.10.1812
      (P), Henry DRAVIS + 1853. One son.
   2d) James Frederick * 31.12.1772 (A) + young.
   3d) John *Frederick,* twin * 31.12.1773.
   4d) John *Christopher,* twin * 31.12.1773, ■ 29.3.1829
      (A), unmarried.
   5d) John *Jacob* ~ 21.7.1776 (C).[71]
   6d) Margaret * 9.8.1778 (A); = ca. 1800, John Just
      MORASH, Cole Harbour, * 11.4.1770 (A). Issue.
   7d) Ann *Catherine* * 11.3.1780 (A) + 11.2.1856 (A);
      = 18.11.1798 (A), Joseph Nicholas COUNTWAY
      * 8.11.1774 (A) + 17.6.1859 (A). Issue.
   8d) Sophia * 29.10.1782 (A); = 24.2.1805 (C), John
      Matthias BLEISTEINER * 1779 + 5.8.1811 (L).
   9d) John George * 3.3.1785 (C) + young.
   10d) Mary *Elizabeth* * 1.3.1787 (C); = 12.1.1828 (C),
      John GAULD.
   11d) George Frederick * 26.8.1789 (C) + young.

---

[71] His baptismal entry does not state the mother's name.

12d) *Hanna* Sevilla * 20.8.1789 (C), living 1828.
6c) **Jean-Jacques** * 21.1.1752 at Allondans + summer
   1752 at sea; youngest child of the first marriage.
7c) Catherine-Elizabeth ~ -.10.1753 (A).
8c) Elizabeth ~ 7.3.1756 (A).
2b) Jean-Jacques ~ 29.9.1709 + young at Allondans.
3b) Marguerite ~ 9.9.1711 at Allondans.
4b) Marie-Catherine ~ 2.4.1713 at Allondans.
5b) Elisabeth ~ 9.1.1715 at Allondans ; = 27.12.1735 at
   Couthenans, Jacques DORMOI. Issue.
6b) Jacques-Christophe ~ 2.11.1717 at Allondans.
7b) Jean-Jacques, tailor ~ 7.6.1720 + 18.9.1782 at Allondans;
   = Anne-Catherine LODS. Issue.
8b) Pierre-Jacques ~ 12.4.1722 at Allondans.

JEAUDRY-II

Jacques JODRY = 19.11.1715 in Montbéliard Town = Susanne
COULOMB, and had issue, two sons:
1. Pierre, weaver ~ 8.8.1723 in Montbéliard Town; = 9.11.1745 at
   Temple St.-Martin, Montbéliard Town, Anne MATHIOT of Dasle.
2. **Marc-Élie** ~ 22.4.1726 in Montbéliard Town; a shoemaker by trade,
   he emigrated to Nova Scotia in the *Betty* in 1752, a single man. He
   was ■ 30.3.1756 (P). The burial register calls him "Mark Jodrith".

JEAUDRY-III

Jean-Jacques Jeaudry * 1698 at Bavans; a farmer, he emigrated
to Nova Scotia in the *Betty* in 1752, with a household of 1.3.1.0. His
two older sons appeared on the passenger list separately, as single
men. Jeaudry + at Halifax Aug/Oct. 1752; = 8.7.1721 at Longevelle,
Catherine-Marguerite ~ 26.12.1698 at Longevelle + at sea in
the summer of 1752, dau. of Antoine and Claudine (Humbert)
CERTIER.[72] Issue:

---

[72] Catherine-Marguerite Certier was the aunt of three other immigrants, namely Étienne Certier, and the Dauphiné brothers, Jean and David.

1. **Anne-Catherine** ~ 28.11.1721 at Longevelle, ■ 28.12.1752 (P).
2. **Jacques**, farmer, ~ 28.12.1723 at Longevelle; = 20.6.1754 (A),
   Elizabeth ~ 17.1.1736 at Chenebier + 30.1.1785 (A), dau. of Jean-
   Frédéric MAILLARD. Issue:
   1) Peter * 1756, living 1770 at Lunenburg.
   2) Susan Catherine ~ 5.1.1758 (A).
   3) Joan ~ 12.3.1759 (A).
   4) Elizabeth Catherine ~ 26.5.1760 (A).
   5) John James ~ 26.6.1761 (A).
   6) Margaret ~ 20.3.1763 (A).
   7) *John* Stephen ~ 18.12.1768 (A), living 1801 at River John, NS;[73]
      = a dau. of Matthew LANGILLE.
   8) George * ca. 1771, living 1815 with 7 children, Earltown, NS.
3. **Judith** ~ 14.4.1726 at Longevelle; = (I) 31.8.1752 (P), Pierre-
   Anthoine JOLIMOIS, ■ 20.10.1786 (A), and had issue.
   She = (II) 16.5.1790 (C), Jean-Urbain JEANPERRIN.
4. **Jean-George**, farmer, ~ 23.1.1728 at Longevelle, living in 1790
   at River John, NS; = ?? and had four or more children.
5. **Anne-Marie** ~ 27.9.1733 at Longevelle + before 1752.
6. **Susanne** ~ 16.10.1736 at Longevelle + before 1752.
7. **Joseph** * ca. 1738, ■ 26.10.1752 at Halifax.

J E A U N É [74]

Jacob JONEY = Elisabeth RAŸOT of Issans had issue, among others:
1. **Jean-Pierre** * ca. 1720; a farmer, he emigrated to Nova Scotia in the
   Speedwell in 1752, with a household of 2.1.2.2.[75] In 1768 he moved

---

[73] John Jodry was granted land at River John ca. 1801 (NSA, RG 1, Vol. 224, doc.150).

[74] This name is variously given as Jeauné, Josnet, and Joney. In New Brunswick it took the form JONAH, which is still in use.

[75] The Jeauné family accounted for 1.1.0.2. The remainder – 1.0.2.0 – were Mrs. Jeauné's children by her first husband, Jean-Urbain Rigoulot (*q.v.*).

to Hillsborough, in what is now New Brunswick,[76] where he died between 1784 and 1803; He = (I) 1.10.1748 at St.- Julien, **Charlotte-Elisabeth** * ca. 1719, ■ 15.1.1756 (A), dau. of Simon LOVY[77] and widow of Jean-Urbain RIGOULOT, and had three children:

1) **Jean-George** * 5.8.1749 at Issans; carried off by Indians 8.9.1758; his fate is unknown.
2) **Samuel** * 25.3.1751 at Issans + Aug/Oct. 1752 at Halifax.
3) Anne-Charlotte ~ 7.1.1755 (A) + young at Lunenburg.

Jean-Pierre Jeauné = (II) 30.3.1756 (A), Alexandrine-Marguerite, dau. of Jean-Pierre ISELIN and had seven children:

4) Peter ~ 23.8.1758 (A).
5) Peter James ~ 27.5.1760 (A).
6) John James ~ 20.4.1763 (A) + 1830;[78] = Sarah REYNOLDS. Issue
7) Mary Catherine ~ 28.4.1765 (A).
8) George Frederick ~ 17.7.1767 (A), living 1803; = Ann KAY.
9) Martin * 1769 at Hillsborough + 1842/48 at Hillsborough; = ca. 1793, Sophia * ca. 1776 + by 1848, dau. of Peter LUTZ, Sr. Issue.

---

[76] He sold his farm lot A-37 at Northwest Range, 21.11.1768. Gray's Memorial of 26.8.1786 says that Peter Jonah was brought from Halifax to Hillsborough in 1768. (NSA mfm. 13861: CO 217, Vol. 59).

[77] The Lowy connexion links four of the families who came to Nova Scotia from Montbéliard in 1752. Nicolas Lovy [Loew], an Alsatian * 1645 + 25.1.1698 at St.-Julien; = Susanne Josnet/Jeauné and had ten children, one of whom, Simon Lovy * -.2.1679 + 2.3.1740 at St.-Julien; = 29.8.1702 at Issans, Henriette * -.2.1679, dau. of Jean Marçonnet. They had eight children, the two youngest of whom emigrated to Nova Scotia: Elisabeth-Charlotte * ca. 1719, wife of (I) Jean-Urbain Rigoulot, and (II) Jean-Pierre Jeauné; and Catherine-Elisabeth * 1722, wife of (I) Jean Carlin, and (II) David Banvard.

[78] He served in the Royal Fencible Americans Regt. John Joney, Sr., of the Parish of Hillsborough, Westmorland Co., NB, made his will in Oct 1830, proved 1.12.1830, in which he names his children: Joshua JONEY, John Nathaniel JONEY, Lydia [Mrs. Harper] WILSON, Sarah [Mrs. Henry] OGDEN, Jane BOYD, Ann [Mrs. Robert] PERRIGO, Mary [Mrs. Zachariah] LUTZ, Clarasa BOYD, Matilda JONEY, Eunice LUTZ, George Benjamin JONEY, and Henry JONEY.

10) Henry * 1771 at Hillsborough + 15.11.1842 at Hillsborough; = ca.
    1797, Mary Pauline "Polly" * ca. 1778 + by 1842, dau. of Peter
    LUTZ, Sr. & Mary RICKER. Issue.
2. Jacques ~ 25.4.1732 + 1.2.1733 at Issans.

JOLIMOIS[79]

Étienne JOLIMOIS, a weaver at Belverne + 21.1.1716, age ca. 80; = (I)
—NN----, and had a son. He = (II) 3.5.1702 at Étobon, Elisabeth - - - -.
His son,

1. Jean, weaver at Belverne * ca. 1677 + 19.8.1762 at Belverne; = ca.
   1698, Catherine * 27.2.1676 + 31.3.1742, dau. of Nicolas HERTÉ.[80]
   Issue:
   1) Marie * 29.9.1699 at Belverne, living 1739; = 21.11.1724 at
      Étobon, Jean Pierre PERRENON, labourer at Belverne. Issue.
   2) Jérémie * 25.10.1702 at Belverne.
   3) **Pierre-Anthoine** * 10.12.1703 at Belverne; a weaver by trade, he
      emigrated to Nova Scotia in the *Betty* in 1752, with a household
      of 1.0.2.0. He was burned to death in a house fire, and
      ■ 20.10.1786 (A). He = (I) 5.3.1737 at Étobon, Elisabeth
      * 16.4.1709 at Étobon + 13.4.1745 at Belverne, dau. of Jean
      MIGNERÉ, Mayor at Étobon. Issue:
      1a) Marie-Elisabeth ~ 15.2.1741 at Étobon + 3.4.1741 at
          Belverne.
      2a) **Pierre** ~ 2.4.1742 at Étobon ■ 10.3.1753 at Halifax.
      3a) **Jean-Nicolas** ~ 17.12.1743 at Étobon ■ 9.5.1753 at
          Halifax.
      4a) Elisabeth ~ 13.4.1745 at Étobon + 30.4.1745 at Belverne.

---

[79] This family originated in Switzerland. The *Jolimay* family
had citizenship in the community of Goumouens-la-Ville, Canton of Vaud
(*Familiennamenbuch der Schweiz*, II, 928).

[80] Catherine Herté was a dau. of Nicolas * 1646 ■ 20.6.1682
"ayant être trouvé dans l'estang de la forge de Chagey" (son of Nicolas Heritel,
church elder at Chenebier, and his wife, Jeanne Jeanmaire), who = 25.5.1668
at Étobon, Judith ~ 27.12.1648 (dau. of Pierre Blanchard, mayor at Étobon, and
his wife, Jeannette Visol).

Pierre-Anthoine = (II) 14.9.1745 at Étobon, Marie-Elisabeth
* 3.10.1702 at Belverne + 20.9.1762 at Belverne,[81] dau. of
Jean PERRENON, and widow of Jean-Jacques FAINÔT, carpenter
at Frédéric-Fontaine. Pierre-Anthoine = (III) 31.8.1752 (P), Judith
~ 14.4.1726 at Longevelle, living 1790, dau. of Jean Jacques
JEAUDRY. Issue:

5a) Jeanne-Marie ■ 25.10.1753 (A), an infant.
6a) *James* Louis ~ 26.6.1754 (A) + 30.1.1834 at Chester;
    = 27.10.1777 (A), *Catherine* Margaret ~ 1.1.1760 (A) + 1849
    at Chester, dau. of David-Joshué ROBERT, and had issue:
  1b) Christian * 30.6.1779 (A) ■ 5.11.1858 at Hubbards, NS;
    = 13.11.1806 (A), Catharine Margaret * 1.7.1786 (C)
    ■ 5.9.1863, dau. of John Conrad WESTHAVER. Issue.
  2b) Catherine Elizabeth * 3.8.1781 (A) + 31.8.1783 (A).
  3b) John *George* * 13.9.1785 (A), living 1838 at Ingram River;
    = ca. 1810, Sophia, dau. of Jacob SLAUENWHITE. Issue.
  4b) Catherine *Elizabeth* * 20.4.1788 (C) ■ 14.5.1869 at St.
    Margarets Bay; = 27.4.1807 (A), John BRIGLEY. Issue.
  5b) *Catherine Margaret* * 8.11.1791 (A), living 1834, unm.
  6b) Susan * 13.5.1794 (A) + 1821/29; = 26.6.1821 at Chester,
    James Frederick BOUTILIER.
  7b) Mary Margaret * 25.8.1799 (A), living 1871; = 31.3.1817
    at Chester = Peter ROY, Hubbards * 1794 at Montréal. Issue.
  8b) *John* Christopher * 7.2.1802 (A), living 1850 at Hubbards;
    = 4.2.1828 at Chester, Mary Elizabeth * 23.7.1807 (A)
    + 1867, dau. of John Frederick SLAUENWHITE. Issue.
  9b) John *James* * 8.8.1805 (A) ■ 8.1.1857 at Chester;
    = 22.12.1825 at Chester, Elizabeth BOUTILIER. Issue.
7a) Peter James ~ 14.4.1756 (A) + young at Lunenburg.
8a) Catherine Elizabeth ~ 15.5.1758 (A) + 1850 at River John;
    = 22.10.1782 (A), Jean-George JEANPERRIN ~ 6.9.1754 (A),
    living 1800 at River John. Issue.

---

[81] Marie-*Elisabeth* was buried at Belverne by the Pastor of
Étobon, 21.9.1762. The register is unambiguous in describing her as
"*une femme delaissée*", an abandoned wife. The Nova Scotian marriage
of her husband was, in fact, a bigamous union.

9a) Judith *Margaret* ~ 11.8.1760 (A), living 1812; = 26.7.1785 (A), John VIENOT ~ 15.6.1762 (A) ■ 8.5.1814 (A). Issue.

10a) *George* Frederic, master mariner, Northumberland Strait[82] ~ 5.6.1763 (A) + 15.1.1822 at Halifax; = 15.10.1788 (P), Catherine ~ 6.11.1768 (A) + 1855, dau. of Jean and Anne-Marie (Ménégaux) MAILLARD. Issue (with seven others):

1b) George * 21.12.1789 (A).

2b) Catherine Margaret * 11.8.1791 (A).

3b) John George * 17.7.1793 (A).

4b) Margaret * 16.9.1796 (A) + 9.8.1876 at Tatamagouche.

11a) Susan Catherine ~ 2.11.1766 (A), living in 1812 at St. Anns Bay, Cape Breton; = 25.4.1791 (A), James DAUPHINEE ~ 8.11.1767 (A), living 1812. Issue.

4) David * 14.12.1706 at Belverne.

5) Françoise * 11.12.1709 at Belverne.

6) Jean, a twin * 11.6.1712 + young at Belverne.

7) Pierre, twin * 11.6.1712 + young at Belverne.

8) Jean * 15.5.1715 + 1-.5.1740 at Belverne, unmarried.

9) Elizabeth * 11.1.1719 at Belverne; = 20.10.1739, Jean-George ISELIN, nailmaker at St.-Valbert, and at Belverne had issue. They emigrated to Massachusetts in 1752/53.

10) Anne-Marie-Marguerite * 2.3.1721 at Belverne; = 21.1.1744 at Étobon, Jean-Pierre AUBAIRT, miller at Belverne + 7.8.1747 at Belverne. Issue.

LAGARCE-I

Pierre LAGARCE * ca. 1709/10 in the Principality of Montbéliard; a farmer, he emigrated to Nova Scotia in the *Pearl* in 1752, with a household of 1.1.1.0, and was ■ 12.3.1753 at Halifax; = **Elisabeth-Ann "Nanette"** - - -, who = (II) 5.12.1753 (A), Joseph CONTOIS, a baker from Switzerland, and + 1755/56. Issue:

---

[82] He was granted land at River John ca. 1801 (NSA, RG 1, Vol. 224, doc. 150), and had resided there from at least 1798 (NSA, V/F, Vol. 267 # 10).

1. **Anne-Marie** * 1735 ■. 19.7.1777 age 42 (A); = (I) 13.10.1752 (P), John Caspar SHAFFELBERG. Issue. She = (II) 11.5.1756 (A), John Jacob HIRTLE and had a large family.
2. Frédéric, victualled in 1755 with the Contois.[83]

LAGARCE-II[84]

Jean Lagarce of Désandans * ca. 1719; a tailor, he emigrated to Nova Scotia in the *Betty* in 1752, with a household of 1.1.0.1.; living in 1769 at Lunenburg; = **Anne- Marie** - - - -. Issue:
1. **Elisabeth** * ca. 1751 ■ 14.4.1753 at Halifax.
2. Mary Elizabeth ~ 19.6.1754 (A), living 1757.
3. Catherine Margaret ~ 30.8.1755 (A), living 1757.
4. John Frederick ~ 26.11.1758 (A).
5. Barbara ~ 5.3.1761 (A) + 2.6.1817; = John MORTON. Issue.

LAGARCE-III

Jean LAGARCE of Désandans had issue, a son:
1. **Nicolas** * ca. 1728; a farmer, he emigrated to Nova Scotia in the *Betty* in 1752, with a household of 1.0.0.1.; living in 1763 at Lunenburg; = (I) 31.12.1748 at Désandans, Marie-Magdeleine + 5.1.1751 at Désandans, dau. of Leonhard VEUILLEMET of Désandans.[85] Issue:
   1) male baby */+ 31.3.1749 at Désandans.
   2) female baby */+ 30.1.1750 at Désandans.
   3) **Anne-Elisabeth** * 5.1.1751 at Désandans + at sea in 1752.
   Nicolas = (II) 24.10.1752 (P), Anne-Catherine RICHARD ■ 19.4.1760 (A). Issue:

---

[83] This child was either born at sea in 1752 or within months of their arrival at Halifax. It looks very much as if Nanette was Lagarce's second wife, given the gap between the births of his two known children. The name Contois became anglicized in Nova Scotia as Countway.

[84] This man and the next were related, possibly brothers. If so, Lagarce II and III form an extended family group. Through his daughter Barbara, Jean Carlin II was an ancestor of Dr. Winthrop P. Bell.

[85] She was a sister of the immigrant Léonard Vuillemet (*q.v.*).

4) Anne-Catherine ~ 5.4.1755 ■ 24.4.1755 (A).
5) James Frederick ~ 1.4.1756 (A).
6) Catherine Elizabeth ~ 6.2.1758 (A) + 22.10.1815 (L);= 5.3.1776
   (L),[86] John Frederick RAFUSE, Martins Brook ~ 3.1.1754 (A)
   + 27.7.1840 (L). Issue.
Nicolas = (III) 22.7.1760 (A), Anne-Elizabeth, ■ 4.4.1800, age 86 (A),
widow of Johann Georg SCHRUM, who + 1758/59.

LANGILLE

Part of the passport of brothers David and Léopold Langille,
Dampierre-les-Bois, 3 April 1752

(NSA, MG 4, Vol. 99 #6a)

---

[86] The marriage record states that her father was then deceased.

LANGILLE

General Note: Several stories have been told about the origins of this family, but I find little reason to doubt its source is the community of Courtelary in Canton Bern, Switzerland. All the Langilles who emigrated to Nova Scotia in 1752 descended from Daniel Langille * ca. 1630. His family appears in Dampierre-outre-les-Bois from ca.1680. Eleven Langilles came to Nova Scotia, represented by five names in the passenger lists, three in the *Betty* and two in the *Sally*. There follows a general treatment of the family down to the emigrating generation which separately follows the descendants of two brothers, grandsons of Daniel.

Daniel LANGEL * ca. 1630 was the father of:

1. Marie * ca. 1653 in Switzerland; = Jacques SANDOZ.
2. Jean-Pierre * 23.5.1655 in Switzerland + 20.9.1735 (■ Temple St. Martin, Montbéliard Town); = Anne LeCLERC. No issue.
3. Daniel * 4.2.1651 in Switzerland, living 1718; = Françoise PERRENOT * 9.4.1654 at Brognard, and had six children who lived at Dampierre:
    1) Marguerite * 15.9.1681 at Dampierre; = 14.10.1704 at Dampierre, Jean LeCLERC, labourer * 20.2.1674 at Dampierre. Issue.
    2) Françoise * 11.9.1683 + 24.9.1755; = 27.11.1708 at Dampierre, Mathieu PECHIN * ca. 1683. Seven children.
    3) Daniel * 26.5.1687; = 2.12.1711 at Dampierre, Anne BRAN, widow of . . . . HERMAN. Six children:
        1a) Anne * 18.12.1712 at Dampierre, living 1723.
        2a) **David** * 19.1.1715 at Dampierre [LANGILLE - I, *infra*] ~~next pg~~
        3a) Léonard * 20.11.1718 + 3.4.1721 at Dampierre.
        4a) Daniel * ca. 1721; = 28.4.1748 at Dampierre, Marie-Barbe HAUSSERER. Son:
            1b) André * 23.9.1749 + 23.1.1750 at Dampierre.
        5a) **Mathieu** * 4.7.1724 at Dampierre [LANGILLE - I, *infra*]
        6a) Pierre * ca. 1727 + 2.2.1747 at Dampierre.
    4) Jean-Pierre * 25.9.1694 + 10.9.1759; = 13.11.1727, Anne JAPY of Beaucourt.
    5) David * 24.2.1696 + 13.5.1765 at Dampierre; = (I) ca. 1720, Catherine-Marguerite BOUTHENOT, who + 11.1.1750, age 51, at Dampierre. He = (II) 3.7.1753 at Dampierre, Anne-Elisabeth DROZ. Six children, all by Catherine:

1a) **David** * 29.6.1721 at Dampierre [LANGILLE - II, *infra*]
2a) **Léopold-Frédéric** * 26.6.1728 at Dampierre [LANGILLE - II]
3a) Catherine-Elisabeth * ca. 1731; = Benoît, son of George PEUGEOT, and had issue, Georges-Frédéric Peugeot.
4a) Jacques * ca. 1738 + 23.1.1798 at Dampierre; = (I) 31.1.1769 at Dampierre, Anne-Judith HAUSER. He = (II) 9.4.1794 at Dampierre, Anne-Marie CRAMOTTE, a widow, and had:
1b) Pierre-Frédéric * 14.10.1797 at Dampierre; = Catherine BARRE, and had issue at Dampierre.
5a) Françoise * ca. 1743 + 9.2.1777 at Dampierre; = ca. 1770, Abraham PARROT.
6a) Frédéric * 25.10.1745 + 4.6.1752 at Dampierre.
6) Jean-Pierre * 10.6.1700 at Dampierre, living 1718.

L A N G I L L E - I (sons of Daniel)

Two sons of Daniel, * 1687, came to Nova Scotia:
2a) **David** * 19.1.1715 at Dampierre; a farmer. He emigrated to Nova Scotia in the *Sally* in 1752, with a household of 1.1.1.2,[87] and + -.7.1804 at Lunenburg; = (I) Marie-Catherine ---- + ca. 1750. Issue:
1b) **Jean-Jacques** * ca. 1736; a farmer, he emigrated to Nova Scotia in 1752 in the *Sally* as a single man, and living in 1795 at Frederick River, River John, having moved to that area in 1772. He seems to be the "James LANGEAL" who was at Tatamagouche in 1817;[88] = 4.5.1763 (P), Eve, dau. of George LEAU and had issue:
1c) John George ~ 17.3.1765 (A), living 1818; = Mary HAYMAN. They had ten children by 1818,
2c) Mary Catherine ~ 26.7.1767 (A) + young.
3c) John David ~ 1.10.1769 (A) + 14.9.1844 at River John; = Mary MILLER. Issue.

---

[87] The two children below the age of 4 cannot be accounted for, unless they were issue of his newly-wed second wife and possibly surnamed DAVID. Existence of **two** boys named Jacques further muddies the waters. The Jean-Jacques born about 1736 is listed separately on the passenger list.

[88] NSA, RG 29, Series "A".

4c) Mary Magdalen * 27.2.1772 (A).
5c) James * 1773 + 1861; = Agnes Nancy, dau. of John-
George PATRIQUIN. Issue.
6c) Joseph * 1775 + 1835; = Phoebe, dau. of John-George
PATRIQUIN. Issue.
7c) George-Frederick * 1777 + 1835; = Susan Catherine, dau. of
John-George PATRIQUIN. Issue.
2b) Jean-George * 1738 + 30.10.1749 at Dampierre.
3b) **Jean-Jacques** [II][89] * ca. 1743 + 1818 at Brule Point; = Jane
- - - , and had issue:
1c) Mary Ann; = Peter, son of John George MATTETALL. Issue.
2c) Isaac * 1788 + 10.9.1865; = Margaret, dau. of James DUNN.
Issue.
3c) Thomas * 1792 + 10.7.1876; = Mary, dau. of William
SALISBURY. Issue.
4c) David * 1793; = Mary JOUDREY. Issue.
5c) Nicholas * 1801; = Ruth, dau. of James DUNN. Issue.
David = (II) -.5.1752 at Dampierre = **Marie-Catherine** DAVID, who
■ 29.9.1752 at Halifax. Child:
4b) Marguerite * 16.9.1752 ■ 23.9.1752 at Halifax.
David = (III) 3.12.1753 (A), Marie-Catherine * 1735, living 1775, dau.
of Jean-George BESANÇON. They had twelve children:
5b) John Nicholas ~ 28.6.1755 (A); moved to the U.S.A.
6b) Catherine ~ 24.5.1757 (A).
7b) Marie-Madeleine ~ 4.10.1758 (A); = 24.12.1778 at Truro,
Samuel FISHER * 1750 in New Hampshire + Musquodoboit, NS.
Issue.
8b) Marie-Elisabeth ~ 22.5.1760 (A), living 1805; = 1783/84,
George TATTRIE * 1721 + 1805. Issue.

---

[89] Although this person was consistently called "Langille", it seems quite possible that he was a stepson of David Langille, and a son of Langille's second wife. Also noted is Lewis DAVID, Halifax labourer, who sold land at Lunenburg Common, 25.9.1766. (Lunenburg Co. Deeds, 1, ƒ 275 #659). Was he related to Marie-Catherine David, second wife of David Langille?

9b) John Frederick[90] ~ 21.11.1761 (A); = ca. 1785, Susan-
Catherine ~ 19.3.1769 (A), twin dau. of Jean-George
MATTATALL. Known issue were:
1c) Mary * ca. 1787 + 1877; = George FOSTER.
2c) Frederick * 1790; = Mary Elizabeth, dau. of John
Frederick PATRIQUIN. Issue.
3c) Edward * 1794; = Elizabeth, dau. of Matthew MINGO.
Issue.
4c) John * 1798 + 28.10.1876; = Susan, dau. of Henry
HEIGHTON. Issue.
5c) Isaac; = Susan, dau. of John George BIGNEY. Issue.
6c) Samuel * 1804.
7c) Christopher * 9.6.1808 + 29.5.1890; = Lucy, dau. of
James and Agnes LANGILLE. Issue.
8c) George * 1809.
10b) Mary Catherine ~ 6.1.1764 (A).
11b) Margaret ~ 17.11.1765 (A); = Peter HINDS, River John.
Issue.
12b) Catherine-*Margaret* ~ 25.3.1767 (A) + 1854; = 8.6.1786 (St. Marys
River), James MARTIN * 25.12.1757 (Philadelphia). Issue.
13b) Susan Catherine ~ 25.10.1769 (A).
14b) John *David,* Tatamagouche ~ 25.8.1771 (A); = Catherine *Louisa*
* 21.3.1782 (A), dau. of John Christopher JEANPERRIN. Issue:
1c) James * 7.5.1799 + 20.8.1820, unm.
2c) Christopher * 11.2.1801 + 27.2.1876; = Jane JOUDREY. Issue.
3c) Jacob * 1805 + 1887 in Ontario; = Eleanor PATRIQUIN. Issue.
4c) Lucy * 3.2.1809; = George JOLLIMORE. Issue.
5c) David * 1810. Issue.
6c) Susan * 1811 + 1891; = Abram TATTRIE. Issue.
7c) Mary * 1814 + 19.1.1874; = 2.9.1831, Henry DWYER. Issue.
8c) Isabella * 1816; = George LOGAN. Issue.

---

[90] A "John Frederick" Langille ■ 29.3.1767 (A) is almost certainly
an entry intended to refer to the burial of *George* Frederick, the 4-year-old
son of Mathieu Langille (*infra*).

9c) Catherine * 23.10.1818 + 28.11.1895; = Christopher, son of
   James and Nancy LANGILLE. Issue.
10c) George * 26.4.1821 + 1882; = Margaret BURNS. Issue.
11c) Hannah * 1822; = George BIGNEY. Issue.
15b) John George, River John * 1773 at Northumberland Strait
   + 1864; = Marie Catherine * 27/28.12.1780 (A) + 1849, dau. of
   John Christopher JEANPERRIN. Issue:
   1c) Elizabeth * 1799 + 19.7.1874; = Louis * 1799, son of John
      George and Mary LANGILLE.
   2c) Ephraim * 1801 + 9.3.1869; = Elizabeth, * 1811 + 19.7.1896,
      dau. of Joseph and Phoebe LANGILLE. Issue.
   3c) Catherine * 1802 + 7.10.1874; = James, son of David
      LANGILLE.
   4c) Mary * 1804 + 1866, unm.
   5c) Nelson * 1806 + 10.6.1876; = Grace ROGERS. Issue.
   6c) Sarah * 30.3.1807 + 25.4.1884; = James Louis LANGILLE.
      Issue.
   7c) Abraham * 1.4.1810 + 2.2.1887; = Phoebe, dau. of Joseph
      and Phoebe LANGILLE. Issue.
   8c) Isaac * 1811 + 3.1.1877; = Susan, dau. of John Louis
      LANGILLE. Issue.
   9c) Susan * 1817 + 1904; = Louis, son of John Louis
      LANGILLE. Issue.
  10c) Lucy * 1820; = William, son of John Louis LANGILLE. Issue.
16b) John Louis, Tatamagouche * 1775 + 1860; = 1800, Mary
   Margaret * 23.12.1784 (A) + 1860, dau. of John George
   JEANPERRIN. Issue:
   1c) Robert * 1801; = Mary, dau. of Louis TATTRIE. Issue.
   2c) George * 1802; = Elizabeth, dau. of Louis TATTRIE. Issue.
   3c) David * 1803 + 29.9.1889; = Catherine, dau. of John
      Frederick PATRIQUIN. Issue.
   4c) Alexander * 1805; = Margaret TEED. Issue.
   5c) James Louis * 12.10.1807 + 1883; = Sarah, dau. of John
      George LANGILLE. Issue.
   6c) Susan * 1809 + 1893; = Isaac, son of J. George LANGILLE.
      Issue.

7c) William * 1811; = Mary, dau. of John George LANGILLE.
　　Issue.
8c) Louis * 1818 + 1890; = Susan, dau. of John George
　　LANGILLE. Issue.

5a) **Mathieu** * 4.7.1724 at Dampierre; a farmer, he emigrated to Nova
　　Scotia in the *Betty* in 1752, as a single man, and was living 1801 at
　　River John; = 14.3.1758 (A), Susanne-Catherine * ca. 1734,
　　■ 19.4.1786 (A), dau. of Jean-George MÉNÉGAUX. Issue:
1b) Mary Catherine ~ 7.8.1760 (A); = John George PATRIQUIN.
　　Issue.
2b) Agnes * 1761 + 1842; = John George BIGNEY. Issue.
3b) George Frederic ~ 4.1.1763 (A)■ 29.3.1767 (A) as *John
　　Frederick*. [See footnote 90]
4b) Mary Catherine ~ 5.2.1765 (A) + 1836; = John James GRATTO.
　　Issue.
5b) Marguerite ~ 24.2.1767 (A); = John George MATTATALL. Issue.
6b) John Peter ~ 27.3.1769 (A) + young.
7b) Susanne Catherine ~ 25.8.1771 (A), living 1810.
8b) a daughter; = John JOUDREY.

L A N G I L L E - II (sons of David)

Two sons of David (1696-1765; p. 116), came to Nova Scotia:
1a) **David** * 29.6.1721 at Dampierre; a joiner, he emigrated to Nova
　　Scotia in 1752 in the *Betty* as a single man; = (I) 12.4.1746 at
　　Dampierre, Catherine QUAISLET + 1751, and had two children:
　　1b) Jean-Jacques * 17.2.1747 + 1751/2 at Dampierre.
　　2b) Marguerite * 7.4.1749 + 1751/2 at Dampierre.
　　David = (II) 31.8.1752 (P), Catherine ■ 21.3.1753, age 23, at Halifax,
　　dau. of Pierre AMÊT. No issue. David seems to have left the province
　　in the mid-1750s; possibly he enlisted.
2a)**Léopold-Frédéric** * 26.6.1728 at Dampierre; a joiner, he emigrated
　　to Nova Scotia in the *Betty* in 1752, with a household of 1.1.0.1, and
　　+ 17.9.1819 (A); = (I) 11.5.1751 at Dampierre, **Marguerite**
　　* 29.12.1730 at Dampierre + 25.5.1775 (A), dau. of Jacques and
　　Marie-Madeleine (Amêt) SANDOZ. Six children.

Léopold-Frédéric = (II) 27.8.1775 (A), Susan ~ 30.1.1721 at Champey + 19.4.1786 at Lunenburg, dau. of Jean-Jacques JACOT, and widow of Nicolas DARÉ. No issue of this marriage. Léopold-Frédéric = (III) 20.5.1786 (P), Catherine ~ 3.7.1761 (A) + 21.8.1814, dau. of Jean- Nicolas BOUTEILLIER, and had six more children. Issue:

1b) **Catherine** * 28.4.1752 en route to Halifax [cf., page 14, note 21], living 1812; = 20.10. 1772 (A), Jacques DARÉ ~ 1.5.1746 at Trémoins, living 1795. Issue.

2b) John Peter * 17.7.1754 (A) + 1829/30; = 18.4.1775 (A), *Joanna* Elizabeth ~ 25.4.1754 (A), dau. of Johann Jacob CROUSE. Issue.

  1c) James Frederick * 7.8.1778 (A); = 13.5.1801 (C), Mary Elizabeth * 5.9.1781 (C) + 1858, dau. of John BACHMAN. Issue.

  2c) *John* Leonard * 31.10.1780 (A) + 13.3.1852; = 19.4.1807 (A), Catharine SMITH. Issue.

  3c) *Mary* Catherine * 27.2.1783 (A); = 30.10.1804 (L), William *Charles* DEMONE * 4.7.1781 (L). Issue.

  4c) John *David*, twin, Tancook Is. * 16.5.1785 (A) + 20.3.1820 (C); = 16.12.1806 (A), *Mary* Catherine * 5.8.1785 (A), dau. of Thomas BOUCHER. Issue.

  5c) Leopold *Paulus*, a twin, deputy surveyor of lands for Lunenburg County * 16.5.1785 (A) + 19.11.1858 at Lower New Cornwall; = 26.2.1811 (A), Ann Judith * 24.5.1790 (C), dau. of George Frederick DAUPHINÉ. Issue. From 1830 to 1846 he was a Baptist deacon.

  6c) Ann Margaret * 2.10.1787 + 29.6.1791 (A).

  7c) Catherine Elizabeth * 18.6.1790 (A) + 1.8.1791 (A).

  8c) John Peter * 4.6.1792 (A) + 20.1.1864 at Northwest Range; = 3.10.1816 (C), Mary *Elizabeth* * 1.4.1795 (C), dau. of John Nicholas EISENHAUER.

  9c) *Sophia* Elizabeth * 23.12.1794 (A); = 11.11.1817 (L), Conrad WENTZEL * 23.11.1794 (L). Issue.

3b) George * 20.6.1756 (A), living 1817; = (I) 25.4.1775 (L), Ann Elizabeth ~ 2.4.1755 (A) + 13.11.1775, dau. of John Caspar MEISNER. Issue:

  1c) Ann Catherine * 29.10.1775 + 8.11.1775 (L).

George = (II) 27.2.1776(A), Ann-Catherine ~ 24.10.1758 (A),
■ 19.11.1814 at Blandford, dau. of John George KAYSER. Issue:
2c) Catherine Elizabeth * 19.11.1776 (A).
3c) Catherine Barbara * 28.9.1778 (A).
4c) Margaret Barbara * 11.2.1781 (A) + 15.4.1865 at Blandford;
  = Frederick Ott BEAMISH of Halifax + 19.2.1821. Issue.
5c) Matthew * 23.5.1783 (A).
6c) Leopold Frederick * 3.11.1785 (A).
7c) George Frederick * 31.1.1788 (A) + 5.3.1873 at Liscomb, NS;
  = 31.8.1814 (A), Mary Ann RILEY and had issue.
8c) William "LONGEAL", butcher at Halifax ~ 13.12.1792 at
  Halifax; = 14.5.1816 (P), Rachel Abigail * 1798, dau. of Ezekiel
  William RUMRELL and had eleven children. Some of this
  branch of the family used the form "Longueil" in Halifax.
4b) Jeanne Margaret ~ 15.4.1758 (A) + in infancy.
5b) James * 8.5.1760 (A) + 16.11.1844 at Martins River; = 12.12.1780
  (A), Ann Barbara ~ 1.1.1760 (A) ■ 30.3.1845 at Martins River, dau.
  of Johann Georg BOEHNER. Issue:
1c) Catherine Margaret * 4.3.1782 (A) ■ 28.9.1833 (A); =
  18.1.1803 (L), John Henry LANTZ * 30.10.1776 (L). Issue.
2c) John Frederick * 25.5.1784 (A).
3c) John George, Martins River, * 9.8.1785 (A) ■ 26.4.1845
  (Mahone Bay); = 27.1.1810 (L), Mary Catharine * 15.8.1791 (C),
  dau. of George Melchior ZWICKER, and had issue.
4c) Catherine Elizabeth * 6.1.1788 (A) ■ 16.2.1801 (L).
5c) Catherine *Regina* * 18.7.1790 (A) + 5.11.1812 (L), unm.
6c) Hannah * 29.4.1793 (A); = 2.5.1815 (L), John William
  ERNST.
7c) Mary *Catherine* * 8.6.1796 (A) + 1884; = 27.5.1817 (L), John
  George EISENHAUER. Issue.
8c) John William * 17.12.1799 (A) + 29.5.1873; = Mary Catherine
  * 28.3.1802 (A) + 6.2.1891 at Chester, dau. of John William
  KEDDY. Issue.
9c) John Jacob * 22.8.1803 (L) + 11.12.1877; = (I) Jane Margaret
  ~ 13.6.1801 at Chester + 1851, dau. of Michael FLEET. Issue.
  John Jacob Langille = (II) 7.2.1858 (Mahone Bay), Elizabeth,
  dau. of John BERRINGER, widow of John YOUNG.

6b) Charles ~ 14.9.1766 (A) + in infancy; youngest child of first
marriage.

7b) Jacques-Frédéric * 3.4.1787 at Dampierre-les-Bois + 1850. Issue

8b) John Peter * 25.7.1788 (A) + 9.10.1865; = 3.10.1816 (C), Mary
Elizabeth* 1.11.1795(C), dau. of John Philip EISENHAUER. Issue

9b) John Nicholas * 24.9.1790 (A) + -.3.1871 at Blockhouse;
= 14.1.1816 (A), Ann Margaret * 25.9.1793 (L), dau. of Johann
Frederick BOEHNER. Issue.

10b) Léopold Frederic * 14.1.1795 (A) + drowned in 1821.

11b) George Christopher * 8.6.1798 (A) + 20.2.1877 at Hubbards;
= 31.8.1824 at Chester, Mary Ann ~ 6.6.1796 at Chester, dau. of
John George RILEY of Blandford. Issue.

12b) Catherine Elizabeth * 28.3.1801 (A); = 3.4.1828 (C), John Jacob
EISENHAUER * 18.4.1801 (C).

LAURILLARD

George-Jacob LAURILLARD, pastry cook * 14.1.1676; = 30.1.1700 at
Temple St.-Martin, Montbéliard Town, Susanne-Marguerite * 13.3.1679,
dau. of Jean and Elisabeth (Mathiot) FALLOT and had issue, including:

1. **Jean-Christophe** ~ 5.7.1704 at Montbéliard Town; a tailor, he
emigrated to England and came to Halifax in 1749 in the *Beauport*.[91]
He was ■ 16.8.1786 (P); = **Anne** - - - - * ca. 1710/11, ■ 12.5.1769 (P).
They had three children:

1) **Elisabeth** * ca. 1733, ■ 3.12.1799 (P); = 21.11.1763 (P), John
GOSBEE, brewer * 1720 in England + 16.4.1777 at Halifax.[92]
They had five children.

----

[91]The Laurillards were not among the Foreign Protestants brought
to Nova Scotia through the agency of John Dick. The family appears to have
lived in England for several years before coming to Nova Scotia as members of
the founding party at Halifax in the summer of 1749. It is probable that some or
all the children had been born in England. A genealogical article about this
family will appear in the 2015 *Journal* of the Royal Nova Scotia Historical Society.

[92] Gosbee, his first wife Mary and child, came to Halifax in the
Alexander as part of the town's founding party in the summer of 1749. His
first wife died in March 1755, and their child, Jane, died in Dec 1749.

2) **John Henry** + 4.5.1816 at Rawdon, NS; = Sarah, dau. of Caleb and Patience LAKE. No issue.

3) **George,** shipwright * 1746/47 + 6.8.1815 at Halifax; = (I) 4.1.1777 (P), Mary FITZHARRIS + 21.2.1788 at Halifax, age 31. Issue. He = (II) 13.7.1788 (P), Mary FORD + 26.7.1816 at Halifax, age 49. George Laurillard had fifteen children:

1a) Thomas Hardwell, shipwright * 1777 + 7.11.1830 at Halifax; = 23.6.1800 (P), Mary Ann STOKES + 4.1.1826, age 51, widow of Warren LITCHFIELD. No issue.

2a) Ann ~ 16.5.1779 (P) + 14.2.1836 at Halifax, unm.

3a) Mary ~ 5.11.1780 (P) + -.12.1780, age 1 month 14 days (P).

4a) John George Lewis ~ 30.12.1781 (P), drowned in Halifax Harbour, 18.6.1793.

5a) William Hardwill, shipwright ~ 20.1.1785 (P) + 21.3.1862 at Halifax; = 19.12.1809 (P), Elizabeth SCOTT * 1787 + 29.6. 1843 at Halifax They had six children.

6a) Henry, sailmaker * 9.2.1786 (P) + 16.9.1834 at Halifax; = 25.12.1809 (P), Sarah MINNS * 1780 + 17.8.1870, widow of Thomas GODFREY. They had five children.

7a) Mary * 14.5.1789 (P) + 18.6.1793, drowned in Halifax Harbour; eldest child of George Laurillard by Mary Ford, his second wife.

8a) Christopher, shipwright * 26.12.1790 (P) + 29.8.1834 at Windsor, NS; = ca. 1813, Grace - - - -, and had five children.

9a) Edward ~ 9.9.1792 (P) ∎ 25.7.1793 (P).

10a) Maria ~ 11.6.1794 (P); = 30.5.1812 (P), George SOUTH, Jr., tailor * 1791 + 25.3.1843 at Halifax. They had eight children.

11a) Sarah ~ 18.3.1796 (P) + 17.8.1870 at Halifax, unm.

12a) George Edward, shoemaker at Lunenburg ~ 12.2.1799 (P) + 17.7.1888 at Halifax; = 12.7.1832 (G), Mary Ann * 14.1.1811 + 12.7.1873, dau. of John Adam HECKMAN, and had issue.

13a) James ~ 30.10.1800 (P) ∎ 14.1.1801 (P), died of smallpox.[93]

14a) David ~ 3.8.1803 (P).

---

[93] James died of smallpox during an epidemic in Halifax at the time. The burial record at St. Paul's Church indicates that he had not been vaccinated.

15a)John Gosbee, blockmaker, Dartmouth ~ 2.2.1806 (P) + 21.5.1882
at Halifax; = 24.5.1840 (B), Susan Ann * 14.11.1804 at Oak Island,
NS, + 5.5.1897 at Halifax, dau. of John SMITH. Three children.

L E A U - I[94]

Jacques, labourer, son of Pierre LODS, shoemaker at Héricourt;
= 24.2.1685 at Héricourt, Jeanne * 1665 + 28.10.1733, dau. of Jacques
and Anne (Pfister) DEBARD. Their issue included
1. Jacques, master mason ~ 19.12.1700 at Chagey + 27.5.1770; =
   20.1.1728 at Héricourt, Marie + 19.3.1763, age 63, dau. of Pierre
   CHEVALLIER, tailor at Exincourt. Issue:
   1) **Jean-George**, farmer, ~ 15.3.1731 at Héricourt; emigrated to Nova
      Scotia in the *Speedwell* in 1752, as a single man. He + by 1766; =
      (I) 26.5.1753 (P), Anne CURIER, but had no known issue. She =
      (II) 21.3.1766 (A), Jean RENAUD from Switzerland and had issue.
   2) Étienne ~ 4.2.1733 + 11.5.1786 at Héricourt; = Catherine BOILLOU
   3) Pierre-Anthoine ~ 28.8.1735 at Héricourt + 29.4.1792. Issue.
   4) Gabriel ~ 4.12.1739 at Héricourt.
   5) Pierre ~ 2.4.1743 at Héricourt.
2. Daniel ~ 27 Jan 1704 at Chagey.

L E A U - II

François LODS, Chenebier + 28.1.1727; = Catherine DRECH
+ 10.1.1741, age 81. They had issue:
1. **David,** a charcoal burner at Chenebier * ca. 1690;[95] emigrated to Nova
   Scotia in the *Speedwell* in 1752, with a household of 1.1.0.0;
   = 18.10.1712 at Étobon, Elisabeth ~ 25.4.1687 at Étobon + by 1752,
   dau. of Adam & Claudine (Plançon) GOUD. Issue:
   1) Pierre * 21.3.1715, confirmed 1731 at Étobon.

---

[94] The name in Montbéliard was written LODS or LODZ. In Nova
Scotia the four LEAUs of the passenger lists became LOW and LOWE.

[95] Another instance of a man claiming to be younger than he
was, lest he not be allowed to accompany his younger relatives to Nova Scotia.
David Leau appears in the passenger list as being "46", whereas he was at least
60. David seems to have died at sea in summer 1752.

2) **Jean-George** * 17.3.1717 and confirmed in 1733 at Étobon; a joiner, he emigrated to Nova Scotia in the *Speedwell* in 1752, with a household of 1.1.0.2, and was buried 21.4.1796 age 76 (A);[96] = (I) **Marie-Madeleine** - - - -, ■ 8.2.1753, age 39, at Halifax.[97] They had issue:

1a) **Eve** * ca. 1747/8, living 1777; = 4.5.1763 (P),[98] Jean-Jacques LANGILLE * ca. 1736 + 1818, and had issue.

2a) **Frédéric** + summer 1752 at sea.

3a) George-Louis ~ 9.1.1753, ■ 29.3.1753 at Halifax.

Jean-George = (II) 20.5.1753 (P), Eve * ca. 1706 ■ 29.11.1787 (A), widow of Abraham JACQUES. Jean-George = (III) 23.3.1788 (A), Anne-Catherine-Marie ~ 19.4.1737 at Allondans ■ 16.1.1825 (A), dau. of Jean-Christophe JODRY, widow of John Peter WAMBOLT.

3) **Anne-Catherine**, twin * 4.4.1722 at Étobon, ■ 18.3.1791 (C); = (I) 14.2.1753 (P), Abraham DUTOUR * 1697 at Vevey, canton of Vaud, Switzerland ■ 6.12.1756 (A). No issue. She = (II) 31.5.1757 (A), John Leonard MADER ■ 12.7.1771 (C) and had three children.

4) **Françoise**, twin * 4.4.1722 at Étobon.

5) Marguerite * 24.1.1725 at Étobon.

6) Jacques-Frédéric * 22.3.1727 at Étobon.

---

[96] His baptism record has him born in 1717, his age on the ship list, 30, makes it 1721/22, while his burial record works out to 1719/20. Since his father took nearly 15 years off his admitted age in 1752, it would not be a surprise if the son knocked off five years! A less likely identification than that which is presented above is that Jean-George was **not** so closely related to David Lods/Leau. There was a Jean-George ~ 4.4.1723 at Héricourt, the son of Pierre Lods + 29.4.1761, who = 6.1.1722 at Héricourt = Eve + 29.1.1757 at Héricourt, dau. of Jacques Surleau of Héricourt. A list of emigrants from there in 1752 includes "Georges Lods, agé de 28 ans, tailleur, sa femme et une fille de sa femme, pauvres gens."

[97] She was almost certainly a widow when she married Lods, an impression somewhat supported by the fact that she was at least three years older than he was.

[98] Date of license to "John Jacob Laungail" and "Avalley Lau"; no marriage record seen.

2. Pierre-Jacques, labourer at Chenebier * ca. 1692, living 1748; = (I)
   14.5.1715 at Étobon, Elisabeth, dau. of Christoph BONHÔTAL. One
   child. He = (II)14.11.1719 at Étobon, Marguerite * 3.1.1690 at
   Chenebier, dau. of Étienne LAFERTÉ, and had four children.
3. Susanne * ca. 1695, living 1733; = 25.5.1717 at Étobon, David
   REGEOT, labourer at Chenebier, * 4.8.1695 at Chenebier, and had
   issue.
4. Elisabeth * ca. 1701 + 29.4.1762, age 60, at Étobon; = (I) 24.6.1732
   at Étobon, Jérémie MONNIER,[99] weaver at Chenebier, ■ 7.4.1745 at
   Étobon, and had issue. She = (II) 7.8.1753 at Étobon, Abraham
   CHAMOT, weaver at Frédéric-Fontaine * 1698/99 + 27.4.1759 at
   Chenebier, a widower.

L E A U - III

Jean-Jacques Lods ~ 27.2.1707 at Coisevaux; a mason "age 38",[100] he
emigrated to Nova Scotia in the *Pearl* in 1752, with a household of
1.1.3.1., and was ■ -. 10.1752 at Halifax; = ca. 1732, **Frédérique-Sybille**
~ 27.10.1709 at Champey + at sea in summer 1752, dau. of Pierre and
Claudine (Vurpillot) BILLE. Issue:
1. Jean-George ~ 23.2.1733 + 6.3.1733 at Trémoins.
2. **Jean-George**, farmer ~ 29.8.1734 at Trémoins; emigrated, 1.0.0.0, in
   the *Pearl* in 1752. Killed by the fall of a tree, ■ 30.9.1778 (A) unm.
3. **Étienne** ~ 22.1.1739 at Trémoins, orphan at Halifax 1753;
   ■ 25.2.1758 at Halifax as "Stephen Lord"(P).
4. **Jeanne-Catherine** ~ 1.8.1741 at Trémoins, orphan at Halifax 1753;
   put out to Johann Martin Scharenburg or Scherrenberg in 1753.
5. **Judith-Marguerite** ~ 24.2.1744 at Trémoins + summer 1752 at sea.
6. **Claudine** ~ 25.7.1746 at Trémoins, orphan at Halifax 1753; put out to
   Walter Manning in 1758.[101]

---

[99] Jérémie's brother, Abraham Monnier, emigrated to Nova Scotia
Scotia in 1752 (*infra*).

[100] This is another instance of age reduction. His baptism record
proves his age was 45, yet he is listed as being 38.

[101] The passenger list has her as under 4 years old.

L E A U - IV

Jean L'Eau * 1724/25 in the Principality of Montbéliard; a mason, he emigrated to Nova Scotia in the *Betty* in 1752, with a household of 1.1.0.0, and was dead by 20.2.1779;[102] = **Catherine** - - - - * ca. 1725, ■ 6.6.1792 age 67 (A). Issue:
1. Jean-Pierre ~ 6.5.1755, ■ 7.5.1755 (A).
2. John *Peter*, Fauxbourg ~ 22.8.1756 (A), ■ 25.6.1830 (A);
   = 23.3.1779 (A), Elizabeth ~ 15.6.1762 (A), ■ 13.1.1841 (A), dau. of Christopher James VIENOT. Issue:
   1) Elizabeth *Margaret* * 1.3.1780 (A), ■ 27.5.1826 (A); = 24.4.1804 (C), John *Frederick* JOUDRY * 1.2.1780. Issue.
   2) George *Christopher,* Northwest Range * 15.10.1781 (A) ■ 12.2.1842 (A); = 10.10.1805 (A), Catharine Margaret, * 14.3.1784 (L), dau. of Philip Jacob COLP. Issue.
   3) *Mary* Catherine * 31.8.1783 (A) + 1821/25; = 30.10.1804 (A), John Frederick VIENOT. Issue.
   4) John *Peter* * 20.10.1785 (A) ■ 12.10.1828, a sudden death (A); = 21.2.1809 (A), Hannah Elizabeth DARES.[103] Issue.
   5) *James* Frederick * 4.10.1787 (A) + -.2.1868 at Mahone Bay; = 9.12.1817 (A), Sophia Catherine BOUTEILLIER. Issue.
   6) *Susan* Catherine * 22.1.1790 (A), living 1836; = 30.5.1809 (A), John *George* JOUDRY, Northwest Range * 17.10.1776. Issue.
   7) Ann *Elizabeth* * 7.9.1792 (A), living 1825; = 28.9.1813 (A), James Frederick DARES * 7.5.1789 (A). Issue.
   8) *Catherine* Margaret * 14.7.1794 (A), living 1828; = 28.12.1819 (A), Nathan LEVY, Tancook Island ~ 21.3.1798 at Chester ■ 19.5.1839. Issue.
   9) Ann Catherine * 28.1.1797 (A), living 1841; = 28.12.1819 (A), David LEVY, Tancook Island ~ 15.6.1797 at Chester + -.12.1875 at Sherwood. Issue.

---

[102] Date of the probate act; usually this followed within weeks or a few months of a death.

[103] She is almost certainly the child born 7.2.1792 to Jacques & Catherine DARES and ~ 18.3.1792 without a christian name being entered.

10) Sarah * 17.5.1799 (A) + 25.12.1846; = 16.12.1823 (A), John
Henry STEVENS, Little Tancook Island * 20.3.1805 + 5.3.1875 at
Chester. Issue.

11) *John* George * 24.9.1801 (A), living 1825.

3. Catherine *Margaret* ~ 30.5.1758 (A) ■ 6.4.1781 (A),[104] unm.

4. Elizabeth Catherine ~ 7.10.1759 (A), living 1800; ■ 4.4.1780 (A),
John George BOUTEILLIER ~ 11.3.1756 (A) + 3.1.1831 at St.
Margarets Bay. Issue.

5. *George* Frederick, Northwest ~ 29.11.1761 (A) + 6.3.1818 (L); =
9.11.1786 (L), Mary *Magdalen* ~ 26.2.1762 (A) + 5.5.1852 (L), dau.
of Jacob MOSER and widow of Joseph MARIETTE. Issue:

1) John *Peter*, Fauxbourg * 22.1.1787 (A), living 1828; = 26.1.1813
(A), Catherine Elizabeth, dau. of John VEINOT. Issue.

2) Mary Catherine * 23.9.1788 (A) or 18.9.1788 (C), living 1816;
= 13.11.1804 (L), John Christopher LOHNES * 18.12.1783 (L).
Issue.

3) Mary Magdalen * 12.4.1790 (A), living 1816; = 5.11.1811 (C),
John *Frederick* CORKUM, * 9.3.1788 (C). Issue.

4) Mary Anne * 26.9.1791 (A), living 1833; = 23.10.1810 (A),
James ROBAR * 4.4.1786 (A). Issue.

5) Mary *Catherine* * 23.7.1793 (A), living 1816.

6) Mary *Elizabeth* * 16.3.1795 (L) + 2.2.1818 (L), unm.

LOUIS

François Louis, smith, * ca. 1724/25 in the Principality of Montbéliard,
emigrated to Nova Scotia in the *Sally* in 1752 as a single man, and was
living in Halifax late in 1752. After that he apparently enlisted in the
military and left Nova Scotia.

---

[104] The burial register at St. John's Anglican, Lunenburg, states
that she "died . . . by sinking through the ice at ye 2nd peninsula Arm in going
home by dark, & found only yesterday."

MACÉ

André Macé, baker, * ca. 1731/32 in the Principality of Montbéliard, emigrated to Nova Scotia in the *Sally* in 1752 as a single man, and was living in Halifax late in 1752. After that he apparently enlisted in the militaryand left Nova Scotia.

MAILLARD-I

Pierre MAILLARD, schoolmaster, Chenebier +10.9.1727 age 47 years, less 16 days = 9.11.1706 at Chagey, **Anne-Judith** ~ 27.3.1683 at Chagey, ■ 4.3.1762, dau. of Nicolas BOUTEILLIER.[105] She = (II) 3.12.1754 (A), Léopold VIENOT. Issue:

1. **Jean-Frédéric**, labourer at Chenebier ~ 3.7.1707 at Chagey; as a farmer he emigrated to Nova Scotia in the *Betty* in 1752 with a household of 1.4.3.0. He was ■ at Lunenburg 15.12.1771 (A), "an old man"; = 28.11.1728 at Étobon, **Anne-Judith** * 18.7.1707 at Étobon, dau. of Pierre and Jeanne-Louise (Demougin) SUGUEY of Échavanne.[106] They had issue:

---

[105] Anne-Judith was the dau. of Nicolas Bouteillier ~ 29.12.1650 + 21.6.1688, church elder at Chagey, who = 4.4.1676, Anne * ca. 1656 + 4.10.1712, dau. of Pierre Malrage + 12.7. 1708, age 75, a hammerer at the forges at Chagey, and his wife Judith Macaire + 1.1.1702, age 73, from Ste.-Marie-aux-Mines, in Lorraine. Nicolas Bouteillier was himself the son of Pierre Bouteillier + 17.8.1700, age ca. 73 at Chagey, who = 26.6.1649, Jehannette ~ 16.12.1621 + 24.3.1704, dau. of Regnaud Grandpierre of Chagey by his first wife, Jehanna, dau. of Jehan Haugier of Échenans-sous-Mont-Vaudois. Pierre Bouteillier was a son of Jehan-Guillaume Bouteillier and Bonne Williamier of Chagey. Anne-Judith Bouteillier appears to have =(II) 31.1.1730 at Étobon, Jacques-Christophe METTETAL. However that may be, her remarriage to Léopold Vienot at Lunenburg, 3.12.1754 (A), records her name as Ann-Judith Maillard. Vienot was twenty years younger than she, and a widower. No other explanation offers itself.

[106] Anne-Judith Suguey's father, Pierre Suguey * 1659 + 18.22. 1737 was a son of Pierre Suguey * 1620 + 20.6.1690, of the woods of Chenebier, [presumably a woodcutter or forester] and his wife Marguerite Carray. He had = 30.2.1700 at Étobon, Jeanne-Louise Demougin * 1664 + 24.10.1742, dau. of Pierre Demougin of Frédéric-Fontaine.

1) **Jean-Christophe** ~ 1.12.1729 at Chenebier; came to Nova Scotia in the *Sally* in 1752 as a single man. He had been working in Grünstadt before he emigrated, and served here as a soldier in Lascelles Regiment. He was ■ 30.1.1758 (A); = 27.2.1753 (P), Catherine, dau. of Pierre DUPERRIN and had issue:
    1a) Susanne Catherine ~ 30.6.1754 (A), living 1755.

2) Anne-Françoise ~ 10.2.1731 at Chenebier, living 1777.

3) **Anne-Catherine** ~ 6.12.1733 at Chenebier; living 1791; = 31.8.1752 (P), Jean-George BOUTEILLIER ~ 30.6.1729 at Étobon ■ 14.3.1784 (A). Issue.

4) **Elisabeth** ~ 12.1.1736 at Chenebier + 30.1.1785 (A); = 20.6.1754 (A), Jacques JEAUDRY ~ 28.12.1723 at Longevelle, and had issue. She was confirmed, 19.3.1752, soon before emigration.

5) **Pierre-Christophe** ~ 17.8.1738 at Chenebier;[107] emigrated in the *Betty* in 1752 as a single man, and living in 1795 at Tatamagouche; = 2.5.1769 (A), Marguerite-Elisabeth ~ 30.7.1746 at Montbéliard Town, dau. of Jean-George GRETTEAU.

6) George-Frédéric ~ 3.6.1740 + 26.6.1740 at Chenebier.

7) **Jean** ~ 8.10.1741 at Chenebier, living 1808 at Tatamagouche;[108] = 9.9.1766 (A), Anne-Marie, dau. of Jean-Frédéric MÉNÉGAUX. Issue:
    1a) George Frederick ~ 2.9.1767 (A).
    2a) Catherine ~ 6.11.1768 (A) + 1855 (Sharon Church Cemetery); = 15.10.1788 (P), George Frederick JOLIMOIS. Issue.
    3a) Elizabeth Margaret * 27.4.1774 at Tatamagouche, but ~ 28.5.1774 (A) in Lunenburg; = William SALISBURY. Issue.
    4a) Elizabeth * 10.10.1776 ~ 1.12.1776 (A).

---

[107] In *A History of the County of Pictou Nova Scotia* (1877), 127, Rev. George Patterson repeats oral tradition that Peter Millard was among the "fifty young men" involved in an affray about a church. Millard was not yet 14 when he emigrated in 1752, more than a decade after the celebrated fight at Chagey in 1740. The tale is mistaken. See page 10.

[108] His petition for a land grant in 1808 states that he had served in the British forces at Louisbourg (1758) and Québec (1759), and that he had eight living children. The eight would appear to be accounted for *supra*.

5a) William Caspar * 28.6.1778 ~ 16.8.1778 (A).

6a) Frederick * 9.5.1782 ~ 2.6.1782 (A).

7a) Ann Catherine * 25.2.1786 ~ 5.6.1786 (A).

8a) John * 12.8.1790 ~ 25.10.1790 (A).

8) **Jeanne** ~ 25.8.1743 at Chenebier + by 1776; = 18.12.1766 (P), Jacques BEGIN, a widower from Magny Danigon. No issue.

9) **Susanne** ~ 23.10.1745, living 1786; = 8.3.1768 (A), Pierre-Étienne ISELIN ~ 21.4.1746 at Héricourt + 8.3.1815 at Halifax. Issue.

2. Jacques-Christophe, labourer * 22.10.1710 + 11.2.1745 at Chenebier; = 2.2.1740 at Chenebier, Françoise * 3.9.1716, dau. of Jacques BONHÔTAL, Chenebier. Issue:

1) Anne-Catherine ~ 13.11.1740 + 3.3.1767 at Chenebier; = 2.7.1765 at Chenebier, Jacques Christophe MONNIER, roofer.

2) Jean-Jacques ~ 5.1.1742, living 1745 at Chenebier.

3) Jacques-Christoph, carter ~ 3.8.1743; = 7.3.1771 at Chenebier, Suzanne, dau. of Abraham JACOT, and had five children.

4) Marie-Elizabeth ~ 27.9.1744 + 7.4.1747 at Chenebier.

3. Elisabeth * 9.3.1715 at Chenebier; = 13.6.1736 at Chagey = Jean-George MABILLE, smith at Chagey.

4. Pierre-Christophle, labourer * 25.12.1718 + 22.4.1749 at Chenebier; = 12.11.1743 at Étobon, Anne * 1719, dau. of David POCHARD, church elder at Échavanne, and had issue:

1) Jean-George ~ 6.9.1744 + 13.10.1744 at Chenebier.

2) Pierre ~ 12.1.1746 + 10.1.1781 at Chenebier; = 7.7.1772, Anne, dau. of David POCHARD of Échavanne. They had two children.

3) Marguerite ~ 3.6.1748; = 23.2.1773 at Chenebier, Jean-George PETREQUIN. Issue.

MAILLARD-II

Jean-Frédéric Maillard, Hérimoncourt, stocking maker ■ 16.11.1755 (A); = 18.11.1732 at Abbévillers, **Anne-Catherine** COMTESSE ■ 11.10.1750 at Halifax. They came to Nova Scotia in the *Ann* in 1750, with a household that Bell interpreted as 1.1.3.0. They had issue:

1. Catherine-Elisabeth ~ 2.11.1738 at Hérimoncourt.

2. Anne-Judith ~ 2.6.1741 at Hérimoncourt.

3. Susanne ~ 2.7.1743 at Hérimoncourt.

MAILLARDET

Jeanry or Jean Allery MAILLARDET, 25, farmer from Switzerland, came to Nova Scotia in the *Pearl* in 1751, with 2 women and a child. Their stay in Nova Scotia was brief, as we find them the next year in the Sieur de la Roque's census in summer 1752. He reported at Port La Joye [Charlottetown area in PEI]: "Jean-Henry dit Maillardé, master tailor and ploughman, native of the parish of Orbin, Switzerland, aged 26 years . . . in the country two months, having deserted Chibouctou [Halifax] Married to Anne Barbe, native of the town of Bienne, Switzerland, aged 32 years. They have Henry, their son, aged 17 days."[109] This accounts for himself, his wife and their child. The other woman was his sister, Elisabeth Maillardet, living in 1755; = 24.1.1752 (P), Jean-Jacques MICHAUD, a mason and widower from Switzerland who came to Nova Scotia in the *Pearl* in 1751, age 42. With Jean-Henri Maillardet in 1752 was Abraham LOUIS, "bachelor, workman in cotton print, native of Lideau, in Switzerland, aged 20 years. He has been six weeks in the country."[110]

MALBON

Daniel Malbon was a farmer from Belverne, age 40 in 1752. Although his name is included in the passenger list of the *Betty*, he was not on board. He had crossed to Boston in the *Priscilla*, arriving there on 9.11.1751. The members of this family actually on board the *Betty* account for the 1.2.3.0, as Bell logically has it, but the male over 14 was

---

[109] Orbin or Orvin was in territory then belonging to the bishopric of Basel.

[110] The census was taken at Port La Joye in 1752. This Henry *dit* Maillardé had no connexion to the Maillards in Montbéliard, but sometimes has been confused with them. We know that Elisabeth was Jean-Henri's sister from the record in Switzerland. On 29 April 1751 Maillardet, his sister Elisabeth, and Michaud with his wife and five children requested leave to emigrate without paying a tax, as "the families in question are poor." - Albert B. Faust & Gaius M. Brumbaugh, *Lists of Swiss Emigrants in the Eighteenth Century to the American Colonies* (Washington: National Genealogical Society, 1925), Vol. II, p. 63. The Swiss record suggests that they planned to go to Pennsylvania, but evidently John Dick's agents persuaded them to go to Nova Scotia instead.

evidently the son Jacques, rather than Daniel himself. Malbon wrote a letter to his wife from Boston, dated 19.12.1751,[111] and had a grant of 60 acres in Frankfort Plantation on the Kennebec River, Maine, on 11.7.1753, by which time his family had joined him from Halifax.[112]

Nicolas MALBON, bellows maker at Belverne, had four children, including Abram Malbon, carter + 20.10.1736 age 73, who = Elisabeth DEMOUGIN and had issue, Daniel Malbon[113] * 12.3.1707 at Clairgoutte, living 1753 in Maine; = 19.4.1729 at Clairegoutte, **Jeanne-Marguerite HUMBERT**. Issue:

1. **Susanne-Elisabeth** * 19.4.1737 ■ 17.3.1753 at Halifax.
2. **Elisabeth-Marguerite** "Betsey" * 30.3.1741; = Pierre-Emmanuel, shoemaker ~ 9.11.1742 at Étobon, living 1792 at Dresden, Maine, son of Jean and Jeanne (Monnier) POCHARD.[114]
3. **Jacques** ~ 28.8.1743, living in Maine in 1769. Issue.
4. **Marie-Catherine** * 15.6.1745, living 1753.

Accompanying the family was Daniel Malbon's sister, **Anne-Marie Malbon** * 1705 ■ 5.4.1753, age 48, at Halifax, unmarried.

---

[111] The text of Malbon's letter appears in Jean-Marc Debard, "Les Montbéliardais en Nouvelle-Angleterre. Une émigration protestante au milieu du XVIIIᵉ siècle (1751-1755)," in *Bulletin et Mémoires de la Société d'Émulation de Montbéliard*, LXXX # 107 (1984), 276-277. Malbon came out to Boston in the *Priscilla* in autumn 1751.

[112] The situation is evident from material presented by Charles Edwin Allen, *History of Dresden, Maine* (1931), 139, 140, 142, 149, 193-4, 208-210. Daniel Malbon may have been one of the fifty-four settlers sent to Franckfort township between the Kennebec and Eastern rivers, Maine. Each settler was provisioned for a year and granted 100 acres of land. - Allen, pp. 54, 125.

[113] Daniel Malbon had four children who died young: Suzanne (18.6.1730 - 8.12.1731), Daniel (* 16.2.1732), Elisabeth-Marguerite (4.8.1739 - 26.8.1739) and Jean (* 30.7.1749).

[114] Pierre Pochard was known as Peter Pushard in Maine. His mother's brother was Abraham Monnier, who emigrated to Nova Scotia.

MALMAHU[115]

Jacques Malmahu * ca. 1715/16 at Dasle; a thatcher by trade, he emigrated to Nova Scotia in the *Speedwell* in 1752, with a household of 1.1.0.0, and died sometime after 1770; = (I) **Nanette Catherine - - - -**, who was ■ 16.4.1753 at Halifax. He = (II) 16.10.1753 (A), Elisabeth * 1713, dau. of Jean and Marie (Vernier) JEAND'HEUR, widow of Jean-Pierre ISELIN. They had two daughters:
1. Anne-Catherine ~ 12.4.1754 (A), living 1757.
2. Frances-Catherine ~ 17.4.1756 (A); mother of a natural child,
   1) Ann Catherine ~ 30.4.1775 ■ 27.10.1776 (A).

MARIETTE

Étienne Mariette * ca. 1711/12 in the Principality of Montbéliard;[116] a farmer, he emigrated to Nova Scotia in the *Pearl* in 1752, with a household of 1.1.3.1, and + the autumn of 1784; = (I) **Marie - - - -**, ■ 3.3.1753, age 40, at Halifax. Issue:
1. **Pierre** * ca. 1735/36; a farmer, he emigrated to Nova Scotia in the *Pearl* in 1752 as a single man, but + summer 1752 during the crossing.
2. **Étienne**, living 1753.
3. **Michel**, ■ 28.11.1752 at Halifax.
4. **Daniel**, living 1757.
5. **a child** + summer 1752 at sea during the crossing.
Étienne Mariette = (II) 1.1.1756 (A), *Anne*-Catherine ~ 25.8.1718 at Chagey, ■ 27.10.1796 (C), dau. of Pierre BOUTEILLIER, and widow of Jean-George BESANÇON, and had six children:

---

[115] The surname was properly Malmehuz, a name found in the Town of Montbéliard and at Dasle. The latter location is the more likely in this instance.

[116] The name would properly have been Mairet or Mairot, a surname found in Brevilliers, Héricourt and Étobon. In this case, Brevilliers seems the most likely place of origin. His will was dated 23.8.1784 and proved 8.11.1784. He died between those dates.

6. Mary Margaret ~ 25.5.1758 ■ 2.3.1774 (A).
7. Joseph, Clearland ~ 15.9.1760 ■ 30.12.1783 (L); = 18.3.1783 (L),
   Mary Magdalen ~ 26.2.1762 (A) + 5.5.1852 (L), dau. of Jacob
   MOSER. She = (II) 9.11.1786 (L), George-Frederick LEAU
   ~ 29.11.1761 (A) + 6.3.1818 (L), and had issue.
8. Susan Elizabeth Barbara ~ 6.6.1762 (A) + 6.4.1838 at St. Margarets
   Bay; = 24.10.1780 (A), James BOUTEILLIER. Issue.
9. John George ~ 21.10.1764 (A) + young at Lunenburg.
10. John *Peter* Nicholas ~ 29.11.1765 (A) + 9.6.1838 at Harrietsfield;
   = 5.7.1785 (A), Mary Elizabeth ~ 8.2.1768 (A), dau. of Christopher
   Jacques VIENOT. Issue:
   1) John James * 26.3.1786 (A).
   2) Catherine * 17.12.1787 (A).
   3) *Hannah* Elizabeth * 28.9.1790 (A).
   4) *Susan* Elizabeth * 9.4.1792 (A) + 12.12.1869 at Boutiliers Point;
      = *ca* 1813, John George DAUPHINEE, and had nine children.
   5) Margaret Elizabeth * 18.11.1794 (A) + young.
   6) Elizabeth * 21.5.1797 (A); = 18.12.1831 (P), John HUBLEY.
   7) Sarah ~ 1.6.1800 (P) + 17.5.1827 at Harrietsfield; = 17.12.1823 (P),
      Hugh DUGWELL + 16.5.1838, and had three children.
   8) *Margaret* Elizabeth ~ 6.6.1802 (P), living 1846; = 7.11.1820 (G),
      John David BRUNT, Harrietsfield, * 13.1.1795. Eleven children.
   9) Peter James * 11.1.1805 (A).
   10) John James * 5.4.1807 (A) + 10.5.1857; = 19.1.1836 (P), Mary
      Ann LYNCH. Issue.
   11) Eleanor * 1809/10 ■ 3.12.1840; = 23.2.1830 (G), John BRUNT,
      Harrietsfield ~ 29.10.1802 (L) + 2.7.1852. Issue.
   12) John George ~ 22.5.1812, age 10 months (P), + 1.5.1885;
      = 13.1.1835 (P), Mary Isabella, dau. of Peter TOLER. Issue.
11. *James* Stephen ~ 21.8.1768 (A); = 11.9.1786 (L), Catharine Barbara,
   dau. of Jacob MOSER. Issue:
   1) Jacob * 26.4.1788 (A); = 27.9.1808 (D),[117] Rachel * 30.3.1791 (C),
      dau. of John Peter CORKUM, and had issue.

---

[117] (D) indicates an entry in the records of marriages performed
by Joseph Dimock, an early Baptist minister in Nova Scotia.

2) Catherine Barbara * 8.8.1790 (A); = 27.9.1808 (D), Christopher CORKUM * 22.5.1784 (C). Issue.
3) Mary *Elizabeth* * 26.2.1793 (A), living 1838; = 23.1.1816 (D), Alexander FRIDAY [Freda] * 15.8.1792 at Chester. Issue.
4) Ann *Mary* * 22.6.1795 (L), living 1838; = 14.5.1816 (D), Joseph GREENLAW * 17.7.1793 at Chester. Issue.
5) Catherine Elizabeth * 17.6.1798 ▪ 9.8.1802 (L).
6) John * 12.12.1800 ▪ 22.4.1802 (L).

MASSON

Jean MASSON, living 1673; = Susanne PECHIN and had issue:
1. Jean-Frédéric = 15.10.1715 in Montbéliard Town, Éléanore-Charlotte MOREL, and had two sons who emigrated to Nova Scotia in 1752:
   1) **Jean-Frédéric**, farmer * 21.9.1721 in Montbéliard Town; emigrated in 1752 in the *Speedwell*, with a household of 1.1.2.2, and + 6.8.1776 (A); = (I) ca. 1744, **Catherine - - - -**, ▪ 10.9.1753 (A). Three children by her:
     1a) **Anne Catherine 'Nanette'** ▪ 31.1.1758 (A).
     2a) **Pierre** * 1746 + 16.8.1826 at Masons Island (L); = (I) 6.9.1774 (A), Mary Eva ~ 20.5.1754 (A), ▪15.4.1792, dau. of John Adam WAMBOLT. Nine children. He = (II) 26.8.1792 (A), Catharine Barbara ~ 13.7.1766 (A) + 15.8.1842 (L), dau. of John Andrew YOUNG. Eight children. Pierre/Peter's seventeen children were:
       1b) John Frederick * 16.11.1775 + 9.1.1776 (A).
       2b) *Catherine* Barbara * 23.12.1776 (A), living 1827 at Eastern Passage, NS; = 4.2.1798 (A), John Valentine HATT * 15.2.1769 (A). Issue.
       3b) Ann *Elizabeth* * 23.7.1779 + 10.8.1808 at Mahone Bay; = 8.4.1798 (C), John Henry HEISON * 16.7.1776 (C). Issue.
       4b) John *Frederick*, First Peninsula * 19.10.1781 (A) + 1864/72; = 30.3.1806 (A), Rebecca Elizabeth * 20.6.1786 (L), dau. of John Caspar YOUNG. Issue.
       5b) John *Peter*, Second Peninsula * 29.10.1783 (A) + 24.2.1861; = 13.4.1817 (C), Sarah * 13.4.1797 (A) + 18.9.1858 (A), dau. of George Michael SMITH. Issue.
       6b) George, Tancook Island * 17.2.1785 (A), living 1861; = 23.4.1810 (A), Barbara BAKER.

7b) Ann Mary, twin * 11.5.1787 (A), living 1825; = 26.7.1808 (A),
   Frederick MADER * 19.12.1783 (C). Issue.
8b) John, First Peninsula, twin * 11.5.1787 (A) + 1856/59;
   = 18.5.1812 (A), Elizabeth * 26.4.1793 (C), dau. of John
   Adam HEBB. Issue.
9b) Sophia * 27.2.1790 (A), living 1825; = 29.3.1810 (L),
   John Jacob HIRTLE * 4.6.1783 (L).
10b) Rebecca *Elizabeth*, eldest by second wife *14.10.1793 (A);
   = 24.3.1816 (A), James SMITH * 15.9.1789 (A).
11b) Ann Margaret * 18.8.1796 ∎ 1.7.1803 (A).
12b) Caspar * 10.5.1798 (A) + 22.2.1820, unm.; killed by the
   falling of a tree.
13b) Charlotte Dorothy * 17.9.1800 (A) + 24.2.1801 (?), unm.
14b) Philip, Masons Island * 14.2.1802 (A) + 20.3.1882; = (I)
   1.2.1823 (A), Catharine Dorothy + ca. 1832, dau. of
   Adolph C. NEWMAN and had issue. He = (II) 12.12.1833
   (A), Margaret, dau. of Peter HECKMAN and had issue.
   He = (3) 22.12.1838 (A), Mary Ann SMITH, with issue.
15b) John *Jacob*, Masons Island * 3.7.1803 (A) + 1898;
   = 6.7.1826 (A), Anne Eliza, dau. of George SMITH.
16b) Sarah * 25.5.1806 (A), living 1842; = 20.12.1825 (L),
   John Philip MORASH, Militia Sgt. * 5.7.1801. Issue.
17b) Anne Catherine * 30.1.1809 (A), ∎ 14.3.1809 (A).
3a) **Henriette** * 1748, living 1780 at Chester; = 3.9.1767 (A),
   James WILSON. Issue.
Jean-Frédéric = (II) 17.12.1754 (A), Marie-Marguerite ~ 28.6.1726
at Longevelle, living 1780, dau. of Guillaume GUIGNÉ. Issue:
4a) John *James* ~ 23.6.1757 (A) + 1830 on the Eastern Shore of
   NS; = 20.10. 1784,[118] Frederica Mary ~ 28.2.1762 (A)
   + 4.3.1843 at Popes Harbour, dau. of Frederick HAHN. Issue:
   1b) Margaret ~ 26.3.1785 (P) + 28.5.1864; = 9.8.1807 (P),
   John HOOPER. Issue.
   2b) Elizabeth * 22.4.1787 (P); = 22.8.1807 (P), John HAWES.
   Issue.

---

[118] Date of the marriage license; the marriage record itself
not found.

3b) John * 30.8.1789 (P).
4b) Thomas James ~ 6.5.1795 (P).
5b) Mary ~ 6.5.1795 (P).
6b) Marianne ~ 15.11.1797 (P).
7b) George Frederick ~ 9.6.1799 (P).
8b) William.
5a) John Frederick ~ 14.4.1759 (A), drowned, ■ 16.8.1767 (A).
6a) Barbara ~ 7.10.1760 (A).
7a) Catherine ~ 20.4.1763 (A), living 1795; = 30.11.1784 (C),
   Robert KEDY. Issue.
8a) *Susan* Catherine ~ 6.3.1765 (A), drowned with her brother,
   ■ 16.8.1767 (A).
9a) *George* Frederick ~ 9.11.1766 (A) + 5.1.1827 St. Margarets
   Bay; = 15.11.1792 (A), Mary Gertrude * 1772, dau. of Johann
   Conrad KNICKEL. Issue:
   1b) Hanna Mary, "Polly" * 4.11.1793 (A), living 1822.
   2b) Catherine Margaret * 12.3.1795 (A), living 1829; = 25.6.1817
      (P), John GOWENS and had issue.
   3b) *James* Conrad * 24.6.1796 (A), living 1828; = 26.11.1816 (P),
      Ann "Nancy" HIRTLE. Issue.
   4b) Mary Elizabeth * 2.8.1798 (A), living 1822.
   5b) George Christopher * 28.4.1800 (A), living 1822.
   6b) Catherine Magdalen * 9.12.1803 (L).
   7b) *John* Peter * 29.7.1805 (A) + 1827/28.
   8b) John Martin * 10.7.1807 (A) + 27.5.1879; = 15.12.1828 (P),
      Susanna Elizabeth * 2.8.1811 (A), dau. of Charles Frederick
      FADER. Issue.
   9b) Sophia * -.10.1810 + 24.3.1895; = 29.3.1826 (C), John Jacob
      BAKER, Tancook Island ~ 4.8.1799 (C) + 6.7.1881. Issue.
   10b) Frederick ~ 25.5.1815 age 3 mos (G), living 1822.
   11b) Joseph * 24.3.1817 (P), living 1822.
10a) Anne Barbara ~ 19.11.1769 (A) + 17.8.1844 at Dartmouth; =
   16.12.1787 (L), John Christian BOWES + 14.5.1830. Issue.
11a) Eva Margaret ~ 27.12.1771 (A) + 22.9.1853 (L); = 4.11.1788 (L),
   John Conrad MEISNER ~ 20.10.1764 (A) + 2.12.1827 (L). Issue.
2) **François**, a farmer * 1725/26; emigrated as a farmer and single man
   in the *Speedwell* in 1752, living in late 1752 at Halifax.

MATHIEU

Moïse MATTHIEU dit Prevost[119] of "Lagne", Switzerland + 21.12.1726, age ca. 58, at Échavanne; = 16.12.1703 at Étobon, Claudine ~ 27.2.1670 + 30.11.1738, dau. of Adam and Jeanne (Migneré) POCHARD of Échavanne. Two sons:

1. Pierre * 18.11.1706, living 1753 at Échavanne; = 19.10.1734 at Étobon, Marguerite * 1.8.1711, dau. of Pierre and Catherine (Pourtot) LAMBELET of Belverne and Chenebier, and had nine children, two of whom survived infancy:
   1)Jean ~ 8.2.1739 at Échavanne.
   2)Pierre ~ 14.8.1745 at Échavanne.
2. Jean, mason[120] * 5.11.1708 at Échavanne + early 1737; = ca. 1731, **Anne-Marie** GERMAIN * 1708 + 3.6.1778 (A),[121] who = (II) 19.6.1742 (Étobon), Jean-Jacques COULERUS of Dung * 17.3.1711 + by 1752. She = (III) 5.12.1752 (P),[122] Jean- Jacques GROSRENAULD + ca. 1755, and (IV) 6.7.1756 (A), John Michael KAYSER, widower. Issue:
   1)**Jérémie**, a farmer ~ 7.12.1731 at Échavanne + between Dec. 1753 and July 1754 at Lunenburg.

---

[119] The family Matthey-Prévot had citizenship at La Sagne, canton Neuchâtel, Switzerland. *Cf.*, *Familiennamenbuch der Schweiz*, II, 1187.

[120] Jean Mathieu and Abraham Monnier were first cousins through the Pochards. One of the Pochards who was a nephew of Abraham Monnier emigrated to Maine and married a daughter of Daniel Malbon, providing yet another instance of pre-existing relationships among the emigrants.

[121] As with Malbon, we have here another instance of the named person not being on the vessel. It was the **widow** of Jean Mathieu who emigrated to Nova Scotia in the *Betty* in 1752, with a household of 1.2.1.0. Her son was the adult man, while she and two daughters account for the remaining three persons listed. Françoise was evidently Coulerus' daughter.

[122] The marriage record calls her by her maiden name, Germain. That it was she is borne out by the position of the families in the victualling list of July 1755. Grosrenaulds, nos. 1274 and 1275, are followed immediately by the Mathieus as numbers 1276 and 1277.

2) Jean-George ~ 8.7.1734 + 11.8.1734 at Échavanne.
3) Jean ~ 8.7.1735 + 22.12.1736 at Échavanne.
4) **Ann Marguerite** ~ 6.10.1737 at Échavanne, posthumous child; = 4.5.1756 (A), John George KAYSER and had issue.
5) **Françoise** * ca. 1747/8 + 25.10.1812 at Halifax;[123] = (I) 21.6.1765 (P), Frederick William MUHLIG * 1739/40 at Zschorlau, Saxony + 1774/77 at Halifax. Issue. She = (II) 31.3.1778 (P), John Conrad TURPEL, farmer, east side of Musquodoboit Harbour, ~ 30.5.1752 (P), living 1817, and had six children.

MÉNÉGAUX[124]

Note: The Ménégaux were the progenitors of the Mingo family of River John and Tatamagouche. When Winthrop Bell's *The 'Foreign Protestants' and the Settlement of Nova Scotia* appeared, Mr. Justice Frank H. Patterson of Truro disagreed with Bell's derivation of the Mingo from the Ménégaux. Bell wrote back, 27 June 1964, "...you state in your 'History of Tatamagouche' that the Mingoe family did not arrive until 1790, and came from Switzerland by way of Philadelphia." Judge Patterson, after he had read Bell's rebuttal, admitted in a letter to Bell on 8 July 1964 that he was confused about the origin of the Mingo family, that the 'Philadelphia connection was only tradition'. Bell then explained, in a letter dated 10 July 1964, "The name 'Mingo' was one of the many corruptions the 'Menegaux' name experienced in Halifax-Lunenburg already before 1770. In contrast to many of the honest Montbéliardian peasants, the Menegaux were not illiterate. The men at least wrote fairly good signatures. The Montbéliardians were quite commonly lumped in with 'the Swiss' in Nova Scotia from their arrival. . . . I should not be

---

[123] It is of course obvious that the girl known later as Frances Matthews was *not* the child of Mathieu at all, having been born nearly a decade after his demise. Her surname was probably Coulerus.

[124] It is very difficult to know precisely how the Ménégaux and the later Mingo families connect. The surname Ménégaux or Menegal was long established in the Désandans area.

with 'the Swiss' in Nova Scotia from their arrival. . . . I should not be surprised if it turned out, after all, that the Mingo family of Pictou County derived from the Menegaux who came here in 1752."[125] The family in Nova Scotia begins with two brothers.

Jean-George Ménégaux, weaver,* ca. 1708 at Dambenois, a son of Jacques and Marguerite (Fournier) Ménégaux;[126] emigrated to Nova Scotia in the *Speedwell* in 1752, with a household of 2.2.3.0; and was ■ 19.10.1752 at Halifax, after being killed while 'felling trees on George's Is.' He = **Marie-Catherine** - NN - * ca. 1710 + ca. 1780, who = (II) 2.5.1753 at Halifax, Jean-George TETTERAY, a widower. Issue:

1. **Françoise** * 1732; = 13.11.1753 (A), George-Frédéric FAINÔT
   * 1727, ■ 18.2.1764 or 1765 (A). Issue.
2. **Susanne-Catherine** * 1734, ■ 19.4.1786 (A); = 14.3.1758 (A), Mathieu LANGILLE * 4.7.1724 at Dampierre, living 1801. Issue.
3. **Jean-Jacques**[127]
4. *Jean*-**Nicolas;** appears to be the man known as Jean MINGO or MENIGOS, living at Tatamagouche in 1795; = Catharine - - -, and had issue:
   1) Margaret ~ 11.4.1782 (A).
   2) Susan * 13.10.1785 ~ 5.6.1786 (A).
   3) George Davy ~ 2.4.1793 (P).[128]
5. **Anne-Marie-Catherine;** = 30.12.1766 (A), Jean-Christophe GROSRENAULD ~ 21.5.1743 at Héricourt, living 1792 at Oakland. Issue.

---

[125] NSA, MG 1, Vol. 118, items 2, 3, and 5.

[126] Archives Doubs 25, EPM 532 (*dénombrement population,* 1717, 1723); *ibid.* (*État des pauvres 1750*).

[127] This could be the man later known as John Mingo.

[128] I think the boy was about 10 years old at baptism. George Mingo = 10.6.1803 (date of marriage licence), Mary 'Polly' LANGEL. George Mingo was born 16.8.1782 and died 17.3.1855 at Tatamagouche. This is the most probable link between Ménégaux and the later Mingo families.

Jean-Frédéric Ménégaux, carter and farmer * 1711, brother of the foregoing, emigrated to Nova Scotia in the *Speedwell* in 1752, with a household of 1.2.4.1. He was ■ 3.10.1752 at Halifax.[129] He = **Anne** * 1710 + Aug/Sep. 1752 at Halifax, dau. of George and Marie (Cuenot) GENEY. Issue:

1. **Catherine** * 1737, would appear to have died at sea during the crossing in 1752.
2. **Elisabeth** * 1739, living 1783; = 19.9.1768 at Chester, James BUSHEN. Issue.
3. **Jean-George** * 1741 ■ 3/30.12.1752 at Halifax.
4. *George,* mariner * 1743 + 11.11.1781 (A);[130] = ca. 1773, Anna Barbara ~ 5.8.1755 (A), living 1799, dau. of Johann Asmus THIEL. She = (II) 17.2.1784 (L), John Jacob MYRA + 24.6.1824, age 74, and had further issue. George Mingo's issue:
   1) Mary Gertrude * 12.1.1774 (A), + -.1.1841 in Queens County; = 9.1.1798 (A), Peter BOUTEILLIER * 18.10.1773 (A). Nine children.
   2) Mary Margaret * 10.12.1776 (A) + 1820; = 15.2.1795 (C), John Frederick WEINACHT * 11.1.1772 (A) + -.7.1837. Issue.
   3) Mary Catherine * 28.9.1778 ■ 22.5.1779 (A).
   4) John * 5.3.1780 (A), ■ 8.9.1863 at Liverpool, NS; = 28.11.1815 (L), Mary Barbara * 27.10.1780 (A), ■ 27.3.1853, age 72, at Liverpool, dau. of John Henry WAGNER. Issue.
   5) George Adam * 27.3.1782 (A), posthumously, ■ 6.5.1784 (L).
5. **Anne-Marie** * ca. 1745, living 1790; = 9.9.1766 (A), Jean MAILLARD ~ 8.10.1741 at Chenebier, living 1808 at Tatamagouche. Issue.
6. **Susanne-Marguerite** * 1747 ■ -.10.1752 at Halifax.

---

[129] The father of Jacques Ménégaux was Louis Ménégaux, living at Dambenois in 1725, age 77. Jacques was a weaver * ca. 1680, and his wife Marguerite Fournier was * ca. 1682.

[130] Asmus Deal conveyed land to his son-in-law George Mingo of Lunenburg, mariner, on this date – Lunenburg Co. Deeds, III, ƒ 208, dated 5.2.1782. As Mingo had died in 1781 this must have been the grandfather making provision for his Mingo grandchildren.

METTIN

Nicolas METIN and Claudine MAIGRET of Laire had eight children baptised at Tavey. The second eldest was

2. Samuel * 17.8.1712 + 9.3.1742 at Aibre; = Marie-Marguerite * ca. 1713, dau. of Pierre and Marguerite (Surleau) LANDE.[131] Issue:

  1) **Jean-Nicolas** * 20.11.1735 at Aibre; a farmer, he emigrated to Nova Scotia in the *Sally* in 1752, as a single man, living in 1753.
  2) **Anne-Judith** * 6.5.1739 at Aibre. living 1788;[132] = 3.5.1757 (A), Jean-Nicolas BOUTEILLIER ~ 22.10.1731 at Étobon ■ 17.12.1799 (L). Issue.
  3) Pierre * 12.9.1742 + 30.9.1742 at Aibre.

METTETAL-I[133]

Jean-Pierre METTETAL, weaver + 26.8.1768 in Montbéliard, age ca. 60 = (I) 3.7.1731 at Temple St. Martin, Montbéliard, Jeanne-Louise BOILLOT of Blamont + 17.4.1740 age 40 and had an eldest son,

1. **Jean-George**, a mason, ~ 8.1.1732 (St. Martin, Montbéliard Town); single man, emigrated to Nova Scotia in the *Speelwell* in 1752, lived at Tatamagouche in 1795; = 26.6.1759 (A), Catherine ~ 26.10.1743 at Héricourt, dau. of Jean-Pierre ISELIN of St.-Valbert. Issue:

  1) John George ~ 17.9.1761 (A), living 1821; = Margaret ~ 24.2.1767 (A), dau. of Mathieu LANGILLE. Issue:

    1a) David * 1784/85, living 1818. Issue.
    2a) Ephraim * 1786/87, living 1821. Issue.
    3a) Margaret = 1805, George TATTRIE ~ 16.10.1784 (A) + 1878. Issue.
    4a) Mark, living 1821. Issue.
    5a) Peter * 1794/95, living 1821.

---

[131] Marie-Marguerite = (II) 4.7.1747 at Aibre, Jacques Bouteillier (p. 63), and = (III) 16.8.1763 (A), Adam Bouillon (p. 59).

[132] Anne-Judith was one of the "extra" people who accompanied Jacques Bouteillier, her step-father.

[133] Although all three Mettatal families came out in the same ship, there is no indication in the records that they were closely, if at all, related.

2) Elizabeth Catherine ~ 15.3.1761 + young (A).
3) Mary *Catherine* ~ 30.12.1765 (A) + 9.1.1811; = 29.6.1786 (P),
   Capt. Edward VINT of Halifax + 9.6.1825, age 62. Issue.
4) Peter ~ 18.9.1767 (A), living 1809; = Mary Catherine * 28.4.1771
   (A), dau. of Jacques BIGUENET. Issue.
5) Elizabeth Catherine, twin ~ 19.3.1769 (A) + young.
6) Susan Catherine, twin ~ 19.3.1769 (A); = John Frederick
   LANGILLE ~ 21.11.1761 (A), living 1809. Issue.
7) James * ca. 1771; = ... Issue:
   1a) Cynthia = 27.12.1825 at Remsheg = Jeffery WRIGHT.
2. David-Nicolas ~ 24.7.1738 + 17.8.1738 (Temple St. Martin).
3. Jean-Nicolas ~ 12.2.1740 + 4.6.1740 (Temple St. Martin).
   Jean-Pierre Mettetal = (II) 11.10.1740 (Temple St. Martin), Elizabeth
   + 8.2.1754 age 51, dau. of David LAURENT, and had three children.

METTETAL - II

Jacques-Christophe Mettetal * ca. 1702; a tanner, he emigrated to
Nova Scotia in the *Speedwell* in 1752, with a household of 1.3.1.0,
■ 27.2.1760 (A); = **Judith-Margaret** BOUTEILLIER, living 1771 at
Philadelphia.[134] Issue:
1. **Susanne-Judith** = 24.3.1758 (A), Jacques CALAME, who lived in
   New York from 1762 to 1771, and then in Philadelphia. Issue.
2. **Marguerite** = 7.7.1767 at New York, David DUCHEMIN. Issue.
3. **one other** who + at sea in summer 1752.

METTETAL - III

Jean-Nicolas Mettetal * ca. 1721/22; a farmer, he emigrated to Nova
Scotia in the *Speedwell* in 1752, with a household of 1.1.2.1, and
+ May/Sep. 1757 at or near Lunenburg; = **Lucie-Judith** ~ 1.11.1724 at
Bethoncourt ■ 9.3.1763 (A), dau of Abraham and Judith **MONNIER**.
Lucie = (II) 20.9.1757 (A) , Adam BOUILLON. Issue:

---

[134] Lunenburg Co. Deeds, I, *f* 127, dated 22.5.1762, refers to her
as Judith, widow of Christopher Mettetel, farmer. The widow appears in a
Moravian Church record in New York in 1762, while by the winding up of her
husband's estate in 1771, she was of Philadelphia (NSA, RG 1, Vol. 206, 8).
She seems to have moved, along with her married daughters.

1. **Catherine** ■ 15.12.1772 (C); = 19.7.1763 (A), Johann Nickel HAMM * 14.12.1736 in Saarland, ■ 2.10.1814 (C). Issue.
2. **Marie-Marguerite**, twin ~ 29.2.1748 + summer 1752 at sea.
3. *Anne*-**Catherine**, twin ~ 29.2.1748 at Temple St.-Martin, Town of Montbéliard = 7.12.1766 (A), William SHAW of Halifax.
4. Dorothy ~ 19.12.1753 ■ 11.1.1754 (A).
5. Adam ~ 4.12.1755 (A), mariner at Lunenburg, 1785.

MIGNERÉ

Jean Migneré, a farmer, * 1708/09 in the Principality of Montbéliard;[135] came to Nova Scotia in the *Sally* in 1752, with a household of 1.1.2.0; + summer 1752 at sea; = **Susanne - - - -**. Issue:

1. **Jean-Christophe** * 1734/35; a farmer age 17, he emigrated in the *Sally* as a single man; ■ 28.9.1752 (P), just after landing.
2. **Jean-Pierre** * 1739; orphan at Halifax 27.10.1752; put out the next month to Richard Wenman.[136]
3. **Jacques** * 1744; orphan at Halifax, 27.10.1752; put out to Dr. Baxter, 16.4.1754.

MILIET

Abraham Miliet or **Melet**; a gardener * 1719/20 at Abbévillers or Bethoncourt; came to Nova Scotia in the *Speedwell* in 1752, with a household of 1.2.0.0, last in Halifax in 1753; = **Suzanne-Marguerite - - - -**. With them came his sister, **Clémente Miliet**, living in Lunenburg in 1754; = late 1752 at Halifax, Jean-George QUIDORE, who + 26.2.1753 at Halifax (A). The Melet family did not remain in Nova Scotia.

---

[135] He appears in the passenger list as being from Württemberg, since that space on the list was marked "ditto" the entry preceding it. The son was marked as being from Montbéliard and that territory belonged to the Duke of Württemberg, so we may reasonably infer that Jean was, in fact, from Montbéliard.

[136] I believe that he is the same person as the John *Migoner* who had license to marry Jane Parsons, 9.12.1768.

MONNIER

Daniel MONNIER, schoolmaster and church elder at Chenebier; = Alix JACQUOTTE, and had eight children, of whom:

1. Jeanne ~ 26.5.1673 at Étobon; = (I) ca. 1690, Étienne FERTÉ of Chenebier * 16.7.1661 at Chagey + 31.1.1727 at Chenebier. Issue. She = (II) 16.9.1727 at Étobon, Jean Jacques COULOMB dit Martin * ca. 1666 at Les Verrières, Neuchâtel, Switzerland + 1.6.1746 at Étobon.

5. Charles MONNIER, labourer at Chenebier ~ 13.11.1679 at Étobon + 30.12.1736 at Chenebier; = -.11.1699 at Étobon, Jacqueline * ca. 1678 + 16.2.1745 at Chenebier, dau. of Adam and Jeanne (Migneré) POCHARD of Échavanne.[137] They had nine children:

   1) Isaac, labourer at Chenebier * 1.8.1700 + 6.10.1749 at Chenebier; = 20.1.1739 at Étobon, Françoise * 24.11.1717 at Étobon, dau. of Daniel MERMET, and had five children.
   2) Daniel * 16.11.1702 at Chenebier + 22.5.1771 at Chagey. Issue.
   3) Jeanne * ca. 1706; = 3.1.1730 at Étobon, Jean POCHARD, weaver * 20.9.1706, and had issue. This entire family emigrated to Boston in 1751 in the *Priscilla,* and settled at Franckfort, Maine, in 1752/53.
   4) Jérémie, weaver * 13.1.1708 + 6.4.1745 at Chenebier; = 24.6.1732 at Étobon, Elisabeth * 1702 + 29.4.1762, dau. of David LODS of Chenebier. They had five children.
   5) Marie * 2.5.1711 at Chenebier.
   6) **Abraham** * 15.12.1714 at Chenebier; farmer, emigrated to Nova Scotia in the *Sally* in 1752, with a household of 1.1.3.1. He + summer 1752 at sea; = (I) 27.1.1735 at Étobon, Marie-Madeleine * 11.3.1713 + 18.2.1745 at Chenebier, dau. of Daniel MERMET of Étobon and his first wife, Judith REGEOT of Chenebier.[138] Issue.

---

[137] Jacqueline's elder sister, Claudine Pochard = Moïse Matthieu, whose daughter-in-law and grandchildren emigrated to Nova Scotia in 1752.

[138] Daniel Mermet, labourer at Étobon * 25.5.1689, living 1750, was a son of Daniel Mermet * ca. 1644 at Morrens in the Baillage de Lausanne, Switzerland + 21.1.1720 at Étobon, who = 4.4.1673 at Étobon = Elisabeth, dau. of David Goust. Judith Regeot ~ 18.12.1687 + 9.1.1737 at Étobon, was a dau. of Michel Regeot * 1657 + 15.8.1718 of Chenebier, who = 31.1.1682 at Étobon = Françoise, dau. of Jacques de Chezjehan of Chenebier.

Abraham Monnier = (II) 6.7.1745 at Étobon, his first cousin, **Anne-Françoise** * 18.6.1712, dau. of Jean-Pierre JEANMAIRE *(infra).*[139]
Three children. Abraham's issue were:

1a) Elisabeth ~ 6.4.1736 ■ 12.2.1737 at Étobon.

2a) **Isaac** ~ 24.11.1737 at Étobon; a farmer, he emigrated to Nova Scotia in the *Sally* in 1752, as a single man; placed in the Halifax Orphanage 25.9.1752 age 14 [sic]; ■ 19.4.1761 at Halifax, under the name Isaac MONRIE.

3a) Pierre-Christoph ~ 17.1.1740 + 22.1.1740 at Étobon.

4a) Elisabeth ~ 19.2.1741 + 18.10.1741 at Étobon.

5a) Jacques ~ 10.10.1742 + 17.1.1743 at Étobon.

6a) **Jean-Jacques** ~ 8.12.1743 at Étobon; placed in the Halifax Orphanage 25.9.1752, and put out to John Coddman, shopkeeper 18.1.1753.

7a) **Susanne** ~ 3.6.1746 at Étobon, living 1780; = 10.4.1765,[140] Owen JONES * -.11.1733 + 10.9.1790 at Halifax. Issue.

8a) **Jeanne** ~ 19.12.1747 at Étobon + summer 1752 at sea.

9a) **Anne-Catherine** * 29.9.1751 at Chenebier + summer 1752 at sea.

7) Elisabeth * 8.10.1715 at Chenebier.

8) Pierre-Jacques * 25.4.1719 at Chenebier, confirmed 1735 at Étobon.

9) Jean-Frédéric * 6.1.1725 at Chenebier, confirmed 1740 at Étobon.

8. Elisabeth ~ 12.7.1685 at Étobon; = 29.11.1703 at Étobon, Jean-Pierre JEANMAIRE, church elder at Chenebier * 1683 + 30.12.1748, suddenly on the road to Beaume, and had nine children, of whom:

4) Anne-Françoise * 18.6.1712 at Chenebier; = 6.7.1745 at Étobon, Abraham MONNIER, her first cousin *(supra).*

---

[139] Since the surviving children were placed in the orphanage as soon as they reached Halifax, we may take it that both Monnier and his wife perished during the sea crossing in 1752.

[140] Date of marriage license. A marriage record was not found.

MORLEAU[141]

Jean MORLOT from Vieux Charmont = 14.11.1702 at Temple St-Martin, Town of Montbéliard, Alexandrine-Catherine MARÇONNET. Their sixth child and eldest son was:

1. **Jean-Pierre** ~ 10.7.1710 in Montbéliard Town; a tailor and farmer, he emigrated to Nova Scotia in the *Speedwell* in 1752,[142] with a household of 1.1.3.0, and was living in Halifax in 1760; = (I) Hedwig GROSRENAUD and had issue. He = (II) 9.9.1749 at St.-Julien, **Anne-Catherine,** ■ 3.7.1753 (A), dau. of George MARÇONNET of Allon-dans, but had no issue by her. He = (III) 10.4.1755 (A), Anne Frequet PETRE. His three sons by his first marriage were:

    1) **Jean-George** * 28.9.1737 in Montbéliard Town + 28.5.1817 at Halifax; = 18.4.1764 (P), Mary Margaret - - - - * 1733 at Grünstadt + 6.7.1811 at Halifax, widow of Bernard WILT. No issue.

    2) **Daniel** ~ 10.4.1739 in Montbéliard Town + 23.5.1792 (G); = (I) 23.7.1763,[143] Eva Maria ~ 19.11.1741 at Vielbrunn + 2.2.1786 (G), dau. of Johann Peter GEBHART. He = (II) 18.2.1787 (G), Magda-lena Elizabeth * 2.11.1760, living 1811, dau. of Johann Albright LEIZER. Morleau had two daughters by his second wife:

        1a) *Hannah* Dorothy ~ 30.1.1788 (G); = 10.11.1806 (P), William MALONE.

        2a) Sophia Elizabeth ~ 3.2.1791 (G), living 1845; = 11.9.1811 (M), Daniel MITCHELL, farmer * 1782 + 24.5.1845.

    Magdalena Elizabeth = (II) 29.5.1796 (G), Charles OLLENDORF.

    3) **Jean-Pierre** ~ 27.2.1742 in Montbéliard Town, living 1793;[144] = Caroline - - - -. Issue.

---

[141] Thiébault Mourelot (1586) and Antoine Morlot (1609), Huguenots from Fontenoy-en-Vôge, France, became citizens of Montbéliard Town, at those dates.

[142] In 1737 he was a grenadier in the Compagnie du Château de Montbéliard (marriage record states this).

[143] Date of marriage license. Marriage record not found.

[144] He received a 200-acre grant at Hammonds Plains in 1786.

1a) George ~ 25.10.1772 (P).
2a) John Peter ~ 17.11.1776 (P).
3a) Daniel ~ 18.7.1779 (P).
4a) Guildford ~ -.10.1783 (P).
5a) Christian ~ 29.12.1787 (G).
6a) John Simon * -.1.1793 ■ 18.4.1796 (G), as "John Morlon".

NARDIN-I

Jacques Nardin * 1699 at Vieux-Charmont,[145] a basket maker, emigrated to Nova Scotia in the *Speedwell* in 1752, with a household of 3.1.2.0, and was ■ 23.1.1753, age 50, at Halifax; = 27.1.1728 at Ste.-Marie, **Marie-Madeleine** * 2.3.1704 ■ 28.2.1753 at Halifax, dau of Guenin and Magdeleine (Belrichad) JEAIN/GEIN of Ste.-Marie. Issue:
1. Jean-George * 20.3.1729 ~ 21.3.1729 in Montbéliard Town + infancy.
2. **Jean-Isaac** ~ 21.11.1734 ■ 16.3.1753, age 20, at Halifax.
3. **Pierre** ~ 4.5.1738 ■ Dec 1752/Feb 1753, at Halifax.
4. **Susette-Catherine** ~ 25.11.1740; placed in Halifax Orphanage 20.3.1753, put out 21.10.1755 to Lt. Middleton.
5. **Jean-Pierre** * 25.3.1744; placed in Halifax Orphanage 20.3.1753, put out 29.6.1753 to Dr. Grant.

NARDIN-II

Jacques Nardin, farmer,* 1721/22 in the Principality of Montbéliard; he emigrated to Nova Scotia in the *Speedwell* in 1752, with a household of 1.1.0.2, and + summer 1752 during the sea crossing; = **Anne-Judith FINGUEN** * ca. 1721/22 ■ 15.3.1753, age 31, at Halifax. She = (II) 23.1.1753 (P), Jean-George TETTERAY + 1805.[146] Issue:

---

[145] He was 56 in 1752 (passenger list), but 50 in 1753 (burial record. A listing of the poor at Vieux-Charmont in Feb 1750 has his age as 52 - Archives of Doubs 25-EPM 1034. He was perhaps the Jean-Jacques, baptised 14.8.1698, son of Daniel and Marguerite NARDIN, Vieux-Charmont.

[146] While it is possible that the widow Nardin who married Tetteray was the wife of the third Nardin (*infra*), it seems more probable that there would be an interval of a few *months* between the death of one husband and her marriage to another. If the other Nardin widow was the one who remarried in 1753, there were a mere three weeks between burying one husband and wedding another.

1. **Jean-Christophe** * 24.12.1748 at Temple St.-Martin, Montbéliard + 20.3.1753 at Halifax, "aged 9 months."[147]
2. **Françoise** * 1750; placed in Halifax Orphanage in 1753, and was there still on 3.11.1761.

NARDIN-III

Jean NARDIN of Désandans = Catherine GIROLDS and had a son:
1. **Jean-Jacques,** a farmer,~ 22.11.1714 at Désandans; emigrated to Nova Scotia in the *Pearl* in 1752, with a household of 1.1.1.2., and was ■ 1.1.1753 at Halifax; = ca. 1745, **Anne-Judith** NAVION * 1721/22. Issue:
   1) **Marie-Magdalene** * 3.12.1746 at Désandans + summer 1752 at sea.
   2) stillborn child, 23.1.1748 at Désandans.
   3) **Anne-Catherine** * 23.2.1749 at Désandans + summer 1752 at sea.
   4) **Susanne** * 14.9.1750 at Désandans + summer 1752 at sea.
   5) **Jeanne** * 3.2.1752 at Désandans, living late 1752.

PETREQUIN-I

Jean Petrequin,[148] joiner,* ca. 1723/24 in the Lordship of Châtelot; emigrated to Nova Scotia in the *Betty* in 1752, [149] with his sister, **Anne-**

---

[147] Since there were two children below the age of 4 years when the family boarded the *Speedwell* at Rotterdam on 16.5.1752, the child was born before that, making the him more than 9 months old when he died. Given the low accuracy of many early records here, this well could have been the boy baptised in 1748.

[148] Bell, 452, n.6, states that this was the man whose supposed receipt of a letter sparked the Lunenburg insurrection in December 1753. In Nova Scotia the surname evolved into Peterkin, subsequently to Patriquin.

[149] He is most probably Jean ~ 17.12.1724 at Longevelle, a son of Jean and Anne (Vienot) Petrequin, who married there on 2.1.1720.

Marie Petrequin. Jean = 8.5.1753 (A), Anne-Catherine ~ 19.4.1737 at Allondans, living 1788, dau. of Jean-Christophe JEAUDRY. Petrequin was ■ 19.12.1764 (A). She = (II) 20.3. 1769 (A), Étienne CERTIER, and (III) 12.5.1783 (L), Peter WAMBOLT. Issue:

1. John *George* ~ 3.11.1757 (A) + 1850 at River John; = Mary-Catherine, dau. of Mathieu LANGILLE. Issue, with four others:
   1) Phoebe * 1785, living 1871 at River John; = Joseph LANGILLE * 1775 + 1835, and had issue.
   2) David, living 1813
   3) Agnes *Nancy* * 1789 + 1871; = Jacques [James] LANGILLE. Issue.
2. John Urban ~ 27.4.1759 (A) + young.
3. John Frederick ~ 22.11.1760 (A) + in infancy.
4. *John* Frederick ~ 16.10.1763 (A), living 1816; = Catherine ~ 5.2.1765 (A), dau. of Jacques BIGUENET. Issue:
   1) Margaret * 1787.
   2) Nelly * 1789 + 25.12.1862; = Louis TATTRIE. Thirteen children.
   3) Alexander * 1791.
   4) John * 1793 + -.1.1885, leaving a widow (*Truro Sun*, 9.1.1885).
   5) Mary Elizabeth * 1795; = Frederick LANGILLE. Six children.
   6) James * 1797.
   7) Hannah * 1799.
   8) George * 1801.
   9) Danford * 1803; = Susannah *1811, dau. of John George LANGILLE. Issue.
   10) Catherine * 1805 + 1890; = David LANGILLE * 1803 + 1889, and had thirteen children.
   11) Mark * 1807.
5. Mary Catherine, posthumous child ~ 24.6.1765 (A), ■ 26.12.1816 (A); = 28.10.1783 (A), John Peter WAMBOLT, First Peninsula ~ 15.2.1763 (A).[150] Issue.

---

[150] John Peter Wambolt was her mother's stepson by her third marriage.

PETREQUIN-II

Jean Petrequin, a farmer, * ca. 1730/31 in the Lordship of Châtelot;[151] came to Nova Scotia in the *Betty* in 1752, a single man. He was living in Lunenburg in 1755. He enlisted. On 2.7.1763, Jean *Peterquin*, gunner at Halifax, sold Garden Lot E14 at Lunenburg to Philip Knaut for 10 shillings [Lunenburg Co. Deeds, I, *f* 130 # 297.]

QUIDORE

Jean-George Quidore * ca. 1716/17 at Dambenois, a son of Louis, a mason, and Elénore (Mauval) Quidore[152]; Jean-George, a thatcher, emigrated to Nova Scotia in the *Speedwell* in 1752, with a household of 1.1.2.1; = (I) **Elisabeth RACINE** + summer 1752 at sea, and had issue:
1. **Jean-George**, ■ 26.2.1753 at Halifax, age 5.
2. **Jeanne** * 1747 ■ 23.1.1753 at Halifax.
3. **a child** * ca. 1750 ■ 2.1.1753 at Halifax.
Jean-George = (II) late 1752 at Halifax, Clémente MILIET, living 1754.

RICHARD

These two women were obviously of francophone origin, and their marriages suggest that they were among the Montbéliardais who came to Nova Scotia in the 1750s. It is not known in which household(s) they emigrated. Several families had surplus women and teenaged girls in them, so it is most likely that these two women - possibly related to one another - came here under those auspices. They were:

(A) Anne-Dorothy Richard = 18.9.1753 (A), Vernier RIGOULEAU + 1755/56.

(B) Anne-Catherine Richard, ■ 19.4.1760 (A); = 24.10.1752 at Halifax, Nicolas LAGARCE and had three children.

---

[151] There were four possible baptism records in the Lordship of Châtelot for this Jean Petrequin:
(a) Jean ~ 7.1.1730 (St.-Maurice), son of George & Susanne (Laigle).
(b) Jean ~ 3.9.1730 (Colombier-Châtelot), of Pierre & Susanne (Charles).
(c) Jean ~ 26.3.1731 (St.-Maurice), son of Étienne & Judith (Eterneau).
(d) Jean ~ 29.4.1731 (Colombier-Châtelot), son of Jean & Alix (Vauterot).

[152] Archives Doubs 25-EPM 532 for dénombrement population 1723, and état des pauvres, 5 Feb 1750.

RIGOULEAU-I

Jean-Urbain RIGOULEAU, a tailor at Raynans, + 13.1.1746; = 25.8.1739 at St.- Julien, **Elisabeth-Charlotte** * ca. 1720 at Issans, ■ 15.1.1756 (A), dau. of Simon and Henriette (Marçonnet) LOVY of St.- Julien.[153] She = (II) 1.10.1748 at St.-Julien, Jean-Pierre JEAUNÉ * ca. 1720, with whom she and her children came to Nova Scotia in 1752 in the *Speedwell*.[154] Rigouleau's issue:

1. **Pierre-Nicolas** ~ 11.3.1740 at Issans, ■ 21.3.1753 at Halifax.[155]
2. **Jean-Frédéric,** miller * ca. 1742 + 19.6.1810 (L); = 20.10.1771 (A), Maria Louisa * 13.5.1745 in the Palatinate + 5.12.1836 (L), dau. of Johann Nicolaus SILBER. Issue:
   1) Anne Catherine * 10.11.1772 (L), living 1813.
   2) John Nicholas * 11.10.1775 (L) + 4.7.1852 (L); = 4.2.1838 (L), Mary Elizabeth * 13.4.1788, dau. of John Peter KAULBACH.
   3) Mary Elizabeth * 9.12.1777 (L) + 31.3.1853 (L); = 23.5.1802 (L), John Matthew NAAS * 16.12.1772 (L) + 12.6.1843 (L). Issue.
   4) Catherine Louise * -.12.1784 (L) + 6.7.1816 (L); = 3.3.1812 (A), John Nicholas CONRAD * 28.7.1780 (L) + -.3.1853 (L).[156] Issue.
   5) John Frederick * 12.2.1789 (L) ■ 2.11.1790 (L), scalded to death with boiling water.
3. **Jacques** ~ 9.2.1744 at Issans + 10.3.1753 at Halifax.[157]

---

[153] She was a sister of Catherine-Elisabeth Lovy, wife of, first, Jean Carlin (*q.v.*), and second, of David Banvard (*q.v.*).

[154] Her sons by Rigouleau account for three of the members reported in the Jeauné household as enumerated in the passenger list.

[155] The burial record refers to him by his step-father's surname, on 10.3.1753 as Jacques Jeaunais, but on 20.4.1753 as Jacques Joinet.

[156] She was Conrad's second wife. In all he married four times and had fourteen children.

[157] The burial record terms him "Pierre Josnet", attributing to him his step-father's name.

RIGOULEAU-II

Vernier Rigouleau, a farmer, * 1716 in the Principality of Montbéliard, a son of Vernier[158] and Suzanne-Catherine (Coulerus) Rigoulot of Audincourt, came to Nova Scotia in the *Speedwell* in 1752, with a household of 1.1.3.1, and + ca. 1755/56 at Lunenburg; = (I) 1741, **Jeanne** *1716 ■ 6.4.1753, age 36, at Halifax, dau. of Humbert and Marguerite (Calame) JODRY. He = (II) 18.9.1753 (A), Anne-Dorothy RICHARD, living 1756. He had five children, all by the first marriage:
1. **Anne-Marie** * ca. 1739, living 1757.
2. **John *Frederick*,** butcher * ca. 1742 + -.11.1816 (L); = 28.3.1769 (A), Margaret Elizabeth * 24.7.1746 at Brensbach + 11.11.1829 (L), dau. of Johann Friedrich ARENBERG. They had three daughters:
   1) Charlotte * 25.2.1770, ■ 6.3.1770 (A).
   2) Mary Catherine * 18.4.1772 (A) + 2.11.1845 (L); = 26.7.1792 (A), Thomas ENGLISH, sailmaker * 1761/62 at Leith, Scotland ■ 28.3.1822 age 60 (A), having had eleven children.
   3) Ann *Mary* * 8.3.1774 (L); = 10.10.1793 (A), Patrick BURKE, and had four children: Mary, Thomas, John, and Frederick.
3. **Susanne** * ca. 1745, living 1789; = 22.12.1765 (A), Jacques BOUTEILLIER ~ 11.8.1735 at Étobon + -.5.1827 in Cape Breton. Issue.
4. **Marie-*Elisabeth*** * ca. 1747, living 1790; = 16.12.1766 (A), John Jacob SLAUENWHITE, Second Peninsula, * 11.8.1743 at Nordheim, Württemberg, living 1815. Issue.
5. Catherine-Elisabeth * summer 1752 at sea ~ 26.10.1752 at Halifax, ■ 1.7.1753 at Lunenburg (A).

ROBERT-I

Josuë Robert of LeLocle, Valangin, Canton of Neuchâtel, Switzerland, was dead by 1733; = Susanne BRANDT, of LeLocle, who + 15.12. 1733 at Étobon. Issue:
1. Joshué, shoemaker, carpenter and school official at Étobon * 1702 + 1749/52; = 28.8.1731 at Étobon, **Jeanne** * 4.2.1715 at Étobon,

---

[158] The senior Vernier was himself a son of Jean and Elisabeth (Ferrand) RIGOULOT of Audincourt - Archives, Doubs - EPM 237 (Dénombrement, 1 janv. 1713).

■ 6.4.1788 (A), dau. of Pierre RACINE of Échavanne.[159] Jeanne, with her three surviving children, emigrated to Nova Scotia in the *Betty* in 1752, with a household listed as 1.1.2.0. She = (II) 14.8.1753 (A), Jean-Christophe JEAUDRY. Joshué's issue:

1) Pierre-Frédéric ~ 19.3.1732 + 3.5.1737 at Étobon.
2) **David-Joshué** ~ 21.9.1733 at Étobon, living 1785;[160] = 8.6.1756 (A), Marie-Elisabeth * 11.1.1741 at Allenjoie, living 1780, dau. of George-Frédéric ALISON. Issue:
   1a) Charlotte Elizabeth ~ 25.8.1757 (A); = 27.2.1785 at Chester, George GIBBONS.
   2a) Catherine Margaret ~ 1.1.1760 (A) + Feb/Mar. 1849 at Chester; = 27.10.1777 (A), James Louis JOLIMOIS/Jolimore, Hubbards ~ 26.6.1754 (A) + 30.1.1834 at Chester. Issue.
   3a) James Christopher ~ 17.1.1762 (A).
   4a) Mary Elizabeth ~ 2.12.1764 (A).
   5a) Elizabeth ~ 7.12.1766 (A) + young.
   6a) John George ~ 26.12.1768 (A).
   7a) Elizabeth * 11.4.1771 (A); = 27.1.1791 at Sydney, Friedrich Wilhelm WILHAUSEN, Regt. von Lossberg * 1755 Rinteln in Hanover + between 29.4.1829 (will) and 31.10.1829 (probate) at St. Anns, NS. Issue.
   8a) *Peter* Conrad * 18.9.1772 (A), living 1838 at Ingonish; = Bridget
   . . . . .
   9a) *Charles* Nicholas * 28.10.1774 (A), living 1838 at Ingonish.
   10a) Peter *Alexander* * 4.12.1767 (A), living 1838 at Ingonish.
   11a) *John* Christopher * 18.1.1779 (A), living 1838 at Ingonish.
   12a) Hannah ~ 26.12.1780 at Chester.

---

[159] Pierre Racine, labourer ~ 4.5.1684 at Étobon + 2.1.1756 at Échavanne, was the son of Jean Racine of Chenebier * 1649 + 17.4.1724, who = 16.8.1670 at Étobon, Claudine, dau. of Adam LeCrisle. Pierre Racine = (II) Judith Perretgentil of Échavanne, who + 22.12.1737.

[160] Robert/Robar moved to Cape Breton ca. 1785. He was selling his land in Lunenburg, *cf.*, Lunenburg Co. Deeds, III, *f* 163, dated 5.2.1785 and 19.3.1785, probably preparatory to going to Cape Breton Island to live.

3) Catherine-Elisabeth ~ 22.1.1736 + 26.10.1736 at Étobon.
4) Jonas-Frédéric ~ 11.8.1737 + 25.2.1738 at Étobon.
5) Gabriel ~ 17.1.1739 + 22.3.1743 at Étobon.
6) **Anne-Catherine** ~ 11.9.1741 at Étobon, ■ 28.12.1812 (A);
   = 13.4.1761 (A), Christophe-Jacques VIENOT ~ 22.11.1789 at
   Bavans + 13.10.1813 (A). Issue.
7) **Elisabeth** ~ 6.5.1744 at Étobon + 1771/76; = 17.4.1763 (A),
   James COVEY, mariner * ca. 1741 + late in 1823.[161] Issue.
8) Pierre-Frédéric ~ 7.4.1746 + 18.12.1746 at Étobon.
2. Susanne * 1704 at LeLocle + 25.3.1754 at Étobon; = 3.2.1739
at Étobon = Pierre MERMET, wagoner, Étobon * 6.12.1707
+ 15.2.1762 at Étobon. One son.

ROBERT-II

Isaac ROBERT, master mason * 1683 + 2.12.1748 at Brevilliers;
= 11.9.1708 at Brevilliers, Julienne Alexandrine * 26.8.1680
+ 23.11.1748, dau. of Daniel and Ezibel (Jacquot) DEVIN. Issue:
1. Jean-Nicolas ~ 26.2.1709 at Brevilliers.
2. David ~ 22.2.1711 + 28.11.1748 at Brevilliers.
3. Gabriel * 28.4.1715 at Brevilliers.
4. Marie-Marguerite * 25.5.1716 at Brevilliers.
5. Elisabeth-Dorothée * 7.9.1718 + 3.9.1719 at Brevilliers.
6. Pierre-Anthoine * 26.3.1721; = 10.1.1745 at Brevilliers, Anne, dau.
   of Jean-George SANDOZ of Dampierre-outre-les-Bois. Issue:
   1) Marie-Marguerite * 27.1.1746 at Brevilliers.
   2) Pierre * 11.4.1750 at Brevilliers + 25.12.1762 at Brevilliers.
   3) Anne-Marie * 31.1.1753 at Brevilliers.
   4) Jean-Nicolas * 13.3.1756 at Brevilliers.
7. **Abraham** * 5.12.1723 at Brevilliers; a mason, he emigrated to Nova
   Scotia in the *Speedwell* in 1752, with a household of 1.1.0.1, and
   was ■ 2.10.1799 (A); = 31.3.1750 at Brevilliers, **Elisabeth-
   Catherine** * 27.5.1720 at Héricourt + Jan./Mar.1793 (A), dau. of
   Jean and Marguerite (Dormoy) LODS. Issue:
   1) **Elisabeth-Catherine** * 1.4.1751 at Brevilliers, ■ 16.8.1754 (A).

---

[161] His body was the subject of an inquest at St. Margarets Bay,
11.12.1823 (NSA, RG 41, Vol. I).

2) Peter ~ 22.5.1754 (A), ■ 7.7.1801 (A), with no issue. He
   = 16.3.1784 (A), Susanne-Catherine ~ 5.4.1756 (A), dau. of
   John George BESANÇON. She + (II) 11.3.1802 (A), Joseph
   BOUTEILLIER.
3) *John* George ~ 30.4.1756 (A) + 1801; = 27.4.1779 (A), Elizabeth
   Margaret ~ 30.8.1760 (A), living 1801, dau. of Jean-Nicolas
   DARÉ. Issue:
   1a) Catherine Margaret * 2.5.1781 (A) ■ 16.12.1783 (L).
   2a) Sarah Catherine * 18.9.1782 (A), ■ 15.2.1783 (A).
   3a) Catherine Margaret * 14.8.1784 (A), living 1825; = 21.12.1803
      (C), John OICKLE, Northwest Range * 11.5.1785 (A)
      + 27.4.1851 (L) and had issue.
   4a) James * 4.4.1786 (A); = 23.10.1810 (A), Mary Anne
      * 26.9.1791 (A), living 1833, dau. of George Frederick LEAU.
      Issue.
   5a) George Andrew * 19.11.1788 (A) + 1815/16; = 3.1.1815 (A),
      Sophia MOSER and had a daughter. She = (II) 27.5.1817 (L),
      George VIENOT.
   6a) John, blacksmith, Upper Lahave * 15.7.1791 (A), living 1829;
      = 15.11.1814 (A), Catherine DEMONE. Issue.
   7a) John *Frederick* * 10.11.1793 (A) + 10.12.1870 at Lahave;
      = 4.6.1822 (A), Mary Catharine ~ 30.11.1799 (A), living 1839,
      dau. of John OICKLE. Issue.
   8a) Susan Catherine * 5.3.1796 (A).
   9a) James Frederick * 5.5.1798 (C); = Sophia Catherine VIENOT.
   10a) Christian, Big Tancook Island * 7.4.1800 (C), living 1830;
      = 9.9.1824 (C), Ann Catharine ALLEN. Issue.
4) Andrew, Northwest Range * 18.10.1758 (A), living 1800; =
   21.4.1778 (L), Greta *Barbara* ~ 16.6.1755 (A), ■ 22.3.1815, age 59
   years 9 months (A), dau. of the late Georg MOTZ. Issue:
   1a) John Peter * 13.8.1779 (A).
   2a) Catherine * 2.4.1782 (C).
   3a) Mary Catherine * 14.9.1783 (C), living 1816; = 6.10.1811 (L),
      William Christian NAUGLE, Northwest Range. Issue.
   4a) Catherine Margaret * 5.2.1785 (C).
   5a) Mary Elizabeth * 18.4.1786 (C).
   6a) Frederick * 24.6.1788, ■ 2.8.1787 (C).

7a) George * 28.11.1788 (C) + 1871; = 17.12.1815 (A), Hanna
    Susan * 16.3.1796 (L), dau. of Eberhard RAFUSE. Issue.
8a) John, of St. Mary's River, ~ 6.9.1791 (C); = 13.11.1816
    (St Mary's River), Susan REDMAN. Issue.
9a) James, militiaman in 1822 * 21.8.1793 (C); = 21.1.1818 (L),
    Susanna, dau. of John Peter CLATTENBURG. Issue.
10a) Mary Margaret * 7.11.1796 (C).
11a) Catherine Elizabeth * 8.8.1799 (C).
5) Catherine *Margaret* ~ 26.2.1761 (A); = 23.5.1782 (C), John
   Handley RIGBY. Issue.

ROLLAND

Jean-Jacques Rolland * 1692 in the Principality of Montbéliard;[162]
emigrated to Nova Scotia in the *Speedwell* in 1752, with a household
of 1.2.1.1, ■ 26.3.1753, age 68, at Halifax.[163] He = **Catherine** - - - -,
■ 27.10.1752 at Halifax. Their son had died, but his widow, **Anne** - - - -
came, bringing two children:
1. **Jean-George** + 1.6.1753, age 3, at Halifax.
2. **Anne-Catherine** * ca. 1751, ■ 12.3. or 9.10.1753, age 2 yrs. (P).

SERTIER

Pierre ~ 23.10.1686 + 16.3.1739, son of David and Susanne
SERTIER Montbéliard Town; = 4.7.1713 at Temple St.-Martin in
Montbéliard Town, Catherine CORDIER of Pierrefontaine, and had an
elder son:
1. **Jean-Urbain**, a farmer and weaver, ~ 11.1.1718 in Montbéliard
   Town; emigrated to Nova Scotia in the *Betty* in 1752, with a household of 1.1.2.0, and + June 1755/Feb.1756 at Lunenburg; =
   14.2.1741 at Clairegoutte, **Marie-Catherine**, ■ 14.1.1756 (A), dau.
   of Abraham BELOS, a collier at Frédéric-Fontaine. Issue:

---

[162] The surname Rol(l)and was widespread in the territory, but
this particular family was likely of Pierrefontaine, Vandoncourt or Bondeval,
all in the Lordship of Blamont.

[163] This is another case of an emigrant minimizing his true age
in order to be accepted by Dick's clerks at Rotterdam. Since Rolland was
bracketed with the Masson brothers on the *Speedwell*'s passenger list, it
seems likely that he was the father of Catherine, wife of Frédéric Masson.

1) **Jacques-Frédéric** * 26.2.1742 + 1807 (NSA, RG 48, reel 19,882 for his probate) = 6.9.1767 (A), Catherine Louisa, * 1751 in the Palatinate, + 11.6.1841 age 90 (L), dau. of Johann Georg SCHRAM. Issue:[164]

   1a) George Lewis ~ 13.11.1768 (A) + 23.2.1846 (L);= 27.12.1796 (A), Ann Gertrude * 5.4.1772 (L) + 27.6.1826 (C), dau. of John Frederick SLAUENWHITE. Issue.

   2a) Mary Barbara * 2.6.1771 (A); = 11.12.1787 (A), George *Frederick* DAUPHINÉ, First Peninsula ~ 22.5.1753 (A) + 11.12.1831. Issue.

   3a) Elizabeth *Catherine* * 25.12.1773 (A) + 27.9.1826 (L); = 30.7.1797 (A), John George NAUGLER * 1756 + 16.12.1832 at Western Head, Queens County. Issue.

   4a) James Frederick * 20.10.1776 (A) + -.6.1831 (L); = 23.11.1802 (A), *Frances* Margaret * 26.7.1779 (A), dau. of John Philip TANNER. Issue.

   5a) James * 23.6.1779 ■ 28.6.1779 (A).

   6a) Margaret Elizabeth * 23.7.1781 (A); = 8.10.1799 (L), John Jacob Rudolf SLAUENWHITE * 13.10.1774 (L) + 25.4.1848 (L). Issue.

   7a) Louisa * 7.7.1787 (C); = 7.3.1815 (L), John George HENN, Upper Lahave * 18.11.1791 (L), living 1838. Issue.

   8a) Catherine Barbara * 27.5.1790 (A), living 1809.

   9a) Lucy; = 5.12.1809 (A), John Christopher VIENOT * 18.4.1786 (A), living at New Ross in 1861. Issue.

2) **Pierre** * 4.2.1744, living 1757.

S U R L E A U

Pierre Surleau, a farmer, * 1723/24 in the Principality of Montbéliard; emigrated to Nova Scotia in the *Sally* in 1752 as a single man, ■ 26.3.1753 at Halifax.[165]

---

[164] There were probably three other daughters and another son.

[165] The death report gives his age as 21, the passenger list as 28.

TETTERAY

Julius TATTEREI, labourer at Chagey + 6.2.1709, age ca. 60;
= 17.10.1682 at Chagey, Anne ~ 7.3.1652 + 29.9.1719, dau.
of Anthoine and Jehanne (Noblot) MOREL of Chagey. Issue:
1. Anne ~ 13.5.1684 at Chagey; = 2.12.1710 at Chagey, Nicolas
   RICHARD of Chagey + 30.5.1715 at the Wood of Belchamps, age
   30. One son.
2. Pierre ~ 20.2.1687 at Chagey.
3. Jean-Jacques, shepherd at Chagey ~ 1.3.1688 + 31.5.1751 at
   Chagey; = 30.4.1715 at Chagey, Susanne L'ABBET + 28.8.1752,
   age 65, a native of Les Verrières, Canton of Neuchâtel, Switzerland.
   Seven children:
   1) Abraham ~ 24.10.1718 at Chagey.
   2) Jean-George ~ 3.4.1721 at Chagey; = 18.1.1752 at Chagey,
      Elisabeth * 1717, dau. of George VUILLEMENOT of Trémoins,
      and his wife Judith BOHY of Bavans. Issue:[166]
      1a) Jean-Nicolas * 14.4.1752 at Chagey.
      2a) Catherine * 4.11.1753 at Chagey.
      3a) Elisabeth * 15.12.1754 at Chagey.
      4a) Jacques * 8.1.1756 at Chagey.
      5a) Anne-Françoise * 27.9.1758 at Chagey.
   3) Étienne ~ 9.1.1724 ■ 22.6.1730 at Chagey.
   4) Pierre-Anthoine ~ 4.1.1727 + -.9.1731 at Chagey.
   5) Anne-Catherine ~ 15.12.1728 at Chagey.
   6) Anne-Clémence ~ 21.6.1731 at Chagey.
   7) Henriette-Marguerite ~ 15.7.1733 + 4.9.1736 at Chagey.
4. Abram * ca. 1691/92 + 6.8.1762 at Chagey; = (I) 11.7.1719 at
   Chagey, Madeleine + 10.9.1720 in premature birth, dau. of Martin
   DAREL of Coisevaux. Abram = (II) 28.1.1721 at Chagey,
   Catherine + 21.4.1731, age ca. 49, dau. of the late Jean FALLOT
   of Désandans. Issue:

---

[166] The fact that this couple had children born regularly in Chagey
into the late 1750s rules out this marriage as being that of the Jean-George
Tetterai who emigrated to Nova Scotia.

1) **Jean-George** ~ 31.10.1721 at Chagey; a farmer, he emigrated to Nova Scotia in the *Sally* in 1752, with his wife and his sister. He + 1795/1805, when his "widow" is mentioned. His first wife, **NN,**[167] died at sea in summer 1752. He = (II) 23.1.1753 at Halifax, Anne-Judith, ■ 15.3.1753 age 31, at Halifax, widow of Jacques NARDIN. He = (III) 2.5.1753 (P), Marie-Catherine - - - - * ca. 1710 + ca. 1780,[168] widow of Jean-George MÉNÉGAUX, but had no issue by the first three marriages. He = (IV) ca. 1783, Marie-Elisabeth ~ 22.5.1760 (A), living 1805, dau. of David LANGILLE. Issue:
   1a) George ~ 16.10.1784 (A) + 1878; = 1805, Margaret, dau. of George METTETAL. Issue.
   2a) Louis * 1785/86 + 3.1.1855 = Eleanor * 1789 + 25.12.1862, dau. of Jean-Frédéric PETREQUIN. Thirteen children.
   3a) David * 1790 + 2.5.1849; = Catherine * 1792, dau. of John George LANGILLE. Eleven children.
   4a) Susan; = John Frederick LANGILLE. Issue.
2) **Jeanne** ~ 18.6.1724 at Chagey; she emigrated to Nova Scotia in 1752 in the *Sally* with her brother, ■ 22.12.1789 (A); = 1752/53 at Halifax, Jean-Urbain JEANPERRIN ~ 3.3.1717 at Longevelle, living 1800 at River John , and had issue, two sons.
Abram TATTEREI of Chagey = (III) July 1731, Marie GAGNEBIN and had :
3) Marie-Catherine ~ 27.4.1732 at Chagey.
4) Jacques ~ 11.11.1736 at Chagey.

[167] That the second female in his household (1.2.0.0) was his wife is, of course, speculation. No record of either their marriage or of her death has been noted by either Winthrop Bell or the present author.

[168] She was a midwife at Lunenburg in 1764. – NSA, RG 1, Vol. 382, doc. 38.

THOM

Christophle THOMME, a mason = Elisabeth FOSTE [?] and had a son:
1. **Daniel-Frédéric** ~ 3.9.1718 at Temple St.-Martin, Montbéliard Town; a mason, he emigrated to Nova Scotia in the *Speedwell* in 1752, with a household of 1.1.0.0, and was living in Halifax in 1766; = (I) 30.6.1744 at Temple St.-George, Montbéliard Town, **Françoise GUILLERMET** * 1703/04 ▪ 7.5.1753 at Halifax, widow of Jean-Jacques MELET of Bethoncourt. No issue. He = (II) 30.10.1753 (A), Joanna *Sophia* KÖHLER from Hamburg. He had issue by her:[169]
   1) George Caspar ~ 25.4.1758 (A).
   2) Juliana ~ 22.4.1760 (A).

TISSERAND

Jacques TISSERAND, mayor at Coisevaux = (2) 14.4.1722 at Trémoins, Elisabeth, dau. of Jean JEAND'HEUR of Champey and had issue:
1. **Jacques**; a farmer, * 15.4.1723 at Coisevaux ~ 17.4.1723 at Trémoins, came to Nova Scotia in the *Betty* in 1752, with a household of 1.1.1.2; ▪ 1.5.1753 (P); = 18.5.1745 at Chagey, **Anne-Catherine** ~ 25.8.1718 at Chagey, ▪ 27.11.1796 (C), dau. of Pierre and Elisabeth (Vauterin) BOUTEILLIER of Chagey.[170] Issue:
   1) **Pierre** ~ 16.3.1746 at Trémoins ▪ 27.5.1753 at Halifax.
   2) **George** * 1748 ▪ 25.12.1752 at Halifax.
   3) **Jacques** * 3.12.1750 at Semondans, living 1757.
2. Jean-Nicolas * 21.9.1727 at Trémoins = 13.7.1751 at Chagey, Marguerite, dau. of Pierre & Marie-Marguerite LODS and widow of

---

[169] Indications point to a marital breakdown. Thom sold his town lot in Lunenburg to Gottleb Köhler on 15.5.1759, when he was a mason *of Halifax*. The two children seem to be those of Mrs. Thom. The first baptism entry omits the father, while the second calls the child "spurious".

[170] Pierre Bouteillier, school official at Chagey ~ 24.10.1682 at Chagey + 9.1.1723, was a son of Pierre Bouteillier, church elder at Chagey ~ 8.4.1655 + 13.4.1710; = 6.7.1680 at Chagey, Catherine Dormoy + 13.8. 1721, age 69. Pierre = 1.12.1716 at Chagey, Elisabeth ~ 2.5.1684, dau. of Humbert Vauterin * 1643 at Orny in the Barony of La Sarrez, Vaud, = 8.11. 1664 at Chagey, Marie + 15.1.1703, age ca. 63, dau. of Jehann Réguillot or Roquillot of Chaux-de-Fonds, Canton of Neuchâtel, Switzerland.

Louis FALLET of Couthenans.

3. Jean * 5.11.1724 at Trémoins.

Anne-Catherine (Bouteillier) Tisserand = (II) 20.5.1753 (P), Jean- George BESANÇON ~ 18.4.1706 at Dung + July/Dec 1755 at Lunenburg, and had two children. She = (III) 1.1.1756 (A), Étienne MARIETTE * 1711/12 + 1784, and had six children. She is the ancestress of all the present Montbéliardais Bezansons and Marriotts in the province of Nova Scotia.

VALETTE

Pierre Valette * 1715/16 in Württemberg [of which Montbéliard was a territory]; a tailor, he emigrated to Nova Scotia in the *Sally* in 1752, with a household of 1.1.0.2, ■ 20.1.1793 at Halifax; = (I) **Marie-Louise** - - - - + 1756/63. He = (II) 20.3.1763 (P), Abigail DERBOLT, widow, ■ 7.4.1796, age 82 (P). Issue:

1. **Madeleine** + 1752/53 at Halifax.
2. **David**, living 1757.
3. Bruin ~ 21.4.1755 (A), living 1757.
4. Peter Louis ~ 21.11.1756 (A).

VEUILAMET-I

Charles VUILLAMIER, shepherd at Échavanne, a native of Brevillers + 15.6.1740 at Chenebier; = Anne ~ 28.12.1674 at Chagey,[171] dau. of Humbert and Marie (Réguillot) VAUTHERIN , and had issue:

    1.Catherine * ca. 1703 + 17.11.1750 at Échavanne; = 1.12.1738 at Étobon, Pierre RACINE, labourer at Échavanne, a widower ~ 17.7.1683 + 3.1.1756 at Échavanne.[172]

    2.Jean-Nicolas, of Belverne ~ 22.6.1712 at Chagey; = Éléanore * 28.8.1714 at Brevillers, dau. of Michel and Marie GEORGE. Issue:

    1) Jean-George ~ 14.7.1737 at Étobon.
    2) Marie-Elisabeth ~ 11.9.1739 at Étobon.
    3)Claudine-Catherine ~ 16.11.1741 at Étobon.

---

[171] This date is 7.1.1675 (New Style). It notes the family were there *"où l'on étoit réfugiés à cause des bruicts de guerre."*

[172] Pierre Racine's daughter by his first wife, Judith Perretgentil, was Jeanne Racine * 4.2.1715, wife of Josué Robert. She emigrated to Nova Scotia with her children (*supra*).

3. **Isaac** * 5.4.1716 at Échavanne; a farmer, he emigrated to Nova Scotia in the *Betty* in 1752, with a household of 1.2.0.1.[173] He was ∎ 2.8.1752 at Halifax, barely after arriving; = 8.2.1746 at Étobon, **Anne-Catherine** ~ 13.4.1726 at Échavanne,[174] dau. of Jean and Marguerite (Dormois) POSCHARD, labourer. Issue:
   1) Anne-Catherine ~ 11.12.1746 at Étobon + 23.12.1746 at Échavanne
   2) **Anne-Catherine** ~ 16.6.1748 at Étobon, living 1757.
   3) **Judith-Marguerite** ~ 28.9.1749 at Étobon, living 1752.

V E U I L A M E T - II

Nicolas WUILLEMÉ dit Mermet = Claudine GOGUÉ of Désandans.
Issue:
1. Jehanne ~ 4.1.1657 at Désandans.
2. Estienne ~ 14.10.1658 at Désandans.
3. Michel, church elder ~ 9.12.1660 + 30.10.1747 at Désandans; =(I) 12.4.1687, Anne POINSENOT + 14.1.1690 at Désandans. Issue:
   1) Marie-Magdeleine ~ 29.6.1687 at Désandans.
   2) Marguerite ~ 31.11.1688 at Désandans.
Michel = (II) 6.5.1690 at Désandans, Jeanne LAGARCE + ca. 1702/03 and had issue:
   3) Anne-Catherine ~ 12.7.1691 at Désandans.
   4) Leonhard ~ 8.9.1692 at Désandans; = 20.6.1719 at Désandans, Catherine, dau. of Jean-Jacques BERTIGNEY. Issue:

---

[173] While the passenger list indicates two females above 14 and one child below the age of four, the records enable this to be amended to 1.1.0.2., as appears above.

[174] Jean Poschard, labourer at Échavanne ~ 21.2.1686 + 9.5.1745 was a son of Abraham Pochard of Échavanne who = 23.2.1683, Sara Juné. Jean = 29.11.1729 at Étobon, Marguerite dau. of Nicolas Dormois, mayor at Échenans-sous-Mont-Vaudois. A sister of Anne-Catherine (*supra*) was Catherine-Anne * 16.8.1721, who = 1741, Jean-Nicolas Jeanmaire and emigrated with her family to New England in the 1750s.

1a) Elisabeth-Catherine * 21.4.1720 at Désandans.
2a) Marie-Madeleine * ca. 1728 + 5.6.1751 at Désandans; =
   31.12.1748 at Désandans, Nicolas LAGARCE. Issue.[175]
3a) **Léonard** * 22.1.1735 at Désandans; a farmer, he emigrated
   to Nova Scotia in the *Betty* in 1752, as a single man; = Anne-
   Judith PERRON and had issue baptised in the French church
   at New York:[176]
   1b) François * 6.10.1765.
   2b) Jeanne-Marguerite WILMET * 12.1.1768.
   3b) Pierre * 17.9.1770.
5) Pierre ~ 17.3.1696 + young at Désandans.
6) Pierre * 27.1.1698 at Désandans.
7) Judith-Marguerite * 22.7.1701 at Désandans.
Michel = (III) 22.1.1704 at Désandans, Susanne ROSSEL
* ca. 1670.
4. Nicolas ~ 12.2.1665 Désandans.

VEUTILOT

Jean-George Veutilot, a thatcher, * ca. 1709, son of Jean-George and
Catherine (Barbaud) Voitelot, and grandson of Pierre Voitelot who was
76 in 1717 (census of Ste.-Marie) came to Nova Scotia in the *Sally* in
1752, with a household of 1.2.1.1, and died at sea in the summer of
1752; = 9.2.1734 at Ste.-Marie, **Elise VESSEAU**, who also died during
the crossing in 1752, widow of Jean-Frédéric GIRODS of Échenans-sur-
l'Étang. Issue:
1. Jacques ~ 10.11.1734 + 30.8.1736 at Sainte-Marie.
2. Elisabeth ~ 19.8.1736 + 2.5.1742 at Sainte-Marie.
3. **Catherine-Elisabeth** ~ 24.7.1738 at Sainte-Marie; admitted to
   Halifax Orphanage, 25.9.1752, and put out to Richard Wenman
   14.10.1752.

---

[175] Nicolas Lagarce emigrated to Nova Scotia with his surviving
child in 1752 (p. 114).

[176] We hear no more of him being in Nova Scotia after 1754.
His whereabouts between then and the baptism of his son at New York in
1765 are unknown. One explanation would be that he enlisted and served
during the Seven Years War and was discharged afterwards in New York.

4. **Éléanore** ~ 19.12.1740 at Sainte-Marie; admitted to Halifax Orphanage, 25.9.1752, and put out to Capt. John Gallant, 19.6.1753.[177]
5. Catherine-Elisabeth ~ 29.5.1744 + 7.2.1745 at Sainte-Marie.
6. **Catherine-Elisabeth** * 22.9.1748 at Sainte-Marie + summer 1752 at sea.

VIENOT

Claude VIENOT of Glay + by 1685; = Catherine DeTHOUX of Exincourt.[178] Son:
1. Jean Hori, a miller * 1654 at Glay + 22.5.1727 at Blamont; = 14.7.1685 at Glay, Jeanne * 1662 + 27.8.1725, dau. of Richard and Jeanne (Bouvier) MASSON of Blamont. Issue:[179]
    1) Catherine-Elisabeth + 1686/88 at Glay, living 1712.
    2) Jean-Hori * 1690 at Glay, living 1712.
    3) Marie-Marguerite * 1692 at Glay, living 1712.
    4) Jeanne * 1694 at Glay, living 1712.
    5) Jean-Christophe * 1699 at Blamont, living 1712.
    6) Pierre * 1701 at Blamont, living 1712.
    7) **Léopold-Frédéric** ~ 15.10.1704, of whom next.
    8) Marie-Catherine * 1708 at Blamont, living 1712.

7) **Léopold-Frédéric** ~ 15.10.1704 at Blamont; a farmer, he emigrated to Nova Scotia in the *Betty* in 1752, with a household of 1.1.2.0., and + 10.1.1783 (A); = (I) ca. 1728, **Jeanne** ~ 18.10.1704 at Blamont, ■ 20.2.1753 at Halifax, dau. of Pierre MILIET or MELIÈRE, schoolmaster at Blamont, and his wife, Marguerite RAMEL, and had nine children. Léopold = (II) 3.2.1754 (A), Anne-Judith, ~ 27.3.1683

---

[177] This may well be the young woman called Eleanor Whitlon, = 29.12.1760 (P), Morris Brown.

[178] She = (II) Jean Mettetal.

[179] When Jeanne (Masson) Vienot died in 1725, she was survived, according to the burial record, by two daughters and three sons. Census of Blamont, 20.4.1712 (ADD, EPM.395).

at Chagey, ■ 4.3.1762 (A), dau. of Nicolas BOUTEILLIER and widow
of Pierre MAILLARD.[180] By his first wife, Vienot had issue:
1a) Daniel ~ 9.8.1729 at Blamont.
2a) Catherine-Marguerite ~ 30.9.1730 at Blamont.
3a) Éléanore ~ 3.12.1731 at Blamont.
4a) *Jean*-Christophe ~ 11.1.1735 at Blamont, ■ 12.3.1753 at Halifax.
5a) *Jacques*-Christophe ~ 22.7.1736 at Blamont; a farmer, he
    emigrated to Nova Scotia in the *Betty* in 1752 as a single man,
    ■ 25.11.1802 (A); = 8.4.1762 (A), Jeanne ~ 30.4.1744 at Trémoins
    + 26.1.1787 (A), dau. of Jean-Nicolas Daré. Issue:
    1b) James Christopher ~ 28.11.1764 ■ 31.1.1768 (A).
    2b) *Sally* Phillips ~ 6.4.1766 (A), ■ 14.3.1846; = 16.5.1790 (C),
        James *Christopher* DAUPHINÉ ~ 23.4.1756 (A)+ 17.8.1841 at
        St.Margarets Bay. Issue.
    3b) James Frederick ~ 27.3.1768 (A), ■ 25.8.1842 (A); = 6.10.1804
        (A), Catherine Elizabeth ~ 29.4.1759 (A) + 30.12.1837 (L), dau.
        of Anton HALTER and widow of Thomas BOUCHER. Issue.
    4b) John George * 1770 + 15/28.8.1816; = 24.4.1798 (A), Eleanor
        CONNER + 27.5.1823.[181] Issue.
    5b) Jane Catherine, ■ 19.1.1772, age 3 days (A).
    6b) Jane Catherine * 17.8.1773 (A), living 1802; = 19.5.1795 (A),
        her cousin, Joshua Frederick VIENOT ~ -3.1773 (A)
        + 1.4.1815 (A) (*infra*). Issue.
    7b) John Elizabeth ~ 3.10.1775 + 25.12.1775 (A).[182]
    8b) Catherine Elizabeth * 10.11.1776 (A), living 1802.

---

[180] Despite the fact that she was twenty years older than Vienot
there seems no other reasonable identification for the woman among the
Montbéliardais known to have come here. See also note [105].

[181] She = (II) 29.11.1818 (C), George Leÿpoldt [Laybolt].

[182] Unless the minister intended to indicate the baptism of twins,
this unusual pair of names cannot be explained. No unaccountable Elizabeth
Vienot appears elsewhere in contemporary records, so that this must be
considered merely an unusual name.

9b) Susan Catherine * 28.12.1778 (A); = 17.7.1799 (A), John George DARÉ * 12.2.1777 (A) + 1862. Issue.

10b) John Frederick, Northwest Range * 3.3.1782 (A) + 22.4.1862 at Mahone Bay; = 30.10.1804 (A), Mary Catherine * 31.8.1783 (A) + 1821/1830, dau. of John Peter LEAU. Issue.

11b) John Peter, Blysteiners Lake * 23.2.1784 (A), ■ 21.9.1834 (A), died of 'Cholera Morbus' at an alleged age of "about 60 years"; = 7.7.1805 (A), Catherine * 8.12.1781, dau. of Jules-Frédéric JEAUDRY. Issue:

6a) *Christophe*-Jacques[183] ~ 22.11.1739 at Bavans + 13.10.1813; = 13.4.1761 (A), Anne-Catherine ~ 11.9.1741 at Étobon, ■ 28.12.1812 (A), dau. of Joshué ROBERT. Eleven children:

1b) Elizabeth, ~ 20.11.1759 (A), ■ 13.1.1841 (A); = 23.3.1779 (A), John *Peter* LEAU ~ 22.8.1756 (A), ■ 25.6.1830 (A). Issue.

2b) John Elizabeth, a millwright ~ 15.6.1762 (A) ■ 8.5.1814; = 26.7.1785 (A), Judith *Margaret* ~ 11.8.1760 (A), living 1812, dau. of Pierre-Anthoine JOLIMOIS. Issue.

3b) *Sally* Phillips ~ 24.3.1765 (A), living 1813; = 18.11.1783 (A), John *George* DAUPHINÉ ~ 28.10.1764 (A) + -.10.1811 at St. Margarets Bay. Issue.

4b) *Mary* Elizabeth ~ 8.2.1768 (A), living 1813; = 5.7.1785 (A), John *Peter* MARIETTE ~ 29.11.1765 (A) + 9.6.1838 at Harrietsfield. Issue.

5b) Peter James ~ -.10.1770 (A), ■ 21.9.1834 (died of cholera) = 8.11.1791 (A), Ann-Judith ~ 29.4.1770 (A) ■ 26.2.1811 (A), dau. of Jean DAUPHINÉ. Issue.

6b) *Joshua* Frederick ~ -.3.1773 (A) + 1.4.1815 (A); = 19.5.1795 (A), his cousin, Jane Catherine * 17.11.1773 (A), dau. of Jacques-Christophe VIENOT (*supra*). Issue.

7b) John *Christopher* * 8.10.1775 + 27.11.1775 (A).

8b) *Catherine* Eliza * 31.10.1776 (A) + young.

---

[183] The John or Jane Vienot ■ 1.12.1763 (A) could fit into the family of either James Christopher or his brother, Christopher James. Since it must be the burial of an infant child, there is no ongoing genealogical significance as to which family one assigns the infant.

9b) *Catherine* Elizabeth * 28.6.1779 (A), living 1815; = 24.2.1795
   (A), John CERTIER * 6.8.1771 (A), ■ 27.11.1830 at Martins
   River. Twelve children.
10b)George Frederick, of Northwest Range * 3.4.1782 (A), living
   1828; = 10.10.1802 (A), Margaret * 4.1.1785 (A), dau. of
   Jules-Frédéric JEAUDRY. Issue.
11b)John George, of Northwest Range * 12.3.1785 (A),
   ■ 20.2.1860; = 27.10.1807 (A), Sarah Catherine * 3.9.1785 (A),
   living 1824, dau. of William and Catherine-Margaret (Daré)
   LEGGE. Issue.
7a) Jean-George ~ 10.12.1742 at Blamont + young.
8a) Elisabeth-Marguerite ~ 24.9.1747 at Temple St.-George,
   Montbéliard Town + in infancy.

VIRPILLOT

Jean-George VURPILLOT church elder at Champey + 22.3.1733 = Eve
JACQUOT + 5.1.1746 and had issue:
1. Friderique Sybille ~ 21.2.1706 + 2.10.1710.
2. Catherine Elisabeth ~ 25.7.1709.
3. **Pierre** ~ 7.2.1712; a sawyer, he emigrated to Nova Scotia in the
Sally in 1752, with a household of 1.1.1.1, and + Oct/Dec 1752 at
Halifax; = **Marguerite** - - - - + autumn 1752 at Halifax. Issue:
   1) **George** * 1738/47, living 1752 at Halifax.
   2) **a daughter** * 1748/52, who + summer 1752 during the ocean
      passage.

VUILQUET

Pierre VUILQUEL of Bart had a son Simon who = 1 Feb 1687 at
Bavans, Margaret, dau. of Vite EUVRARD of Ste.-Suzanne Their son:
1. *Pierre*-Anthoine a farmer, ~ 4.12.1687 at Bart,[184] emigrated to Nova
Scotia in the *Speedwell* in 1752, with no family. He = 21 Feb 1708 at

---

[184] In 1752, he claimed to be 50 when he was, in fact, 64. The
assumption is that he wished to accompany his son and his family to Nova
Scotia, and, fearful that he might be rejected if he were "too old", he declared
a false age. Several other instances have been noted *en passant*. Similar
tactics were employed by several German and Swiss immigrants.

Bavans, Marie-Madeleine BAILLIF of Ysseri [Essertines], bailliage of Yverdon, canton of Vaud, Switzerland + 25.12.1737, age 50, at Bart. Pierre + in 1752 or 1753.[185] Issue:

1) Jeanne ~ 18.12.1708 at Bart.
2) Marie-Catherine ~ 5.7.1711 at Bart.
3) **Jean-Jacques** ~ 10.6.1714 at Bart; a farmer, he emigrated to Nova Scotia in the *Speedwell* in 1752, with a household of 1.1.4.1, and
   ■ 15.4.1760 (A); = (I) 3 Feb 1739 at Bavans, **Catherine-Marguerite**
   ■ 27.10.1752 (P), dau. of Jean THIERRI of Courcelles. He = (II) 23.1.1753 at Halifax, Catherine ■ 26.8.1772 (A), widow of Jean-Nicolas DUPUIS. He had six children:
   1a) **Pierre Vuilquet** ~ 13 Dec 1739 at Bavans, living in 1760.
   2a) **Elisabeth** [Elizabeth Barbara] **Vuilquet** ~ 26 Feb 1742 at Bavans, living in 1772.
   3a) **Joseph Vuilquet** ~ 5 Nov 1744 at Bavans ■ 14.7.1753 (A).
   4a) **Catherine Vuilquet** ~ 25 Mar 1747 at Bavans + 9.10.1775 (A); = 27.11.1769 (A), John CASHEN and had issue.[186]
   5a) Frédéric Vuilquet ~ 4 Apr 1749 + 21 Nov 1750 at Bart.
   6a) **Susanne Vuilquet** ~ 4 May 1751 at Bavans + Oct. 1752/Feb. 1753 at Halifax.
4) Marguerite ~ 1.7.1717 at Bart.
5) Pierre-Frédéric ~ 4.12.1718 + in infancy at Bart.
6) Pierre-Frédéric ~ 26.1.1721 + young at Bart.
7) Daniel ~ 18.2.1723 + 6.1.1738 at Bart.
8) Pierre ~ 18.5.1727 + 19.12.1737 at Bart.

---

[185] Bell surmised that the older Pierre died in autumn 1752, but I believe that Pierre died in 1753. My reasoning is that there were two Pierres in this family: the old gentleman, and his grandson Pierre. Note that in the later victualing lists, Pierre Vuilquet appears apart from the rest of the family and was the sole male heir alive when Jean died in 1760. The Vuilquet from Montbéliard did not become the Wilkie family in Lunenburg County, which descends from John Wilkie, a native of Fordyce, Banffshire, Scotland, who came to Nova Scotia as a Loyalist from Gloucester County, Virginia.

[186] Catherine's burial entry calls her Catherine O Cashian, which suggests that her husband was Irish. John Cashen, widower = (2) 19.11.1776 (A), Anna Catharina Elisabetha, ■ 30.10. 1779, age 23 (A), dau. of Josef Slagenweit [now Slaunwhite].

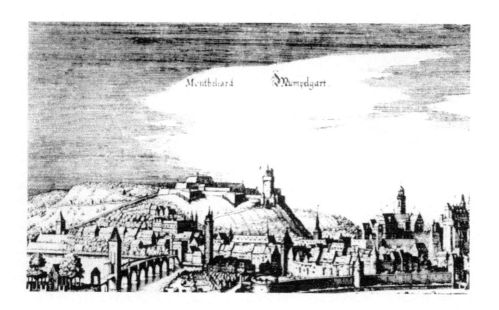

Town of Montbéliard in 1643

BIBLIOGRAPHY

Allen, Charles Edwin, *History of Dresden, Maine.* Lewiston, ME.,1931.

Bell, Winthrop Pickard, *The "Foreign Protestants" and the Settlement of Nova Scotia; the History of a Piece of Arrested British Colonial Policy in the Eighteenth Century.* Toronto, 1961.

Bouvard, André, "Heinrich Schickhardt, technicien des salines au XVIe siècle – Les salines de Saulnot," *Bulletin et Mémoires de la Société d'Émulation de Montbéliard,* LXXIX (1983), 69-77. [Hereafter *Bulletin et Mémoires*]

Brinck, Andreas, *Die deutsche Auswanderungswelle in die britischen Kolonien Nordamerikas um die Mitte des 18. Jahrhunderts.* Stuttgart, 1993.

Canard, Claude, "Chagey, de la zizanie du culte simultané à la construction d'une nouvelle église," *Bulletin et Mémoires, XCIX* (2003), 43-77.

Croissant, Pierre, "La population de la seigneurie d'Étobon du XVIe au XVIIIe siècle," *Bulletin et Mémoires,* LXXXVI (1990), 363-377.

Debard, Jean-Marc, "The Family Origins of Joseph Frederick Wallet DesBarres: A Riddle Finally Solved," *Nova Scotia Historical Review,* 14:2 (1994), 108-122.

_____, "Immigrations, émigrations dans la principauté de Montbéliard du XVIe au XVIIIe siècle - Essai de synthèse," *Bulletin et Mémoires,* XCI (1995), 153-167.

_____, "Les Montbéliardais au Nouvelle-Angleterre; une émigration protestante au milieu du XVIIIe siècle (1751-1755); documents et lettres d'Amérique," *Bulletin et Mémoires,* LXXX (1984), 251-288.

_____, "La Principauté de Montbéliard (XVIe - XVIIIe siècles)," in Roland Fiétier, ed. *Histoire de la Franche-Comté.* Toulouse, France, 1977.

_____, "Réforme et dragonnades à Brévilliers (XVIᵉ - XVIIᵉ siècles)," *Bulletin et Mémoires*, LXXIX (1983), 181-191.

_____, "Tolérance et intolérance; les refugiés huguenots à Montbéliard et dans la Principauté, 1537-1617 (seconde moitié du XVIème siècle)," *Bulletin et Mémoires*, LXXXIV (1988), 47-157.

_____, "Tubingue, université des Montbéliardais (1560-1793)," *Bulletin et Mémoires*, CXI (1998), 393-437.

_____, "Une institution charitable luthérienne 'La Boîte des Pauvres' dans la principauté de Montbéliard. Un exemple paroissial: Saint-Julien au XVIIIᵉ siècle," *Bulletin et Mémoires*, LXXVIII (1982), 197-221.

DesBrisay, Mather Byles, *History of the County of Lunenburg*, 2ⁿᵈ edition. Toronto, 1895.

Familiennamenbuch der Schweiz, 3 volumes. Zürich, 1989.

Faust, Albert B., & Gaius M. Brumbaugh. *Lists of Swiss Emigrants in the Eighteenth Century to the American Colonies, Vol. II*. Washington: National Genealogical Society, 1925.

Hempel, Rainer L., *New Voices on the Shores; Early Pennsylvania German Settlements in New Brunswick*. Toronto, 2000.

Huber, Paul & Eva, "Montbéliard – Principality/Principauté," *European Origins and Colonial Travails; The Settlement of Lunenburg/Steiniger Weg in die Neue Welt; Protestantische Siedler Gründen Lunenburg*. Halifax, 2003, 125-136.

Hurst, Charles W. , "French and German Immigrants into Boston 1751," *The American Genealogist*, 43:3 (July 1967), 168-177; and 44:2 (Apr.1968) 110.

Lassus, François et Jean-Marc Debard, "Une petite ville luthérienne: Héricourt, 1698-1721,"*Bulletin et Mémoires*, LXXXVIII (1992), 299-458.

Macy, Harry, Jr., "Robert Townsend of New York City," in *The New York Genealogical and Biographical Record* (January 1995), 25-34.

Mathiot, Pastor Charles, "Quelques anciens noms montbéliardais de personnes," serialized in *L'Ami Chrétien*, 1982-1983. My English translation of relevant parts may be seen on line at http://web2.uwindsor.ca/library/leddy/people/art/names.html

Mathiot, Charles, et Roger Boigeol, *Recherches historiques sur les Anabaptistes de l'ancienne principauté de Montbéliard, d'Alsace et du territoire de Belfort*. Flavion, Belgium, 1969.

Mittelberger, Gottlieb, *Journey to Pennsylvania*, 1756. Oscar Handlin, Cambridge, Mass., 1960.

Patterson, George, *A History of the County of Pictou Nova Scotia*. Montréal,1877.

Paulsen, Kenneth S., "The Emoneau Family of the Principality of Montbéliard and Lunenburg Township, N. S.," *NEXUS*, 12 (1995), 146-152.

_____, "Settlement and Ethnicity in Lunenburg, Nova Scotia, 1753 - 1800: A History of the Foreign Protestant Community." Unpublished Ph. D. thesis, University of Maine, 1996.

Pegeot, Pierre, "Montbéliard, origines et originalités d'une ville medievale," *Histoire de la Ville de Montbéliard*, Claude Voisin, ed. Roanne, France, 1980.

Punch, Terrence M. , "L'effrayante mortalité des Montbéliardais à Halifax en 1752-1753," *Bulletin et Mémoires*, CXX (1997), 295-303.

_____, "A Genealogy: George-Frédéric Bailly," in *Journal of the Royal Nova Scotia Historical Society*, 5 (2002), 154-168.

_____, "Les Montbéliardais en Nouvelle Écosse: une colonisation par des protestants étrangers au XVIIIe siècle (1750-1815)," *Bulletin et Mémoires*, LXXXI (1985),195-234.

_____, "Les Montbéliardais en Nouvelle Écosse: 1750 - 1815," Paul
& Eva Huber, eds, *European Origins and Colonial Travails; The
Settlement of Lunenburg.* Halifax, 2003, 120-125.

_____, "Montbéliard: An Unknown Homeland," in *Nova Scotia
Historic Review,* 5: 2 (1985), 74-92.

_____, "Montbéliard, 1523-1773; Homeland, Refuge, Way-
Station," *Deutschkanadisches Jahrbuch,* XVI (2000), 147-157.

_____, "Some Surprising 'Foreign Protestants'," *The Nova Scotia
Genealogist,* XXX/I (Spring 2012), 5 - 8.

Renard, Louis, *Nouvelle Histoire du Pays de Montbéliard.*
Montbéliard, 1950.

Smith, T. Lynn, *Demography: Principles and Methods.* Philadelphia,
1970.

Von Hippel, Wolfgang. *Auswanderung aus Sudwestdeutschland:
Studieren zur württembergischen Auswanderung und Auswanderungspolitik im 18 und 19 Jahrhundert.* Stuttgart, 1984.

Wittmeyer, Alfred V., ed. *Registers of the French Church of New York.*
New York, 1886.

Wokeck, Marianne S. *Trade in Strangers; The Beginnings of Mass
Migration to North America.* University Park, PA, 1999.

Wust, Klaus,   "The Emigration Season of 1738 – Year of the
Destroying Angel," *The Report: A Journal of German-American
History,* Vol. 40 (1986), 21-56.

Young, J. Christopher, ed., *Register of the Foreign Protestants of
Nova Scotia (ca. 1749-1770),* 2 vols. Guelph, ON, 2003.

INDEX OF SURNAMES IN THE GENEALOGIES

Acker 61
Alison/Alizon **49**, 157
Allen 77, 81, 159
Amêt **50**, 121
Anderson 56
Andrews 68
Anschutz 89
Arenberg 156
Aubert, Aubairt 64, 113
Bachman, Backman 77, 122
Bailly, Baillif **50-53**, 89, 172
Baker 138, 140
Ballué 92
Banvard **53-54**, 70, 79, 110, 156
Barbaud 167
Barkhouse 68
Barre 117
Bartholet 91
Bataillard 91
Baxter 147
Beamish 123
Begin/Bechin **54-55**, 93, 94, 133
Belos 160
Belpoix 106
Berringer 123
Bertigney 166
Besançon/Bezanson **55-56**, 118, 136, 159, 165
Bidaud, Bidault 51
Biguenet/Bigney **57**, 69, 119-121, 146, 153
Bille 128
Bizés/Bissett **58-60**, 85
Blanchard 111
Bleisteiner 107
Boehner 123, 124
Bohi, Bohy 162
Boillou, Boilloud, Boillot, Boilley 50, 53, 64, 88, 89, 126, 145
Bonhôtal 128, 133
Bonnier 57
Boucher 122, 168

Bouffay, Bouvet, Bovet 58, 85, 91, 103
Bouillon **59-60**, 63, 145, 146
Bourgeois **60-61**
Bourgogne/Burgoine **61-62**
Bourquin 57, 68
Bouteillier 51, 55, 56, 58, 60, **62-68**, 69, 74, 79-81, 93, 98, 112, 122, 129-132, 136, 137, 144-146, 156, 159, 164, 169
Bouthenot 116
Bouvier 68, 168
Bowes 140
Boyd 110
Bran(dt) 53, 59, 105, 116, 156
Bretenier 83
Breuchot 64
Brigley 112
Brothers 59
Brown 168
Brunt 137
Burke 156
Burns 120
Bushen 144
Butler 59
Byers 104
Caburet 92
Cacun 89
Calame 57, 62, **68-69**, 74, 75, 146, 156
Carlin **69-70**, 95, 110, 155
Carmien 90
Carpet 89
Carray 131
Cashen, O Cashian 172
Certier - see Sarty
Chambers - see Jeanbas
Chamot 64, 99, 128
Charlemagne 72
Charles 69, 154
Charpiot 106
Cheaney, Chiney 66
Cherton 59
Chevallier 50, 126

SOME SOURCES OF RESEARCH

At least a working knowledge of French is required to utilize these sources. An additional requirement is an ability to read and decipher ancient handwriting. The registers which have contemporary indexes followed the French practice of entering married women under their maiden names – e.g., Léonard Receveur's wife (died 1736) is recorded under her birth name of Laurillard, rather than Receveur. In church registers the last four months of the year are abbreviated as 7ber (September), 8ber (October), 9ber (November) and 10ber (December). Bear in mind also that there are human errors in the registers, so that a man named Jean may turn up in an index as Nicolas, his full name having been Jean-Nicolas. The registers of the German chapel in the château pose the added difficulty of being in the old German Schrift, rather than in the familiar Latin characters we use.

The département of Doubs offers 556,533 documents of births, marriages and deaths, population lists and miscellaneous documents in its *dépouillement d'actes de l'état-civil* et des registres paroissiaux at

www.doubsgenealogie.fr/genealogie/actes/index/ph

The département of Haute-Saône offers 1,394,279 similar documents available to be examined. As of 25 January 2015, to view these, click on "Dépouillement des Acts" [Examination of records] at

www.servancnaute.fr/

The town of Montbéliard has thousands of birth, marriage and death records on line, based on the registers of the main parish of St. Martin (from 1571), the suburban parish of St. Georges (from 1744-1794), the German chapel in the Château (from 1651), and the Roman Catholic church of St. Maimboeuf (1681-1793). Mennonite records begin 1750. www.rfgenealogie.com/s-informer/infos/archives/l-etat-civil-ancien-de-montbeliard

Several communities or suburbs of the town of Montbéliard were included in the records of Temple St. Martin: Arbouans, Grand and Vieux Charmont, and Souchaux.

The foregoing information was verified as of 10 February 2015.

ON-LINE REGISTERS OPENING BEFORE 1752

	BAPTISMS	MARRIAGES	BURIALS
* Abbévillers	1722	1712	------
* Bavans	1593	1611	1616
* Bethoncourt	1651	1660	------
* Beutal/Brétigny	1678	1677	1677
* Blamont	1683	1684	1685
* Blussangeaux/Blussans	1654	1654	1658
Brevilliers/Mandrevillars	1605	1609	1606
Bussurel	1737	------	
Chagey/Luze	1619	1620	1620
Champey	1724	(1794)	1729
Chenebier	1750	1751	1750
Clairegoutte	1637	1636	1678
* Dampierre-les-Bois	1669	1671	1671
Étobon/Belverne	1646	1647	1655
Frédéric-Fontaine	1647	(1794)	(1792)
Héricourt/St. Valbert	1663	1611	1619
* Hérimoncourt/Thulay	1686	------	1686
* Longevelle	1605	1606	1624
Magny Danigon	1637	(1795)	(1796)
* Mandeure	1648	1673	1669
* Nommay	1723	1723	1723
* Pierrefontaine	1737	1737	1736
* Sainte-Suzanne	1593	1716	1607
* Sainte-Marie	1684	1711	1612
Tavey/Byans	1681	1684	1685
Trémoins/Aibre	1590	1678	1705
* Valentigney	1595	------	------
Vyans/Laire	1616	1624	1617

* indicates those in the département of Doubs. The remainder are in the département of Haute-Saône.

CENSUS 1704 - 1750

* Allenjoie 1717, 1723, 1725
* Arbouans 1704, 1723
* Badeval 1704, 1718, 1723
* Brognard 1717, 1723
* Dambenois 1717, 1723, 1725
* Dampierre 1705, 1717, 1723
* Étupes 1705, 1723, 1725
* Fesches-le-Chatel 1717, 1718, 1723

* Grand Charmont 1719
* Hérimoncourt 1750
* Nommay 1717, 1723, 1725
* Présentevillers 1704, 1717, 1723
* Sainte-Marie 1717, 1719
Trémoins 1717, 1723, 1727
* Vieux Charmont 1717, 1723

POOR FAMILIES 1750

* Allenjoie (15)
* Brognard (8) - Besançon family
* Dambenois (7) - Ménégaux family
* Étupes (13)
* Nommay (11)
* Vieux Charmont (4) - Nardin-1 family

* indicates those in the département of Doubs. Trémoins is in the département of Haute-Saône.

HISTORICAL SOCIETY

Société d,Émulation de Montbéliard
Hôtel Beurnier-Rossel
8 place Saint-Martin   B. P. 251
25204 Montbéliard
France

email: sem.montbeliard@wanadoo.fr

website: www.montbeliard-emulation.fr/

CPSIA information can be obtained
at www.ICGtesting.com
Printed in the USA
LVHW081714170119
604061LV00029B/223/P